Developing Critical Thinking through Science

Book 2

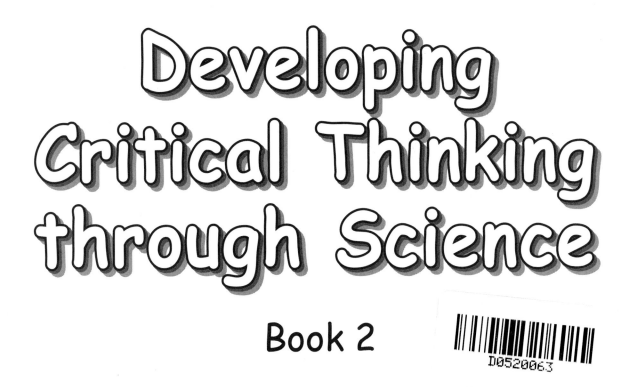

Developing Critical Thinking through Science Series

📖 Book 1 📖 Book 2

Written by
Paul Eggen
June Main

© 2001, 1990
THE CRITICAL THINKING CO.™
www.CriticalThinking.com
Phone: 800-458-4849 • Fax: 541-756-1758
1991 Sherman Ave., Suite 200 • North Bend • OR 97459
ISBN 978-0-89455-422-3

MIX
Paper from responsible sources
FSC® C011935

ABOUT THE AUTHORS

PAUL EGGEN is a Professor of Education at the University of North Florida in the Division of Curriculum and Instruction. He has been a science professor at the university level since 1972; for several years prior to this, he taught science in public school.

He holds a B.S. in Physical Science and Mathematics Education from Northern Montana College and a Ph.D. in Science Education from Oregon State University.

Dr. Eggen is a frequent presenter at national and international conferences and serves as a consultant for effective instruction, school-based staff and curriculum development, the teaching of thinking skills, and the improvement of science instruction all over the world. He gives regional, national, and international workshops on these subjects as well as additional workshops on student motivation and evaluation, classroom management, general teaching techniques, and specific techniques for teaching science and critical and analytical thinking skills.

Dr. Eggen is the author of numerous books and articles about education and science education.

DR. JUNE MAIN, Professor of Education at Jacksonville University in Jacksonville, Florida, taught elementary school children for 13 years. She has taught science education courses at the college level for the past 15 years.

June has made numerous presentations at regional, national, and international conferences focusing on activity-based, constructivist science teaching that emphasizes strategies to develop children's critical thinking skills. She has been a science consultant and presenter for the Association of International Schools in Africa, recently presenting many workshops at annual teacher conferences in Kenya and Namibia.

June is the recipient of many awards for excellence in teaching, including the Carnegie Foundation's *Florida Professor of the Year* award (2001–2002), the *Times-Union EVE Award for Education* (2001–2002), the award for *Innovative Excellence in Teaching, Learning and Technology* (1999), *Who's Who in American Education*, (1990–2002), and the National Science Teacher Association *STAR* Award. She is the author and coauthor of many books, curriculum materials, and journal articles.

TABLE OF CONTENTS

INTRODUCTION

Man's mind, once stretched by a new idea, never regains its original dimensions.

— Oliver Wendell Holmes

Developing Critical Thinking through Science is based on the premise that students apply thinking skills to learning science concepts and principles by:

Doing through direct, firsthand experiences in an interactive, open atmosphere;

Constructing by building their knowledge through guided inquiry;

Connecting by relating their learning to the world around them.

To help students learn science, four major themes are promoted in this book.

1. *Science can and should motivate students toward learning and toward developing curiosity about the world in which they live.*

The contents of this book have been designed to provide teachers and prospective teachers with a variety of science activities that spark this curiosity in students. All of the activities have been tested in classrooms. Each activity includes step-by-step procedures and questioning strategies that help students practice critical thinking while applying it to what they learn in class and to their real world.

These activities can be used successfully with a minimum of science knowledge, preparation time, and science equipment. Most of the materials and equipment are everyday, inexpensive items that can be found around school, home, outside in the environment, or in local stores. Many items can be collected and contributed by the students, thus reinforcing their concept of direct participation in the science activities.

2. *Science is viewed as an active process of developing ideas, or "storybuilding," rather than as static bodies of already-existing knowledge to be passed on to students.*

As teachers, we want our students to develop valid ideas about science, and we want the ideas developed in a spirit of inquiry and investigation. This means that instead of merely describing what is taking place, the teacher guides the students through an inquiry process by asking pertinent, open-ended questions and by encouraging investigative process through demonstration, hands-on opportunities, and extension of experiments. Using this process, students can build and comprehend ideas for themselves.

The story-building components come from the students' own direct observations, previous knowledge, and personal involvement in the activities. Together with the teacher's guidance, this leads to comprehension of meaningful and valid science concepts and principles.

3. *Students are encouraged to observe and describe their observations accurately and completely.*

All student observations and descriptions are considered acceptable no matter how they are stated, for it is from these observations that the information is examined and evaluated for relevancy and organized to build their concept "stories." Students should be encouraged to articulate their observations and ideas using scientific terminology. Scientific terms are defined, demonstrated with concrete examples, then applied and reinforced throughout the activities.

Let's illustrate this process with a model lesson in which students have two different pieces of sandpaper to rub on wooden blocks. Questions can be added to or deleted from this process as the students' ability or pre-knowledge dictates.

Teacher   *Let's compare these two pieces of sandpaper. How are they the same or different?*

Students   *The two pieces are the same size.*

Teacher   *How else might we say that?*

Students	*They have the same area.*
Teacher	*What else is the same or different?*
Students	*One piece is scratchier than the other piece.*
Teacher	*How else might we describe "scratchy"?*
Students	*One is rougher than the other. The pieces of sand are bigger on one.*
Teacher	*Each tiny particle of sand is called a grain. We say that the bigger grains of sand are coarse-grained and the smaller grains of sand are fine-grained. Let's touch them and feel the difference. What does coarse mean?*
Students	*Coarse means the pieces of sand are larger and rougher.*
Teacher	*What does fine mean?*
Students	*Fine means the pieces of sand are smaller.*
Teacher	*What is each particle of sand called?*
Students	*Each piece of sand, or particle, is called a grain.*
Teacher	*Now let's describe the pieces of sandpaper again.*
Students	*One piece is coarse-grained and one piece is fine-grained.*
Teacher	*What else do we observe about the pieces of sandpaper?*
Students	*They both have straight edges. They are both the same shape. They are both rectangles.*

Research and teacher experience indicate that students often have difficulty stating their observations in precise terms such as *area* rather than *size*, or *coarse-grained* and *fine-grained* rather than *scratchy* and *rough*. If the students cannot supply terms such as *coarse* or *grained*, you can initially offer and model such terms for them. Then you can continue to reinforce and expand their use by repeating the terms as you continue to demonstrate other activities. You can also ask students to rephrase their observations and descriptions of science experiences so they express themselves "scientifically." Being able to

practice observing and describing in this way not only aids in their understanding of science topics but also helps their general language growth. These tools will better prepare them for science studies in the future.

4. *An open, interactive atmosphere in the classroom is essential.*

In an open and interactive atmosphere, the teacher and the class, or small groups of students, actively investigate ideas together (compared to a passive learning situation in which students are merely told the problem, given the answers, and expected to memorize the information). The open-classroom atmosphere removes students' fear of giving a "wrong" answer or explanation and replaces it with a less inhibited ability to express what they think is possible based on their experiences at that time.

The open, interactive atmosphere promotes questioning between teacher/student, student/ student, and student/teacher. It encourages prediction, experimentation, and discovery of new dimensions of concepts. It allows examination of "What if?" questions about possible changes in the activity, then allows testing for the results of these changes or *variables*. Activities can be followed as written or expanded. If time allows, the teacher can encourage free expression of students' related curiosities and personal interests and extend an activity by exploring, experimenting, and discussing until all are satisfied. Also, some activities can be repeated for reinforcement using different variables suggested by students.

By becoming involved in these activities through direct observation, hands-on participation, and verbalization of the physical and thought processes, students build a more concrete understanding of the concepts taught in the activities. They are able to relate and apply these concepts to their environment on a more scientific level. With the teacher's help, students can learn to apply these same analytic and problem-solving skills to their other studies and to any classroom or social problems that might arise.

UNIT 1—PROCESS SKILLS

The activities in this unit were developed to increase the basic science processing skills of observing, gathering data, describing, comparing, discussing, classifying, categorizing, making inferences based on observations, giving reasons for classification categories, and generalizing.

Background Information

Observing is the essential, basic skill that builds the foundation for the development of more advanced science process skills. The process of observing is most often confused with making inferences and stating opinions.

Observations are made as students experience their natural environment using one or more of their senses—by looking, listening, smelling, touching, and/or tasting. When they describe what they observe, they should be guided to communicate what they see, hear, smell, touch, or taste from direct observations without making inferences or offering their opinions.

Inferences are made as students explain or interpret events. These inferences need to be based on the observations students have made. An inference can be a conclusion based on an observation when no personal preference or sentiment is involved.

Opinions are different from inferences because they are conclusions based on personal preferences and may or may not be based on observation.

Let's illustrate the differences between the three processes with this picture and the accompanying possible responses from students. List as many observations, inferences, and opinions as you can before you turn to the next page.

Here are some **observations** that students could make about the picture:
- There is a cat and a ball in the picture.
- The CDs are under and behind the cat.
- Some CDs are in a stack.
- The CDs right behind the cat are not in a stack.

Here are some **inferences** that students could make:
- The cat was probably playing with the ball because of the way it's looking at the ball.
- The cat probably knocked down the stack of CDs right behind it because the stack was so close to where it was playing with the ball.
- The cat is probably a kitten because it is not very big in comparison with the CDs.

Some **opinions** that could be expressed by students:
- I like kittens.
- This kitten is cute.

Grouping information for better understanding and retrieval involves three additional processes after initial observations have been made:
- To **compare** is to examine things or events to find out how they are alike and different. For instance, a paper clip, staple and clothespin could be thought of as being alike because each of these three objects could hold things together. They are different in other characteristics like size, shape, and material.
- To **classify** is to put objects or events into groups based on common characteristics or properties. Nails, screws, and thumbtacks could be added to the objects listed above to make a group with similar properties.
- To **label** a group is to choose a name for the group that will fit the characteristics or properties of the specific set of objects or events. The group could be labeled "types of fasteners."

Students need a variety of different experiences in which they observe, compare, classify, and label objects so that they can better understand and access information about the objects, living things, and events in the world. The number of interrelationships or connections that students build among pieces of information directly relates to their ability to be able to retrieve and use the information.

What if we went into a supermarket that had no classification system for arranging food and household items? What if the listings in a telephone book were not in alphabetical order? Would we be able to easily find something we need? Imagine what it would be like if we had not developed a classification system for all of the information we have in our brains. How easy would it be to find one piece of information? How long might that take?

The activities in this unit were written as an introduction to the many ways of categorizing information. With guidance, students can learn to apply these processes in many different subject areas when studying a variety of topics.

The Ping-Pong® ball and the golf ball can go with the index card because they are all white.

9. What can you put with the bolt?

The wing nut.

10. For what reason?

The wing nut could be screwed onto the bolt.

11. Is there any other object that can be grouped with the nut and bolt?

The screwdriver.

12. Tell us your reason.

The screwdriver can be used to tighten the bolt into the nut.

13. Can you think of another way to group some of the objects?

Possible answers: the pencil and the golf tee are both made of wood; the screw, pencil, and golf tee all have sharp points; the pencil could be used to mark the spot to screw in the screw using the screwdriver; the golf ball, screw, and bolt all have rough surfaces; the nut, bolt, screw, and paper clip are all made of metal.

Accept all answers that have logical explanations.

14. Who can make a generalization about how we can group objects?

Objects can be grouped in many different ways depending on how we think about them.

15. What are some different ways we can think about groupings of objects?

Color / shape / size / use of object / texture / type of material

16. All of these ways we use to think about groupings are called PROPERTIES.

A PROPERTY is a characteristic of an object that can be used to describe it.

— Practical Application —

1. Let's think about the way objects can be used. If we have a piece of rope about 12 feet long, how can we use it in P.E.?

We can use it as a jump rope with one person turning it at each end.
We can use it as a rope for tug of war.
We can use it as a starting line for a race.
We can hang it from a tree branch to use as a swing.

List some common animals on the chalkboard, such as horse, donkey, mule, dog, wolf, cat, lion, tiger, walrus, and sea lion.

2. Let's group these animals together. Which ones go together?

   (If the students group dog and cat together because they are both pets, continue by asking question 3.)

3. How do you suppose scientists would group the animals?

   Horse, donkey, and mule would go together.
   Dog and wolf would go together.
   Cat, lion, and tiger would go together.
   Walrus and sea lion would go together.

4. Why would these animals be grouped together?

   They have similar properties or characteristics.

ACTIVITY 3: CLASSIFICATION – ONE PROPERTY

Goal: To understand that objects can be classified into two groups using one property to describe the objects; to understand that there are many properties that can be used to describe objects

Skills: Observing, gathering data, describing, discussing, comparing, classifying, inferring, generalizing

Materials: 8 small bags or boxes (like pencil boxes, lids of shoe boxes)
8 each of different objects so that every bag or box will have the same group of objects.
Some possibilities are:

Paper clips	Pieces of yarn
Shells	Marbles
Buttons	Twigs
Cotton balls	Clothespins
Popsicle sticks	Stones
Pieces of cloth	Bottle caps
Pencils	Crayons

Preparation: 1. Put the objects into bags or boxes so that each has the same set of objects.
2. Divide the students into 8 groups with 3–4 students in each group.

Preparation Time: 5 minutes

Lesson Time: 20–25 minutes

— Procedure and Questioning Strategy —

Explain to the students: "We have eight bags/boxes, one bag/box for each team. Every bag/box has the same set of objects in it. The members of each team are to:
- observe and discuss the similarities and differences of objects.
- decide on one property or characteristic that would include all objects; for example, hardness.
- choose a property that is different from the properties you hear being used by other teams.
- physically divide the objects into the two groups within that property; for example, soft and hard.
- decide on another property with groupings in case the ones you've chosen are mentioned by another team.
- choose one member of your team to tell how the team categorized its groupings and to give explanations to the rest of the class; i.e., 'something is hard when you can't squash it and something is soft when you can.'"

Before beginning the activity, ask students the following questions.

1. What is a property?

    A way of describing something.

2. Give an example of a property.

    It could be size, texture, weight, flexibility, etc.

3. If you were to describe a group of objects using the property of texture and divide the objects into two groups, what two groups could you have?

> A group of smooth objects and a group of rough objects.

Remind students that they need to come up with a property and two groupings that are different from any other team's. Distribute one bag or box of objects to each team. Allow teams ten minutes to decide their properties and groupings. Then ask each team's spokesperson, one at a time, to explain their groupings as you write labels for the groupings on the chalkboard—i.e., rough/smooth, etc. Possible questions and answers follow.

4. What did your team label its two groupings of objects, (student's name)?

> Light and heavy.

5. How did you determine which were heavy and which were light?

> One group has things heavier than the shell; the other group, things lighter than the shell.

6. What property did you use?

> Weight.

7. What are the two groupings your team used, (student's name)?

> Things that bend and things that don't bend.

8. How can we label your groups to put them on the board?

> Flexible and not flexible.

9. How did you test them?

> By trying to bend them—without breaking them—with our hands.

10. What was the property your team used?

> Flexibility.

Continue until all eight groups have shared their properties and groupings.

11. How many properties were used to describe the objects?

> Eight.

12. Did you think of any other properties and groupings?

Add to those already listed on the board.

13. What can we say about the way properties are used to describe objects?

> That there are many properties that can be used to describe objects.

Ask students to do the activity again, choosing properties and groupings that have not already been used by other teams. Have them choose another member of their team to be the team leader for this activity.

ACTIVITY 4: CLASSIFICATION – TWO PROPERTIES

Goal: To understand that objects can be classified into four groups, using two properties to describe the objects

Skills: Observing, gathering data, describing, discussing, comparing, classifying, inferring, generalizing

Materials: The same materials used in Activity 3, "Classification – One Property"

Preparation: 1. Put objects into bags or boxes so that each team has the same set of objects.
2. Divide the students into 8 groups with 3–4 students in each group.

Preparation Time: 5 minutes

Lesson Time: 20–25 minutes

— Procedure and Questioning Strategy —

1. In this activity we are going to use *two* properties to divide the objects into four groups. Who can name two properties?

    Material and texture (students may make other suggestions which can be modeled as follows.)

2. What kinds of materials are you thinking about?

    Those that are natural and those that are man-made.

3. If we were to divide objects into two groups using these two properties, how could we go about doing it?

    We could make two groups first, natural and man-made.

4. What could we do next?

    We could divide the natural objects into two groups using texture as our second property— smooth and rough. Then we could divide the man-made objects into the same two groups.

5. Let's see how we could show that on the board.

    We'd have our set of objects...divide the set by our first property— material—into *natural* and *man-made* objects...then break down those two sets using our second property— texture—into *smooth* and *rough*.

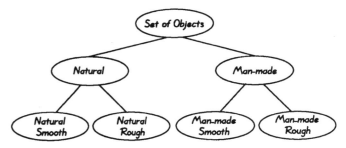

Put the small and large yellow triangles in the overlapping portion of the circles to confirm their conclusion.

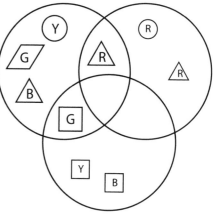

5. Now, we're really going to have to think about what we're doing. This time we're going to have three circles.

Draw the third circle, and place the figures in them as shown to the right.

6. Now your task is to put all the rest of your figures in the proper places. As a group, you decide where they all go and when you're finished we'll discuss them.

Have the students make circles with the string as shown by the drawing on the board, then give them a few minutes to classify the figures into the locations.

7. Now let's look at what we did. We call this CLASSIFICATION.

CLASSIFICATION is the process of putting objects into groups based on common characteristics or properties.

8. Now, how did you classify the figures? What went in here (area 1 in the drawing)?

    Shapes that were large.

9. How do you know?

    It was the only thing they had in common.

10. How about these two (area 2 and area 3 in the drawing)?

    Red objects (area 2) and squares (area 3).

11. And how about here (area 4)?

    Objects that are both large and red.

12. Why?

    This is where the two circles overlap. The shape must be large to fit in the first circle, and it must also be red to fit in the second circle.

13. Now, how about here (area 7)?

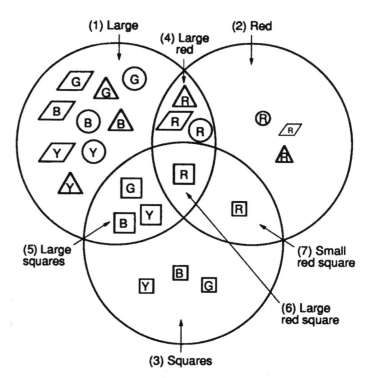

The small red square.

14. **Why not both the red squares?**

The large red square goes in there (area 6).

15. **Why do you think so?**

All three circles overlap there. The shape must be large for the first circle, red for the second circle, and a square for the third circle. Only one shape is all three. It is the large red square.

16. **How about here (area 5)?**

All the large squares except the red one.

At this point you may choose to give the students another problem, such as the one which can be duplicated from the drawing on page 18. The solution to the problem is shown below.

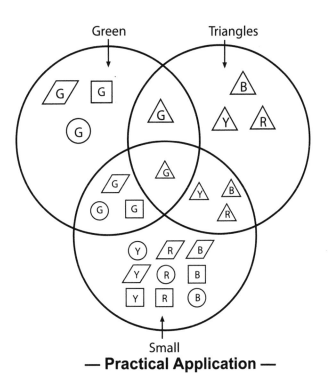

— **Practical Application** —

Select three criteria among the students, such as tall, wearing glasses, and wearing shorts. Without identifying these criteria to the students, select students to go into each of the three categories. Then have them decide what the criterion is for each group and what students would fit overlapping categories, such as a tall student with glasses, or a short person who is not wearing shorts. Any number of problems such as these can be designed to help them practice their classification skills. Avoid any classifications that might embarrass students.

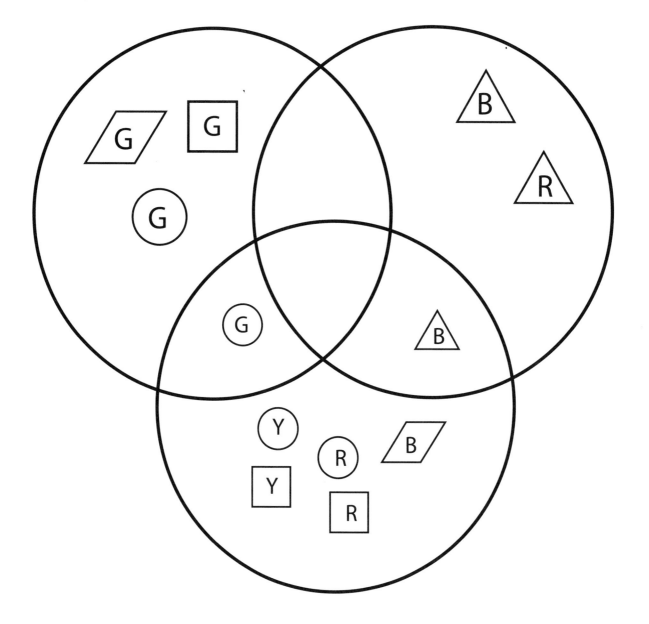

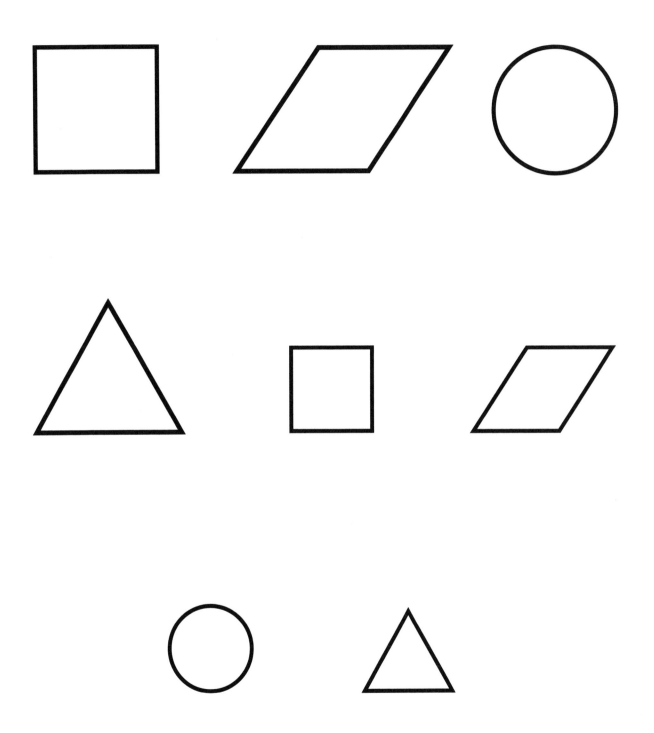

ACTIVITIES 1–5: CONNECTIONS

Goal: To understand the relationships between observation, inference, and classification

Skills: Comparing, explaining, supporting explanations with observations

— Questioning Strategy —

1. Let's see what kinds of relationships we can find between the thinking skills we have been practicing. How are observations and inferences related?

   An inference is supported by observation. The more observations that support an inference, the better chance the inference has of being accurate.

2. How do we know whether or not an observation is accurate?

   We see, hear, touch, taste, or smell to make our observations.

3. Think carefully now. What is the difference between an inference and a guess?

   An inference is a conclusion *based on* an observation. A guess is simply a guess. It has no observation that supports it.

4. What is the difference between an inference and an opinion?

   An inference is based on observation alone. No personal preference is involved. Opinion has some personal preference in it or has some sentiment in it.

5. Which do you think are more closely related: observation and classification or inference and classification?

   Probably observation and classification. When we classify, we are not making a conclusion about the information. We are finding common features in the examples.

6. Are observation and classification the same?

   No.

7. Why do you think they are not?

   When you classify, you pick out one or more properties that the objects have in common so you make some decisions about which property you're going to use for the common one.

8. Let's try an example to illustrate what you're saying. Suppose we had a baseball, a tennis ball, and a marble. What property could we use to group them all together?

   Roundness.

9. What are some properties we might use that would prevent them from being grouped together?

> Objects made of glass. The marble would fit in that category, but the baseball and tennis ball wouldn't.

The students will suggest other examples once you get them started.

10. So how are observation and classification related to each other?

> Classification depends on observation. When we classify, we group or put together the properties that the objects have in common.

UNIT 2—FORCE, MOVEMENT, WORK, SYSTEMS AND WEIGHT

Background Information

Force is generally defined as any push or pull. Most objects can be either pushed or pulled, but some objects require only a push in order to be used in the way they're designed. For instance, a doorbell, computer keys, and musical instrument keys are pushed in order to function. Tug of war ropes, venetian blind or curtain cords, and lawn mower starter cords require a pull.

If an object is pushed or pulled, the object exerts a resisting force, so a force can also be described as an interaction between objects. If an object doesn't move, then the forces exerted on it are equal and the object remains in equilibrium. If the object moves, it moves in the direction of the greater force. So, if people exerted equal and opposite forces on a tug of war rope, the rope would remain in equilibrium. If the people on one side of the rope exerted more force than the people on the other side, then the rope would move toward the people exerting the greater force.

The game of tug of war also illustrates the interaction of forces in a **system.** Each person exerts a force, a pull, on the rope. The feet of the people pulling on the rope are exerting force on the ground; gravity is also exerting a downward force on the rope. A system has parts that are connected in some way. In this example, the parts of the system include the rope, the people, the ground, and gravity. There may also be a piece of cloth tied in the middle of the rope and a cone to show the starting place of the rope at the beginning of the game. All parts of this system are needed in order to play the game.

Students can identify with many different types of systems: school systems, computer systems, stereo systems, and human body systems. All have parts that are connected in some way. The parts of bicycles, skateboards, and cars are connected in systems.

The gravitational system is the pull between two or more objects. We are held down on Earth by the pull of gravity on us. This happens because Earth exerts a greater pull on us than we exert on Earth. When we step on a spring scale, like our bathroom scales, our weight is measured. **Weight** is the measure of the force—the pull—of gravity on the mass of a person or object. When the mass of our bodies is pulled to Earth by gravity and we have a spring scale between Earth and our bodies, the force exerted on the scale compresses its springs and our weight is registered on the scale. The scale measures this force in pounds or in grams. When you step on your bathroom scale to measure your weight, you are part of another system—a measurement system that includes gravity, the spring scale, and your body.

There are also systems within systems. For example, on a grand scale, Earth is a system within the solar system; the solar system exists within the Milky Way Galaxy; the Milky Way Galaxy is a system within the system of the universe.

The exertion of force can also result in **work** being done. The scientific definition of work is the product of the force used and the distance an object moved. So, to a scientist, a force needs to produce measurable movement in order for work to be done. If you push hard on a wall, or if you hold up a heavy object, and there has been no movement of the wall or the object, no work has been done. In both of these instances it would feel as though work had been done; but according to a scientist, if movement can't be measured, it isn't work. The exertion of force would be felt even if no work were accomplished.

So . . . if you were on one of the tug-of-war teams, and the rope moved a measurable distance toward your team, did the people on your team do work? Or was it just a game? If you pushed hard on a stalled car to move it off the road and it didn't move, did you do work?

Unit 2–NATIONAL SCIENCE EDUCATION STANDARDS

- *Unifying Concepts and Processes:* Students should develop understanding and abilities with regard to systems, order, and organization; evidence, models, and explanation; constancy, change, and measurement; and evolution and equilibrium.

- *Science as Inquiry*—Content Standard A: Students should develop the necessary skills to do scientific inquiry and develop an understanding about scientific inquiry.

- *Physical Science*—Content Standard B: Students should develop an understanding of the properties of objects and materials, and of the position and motion of objects.

- *History and Nature of Science*—Content Standard G: Students should develop an understanding of the nature of science and of science as a human endeavor.

ACTIVITY 6: FORCE, MOVEMENT, AND WORK

Goal: **To understand the concepts of force and work**
       To understand that objects move in the same direction as the force that acts upon them

Skills: Observing, comparing, generalizing, explaining

Materials: None

Preparation: None

Preparation Time: None

Lesson Time: 15–20 minutes

— Procedure and Questioning Strategy —

Begin the activity by having a student push on the wall of the room.

1. What is (student's name) doing?
   > Possible answers: leaning on the wall, holding up the wall, pressing against the wall, pushing in the wall.

Now have another student pull a desk, the chalk tray, or anything that will not move.

2. What is (student's name) doing?
   > Pulling on the desk/chalk tray.

3. What do we call any *push* or *pull*?
   > Force.

A FORCE is any push or pull. Supply the term FORCE if students don't know it.

Now pull a student in a chair across the room.

4. What do you observe?
   > You're exerting a force.

To EXERT is to put into action. Supply the term EXERT if students don't know it.

5. How does this force compare to the forces we exerted on the wall?
   > This time the force made the chair move.

6. What do we call the combination of force and movement?

> Work.

WORK is the combination of force and movement. Supply the term WORK if students don't know it.

Now push or pull the student in the chair across the room again.

7. What am I doing?

> Exerting a force. Doing work.

8. What is the direction of the force?

> That way (the direction you're pushing or pulling).

9. What direction is (student's name) moving?

> That way (the same direction as the force).

10. Make a generalization about the direction of force and the direction of movement.

> Objects move in the same direction as the force exerted on them.

— Practical Application —

1. You're outside and the wind is blowing toward the east. Your hat blows off. What exerted the force?

> The wind.

2. What is the direction of the force?

> Toward the east.

3. What direction does your hat blow?

> Toward the east.

4. Why?

> Objects move in the same direction as the force on them.

5. Did the wind do any *work* on your cap?

> Yes.

6. How do we know?

> The wind exerted a force and my hat moved.

Lift up a chair, hold it, and stand motionless at the front of the room.

7. Am I exerting a force?

> Yes.

8. What is the force?

> You're pulling on the chair.

9. Am I doing any work right now?

> No.

10. How can you tell?

> The chair is not moving.

11. When did I do work on the chair?

> When you lifted it up to where it is now.

12. Do we do any work when we walk to lunch?

> Yes.

13. How do you know?

> Our feet push on the ground, which is a force, and we move.

14. Suppose you have a heavy log on the driveway by your house. One of your parents tells you to go out and push it off. You try as hard as you can, but you can't budge it. Do you do any work?

> No.

15. Why not?

> The log doesn't move. (This assumes that the person pushing is also not moving, for instance, their feet sliding as the log is being pushed. Work is being done if the feet slide or move.)

16. Are you exerting a force?

> Yes.

17. Why?

> I am pushing on the log and any push is a force.

18. Will I get tired?

> Yes.

19. Can we get tired even if we don't do any work?

> Yes.

20. How?

> Exerting a force will make us tired even if nothing moves.

ACTIVITY 7: FORCES IN A SYSTEM

Goal: To understand a *system*

To understand that when equal forces are exerted on an object from opposite directions, the object does not move, and when unbalanced forces are exerted on an object, the object does move

Skills: Observing, inferring, predicting, generalizing

Materials: A ring similar to one used to hold cafe curtains
Two pieces of string or twine

Preparation: Attach the pieces of string to the ring.

Preparation Time: 2 minutes

Lesson Time: 10–15 minutes

— Procedure and Questioning Strategy —

Have two students hold the ends of the strings with the ring between them.

1. This is an example of a SYSTEM. What are the parts of the system?

    The ring, two pieces of string, and the hands of the students holding the string.

2. Before I attached the strings to the ring, these parts did not make up a system. What is the difference between a system and something that is not a system?

    A system has parts that are connected in some way.

Ask the students holding the two ends to pull easily on the strings so the ring doesn't move.

3. Is each person pulling on a string?

    Yes.

4. How do you know that?

    If they weren't pulling on the strings, the ring would be lower than their hands.

5. What do you think is the reason the ring is not moving?

    Both students are pulling with the same amount of force.

6. What happens if an object like the ring is pulled with equal force in opposite directions?

    It doesn't move.

Ask one of the students holding an end of the string to pull the string a little harder.

7. What happened to the ring this time?

    It moved.

8. Why did the ring move?

    (Student's name) pulled harder on the string than (other student's name).

9. In which direction did the ring move?

    Toward (student's name).

10. So which person pulled with greater force?

    (Student's name).

11. Let's review. How can we identify a system?

    A system has parts that are connected in some way.

12. What causes an object to move?

    When forces that are not equal pull on an object, the object moves.

13. What have we found out about forces when there is no movement of an object?

    When the forces on an object are equal, the object does not move.

— Practical Application —

1. Think about what we just did with the strings and ring. What about the forces in a tug of war when students are pulling on the rope and the rope is not moving?

    The students on each team are pulling on the rope with the same amount of force.

2. What is happening when the rope moves in the direction of a particular team?

    That team is pulling with greater force than the other team.

3. How can the tug of war be related to what we know about a system?

    It has parts that are connected.

4. What are the parts of the system?

    The rope, the students' hands, their bodies, and the ground they're standing on.

5. How can we relate this to a school system? What related parts are in a school system?

    Teachers, students, principals, counselors, office workers, custodians, cafeteria workers, etc.

6. Can you think of other systems?

    Possible answers: computer systems with connected parts like disk drives, monitors, printers, disks; stereo systems with component parts like receivers, tape decks, compact disc players, turntables, amplifiers, speakers, equalizers.

ACTIVITY 8: EARTH PULL

Goal: **To understand that gravity is a force exerted by Earth's pull**
To understand that our weight is a measure of the force of gravity

Skills: **Observing, supporting inferences with observations, explaining**

Materials: **Bathroom scale**
Tennis ball
Ping-Pong® ball

Preparation: None

Preparation Time: None

Lesson Time: 20–30 minutes

— Procedure and Questioning Strategy —

Hold an object, such as a book, eraser, or piece of chalk, then drop it.

1. **What did you observe?**

    The (object) fell to the floor.

2. **What does that tell us about the forces on the (object)?**

    The force downward was greater than the force upward.

3. **How do we know?**

    The (object) moved downward, and objects always move in the direction of the greater force.

4. **Why did the (object) stop falling?**

    The floor stopped it.

5. **What do we observe about the (object) now?**

    It's on the floor. It's not moving.

6. **What does that tell us about the forces on the (object)?**

    They're equal.

7. **How do we know?**

    It isn't moving, and when an object doesn't move, the forces on it are equal.

8. **What forces are acting on the (object)?**

    The force that pulled it down. The floor pushing it up.

9. How do we know?

> It fell until it hit the floor, then it stopped. The floor stopped it.

10. What do we know about the force that the floor exerts and the force that pulled it down?

> They're equal.

11. How do we know?

> The (object) is not moving.

12. We call the force that pulls objects down GRAVITY. Gravity is a force that pulls objects down to Earth's surface. It's Earth's pull on objects.

13. Now think about the forces acting on all of you as you sit in your chairs. What forces are acting on you?

> Gravity is pulling us down. The chair is pushing us up. (The floor is pushing on the chair, which in turn is pushing on the students.)

14. What do you know about the forces?

> They're equal.

15. How do you know?

> We're not moving.

If the students suggest that air is also exerting a force on them, you can ask the following:

16. What do we know about the force of the air on you?

> It's equal in all directions.

17. How do we know?

> If it weren't equal, we would feel a push one way or another.

— Practical Application —

1. How can we measure the force of gravity?

> Use a scale.

Have several student volunteers weigh themselves.

2. How much did you weigh?

Get a variety of answers.

3. We used a scale to measure the force of gravity, and we used a scale to measure our weight. So what is weight?

> The force of gravity on us.

WEIGHT is the force (pull) of gravity on a person or other object.

4. What do we notice about the pull of gravity on people?

    It isn't the same for everybody.

5. What is the difference?

    It is greater for bigger people.

6. What does that tell us about the force of gravity on us?

    The pull of gravity is greater on bigger people.

If they ask why it pulls harder on bigger people, it is simply because they are bigger. The force of gravity depends on the mass of an object.

7. Now suppose you were standing on this scale on the moon. Would your weight be the same as it is here on Earth?

    No.

8. Why not?

    The moon's pull of gravity is less than the Earth's.

9. What have we seen on television that tells us that?

    When the astronauts walked on the moon, they would take a step and then sort of "fly" up into the air before coming back down.

10. So what do we know about our weight on the moon?

    It's less than here on Earth.

11. Is it *really* less, or does it just *seem* to be less?

    It's really less.

12. Why is it really less?

    The pull of gravity on the moon is really less than the pull of gravity on Earth.

13. Why do you suppose the pull of gravity on the moon is less than it is on Earth?

Accept a variety of suggestions, then show them the tennis ball and the Ping-Pong® ball.

14. Now look at the tennis ball and the Ping-Pong® ball. Let's pretend that the tennis ball is Earth and the Ping-Pong® ball is the moon. What do you notice about them?

    The tennis ball (Earth) is much bigger. (Accept a variety of other answers.)

15. So, why do you suppose the pull of gravity on Earth is greater than on the moon?

    The Earth is much bigger than the moon. It has more mass.

ACTIVITY 9: FORCES IN OTHER SYSTEMS

Goal: To understand that all of the connections between the parts of a system do not need to be actually seen for forces to act in a system

Skills: Observing, predicting, inferring, generalizing

Materials: Ping-Pong® ball or other lightweight ball
Piece of string
Tape
Scissors

Preparation: None

Preparation Time: None

Lesson Time: 10–15 minutes

— Procedure and Questioning Strategy —

Show the students the ball, the string, and the piece of tape, one object at a time.

1. If we define a system as made up of parts connected in some way, is this ball, string, or piece of tape part of a system?

    No.

2. What can we do with them to make them part of a system?

    Attach the string to the ball with the tape.

Attach the string to the ball with tape and hold up the ball by the string.

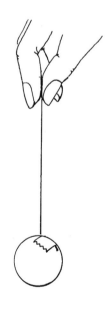

3. What are the parts of this system?

    The ball, string, tape, and hand.

4. Why doesn't the ball fall down?

    The string, the tape, and the hand are holding it up.

5. What do you predict will happen if we cut the string?

    The ball will fall.

Cut the string high up toward your hand.

6. Why did it fall?

    The string was no longer holding it up. It was no longer connected to the system.

7.   What do you think made the ball fall to the floor instead of floating up toward the ceiling or over toward the wall?

Gravity.

pull of string

8.   Now name the parts of this system.

The ball, piece of string, masking tape, hand, and gravity.

9.   Which part of this system didn't we mention when we named the parts of the system earlier?

Gravity.

10.   How do we know gravity was exerting a force in the first system?

The ball was not moving. If gravity weren't exerting a force, the ball would "float" away.

pull of gravity

Hold up the ball on the string again so the ball doesn't move.

11.   What do we know about the force of gravity and the force exerted by my hand?

They're equal.

12.   How do we know?

The ball isn't moving. When an object isn't moving, the forces on it are equal.

13.   So, do all of the parts of our system have to be visible?

No.

14.   How do we know?

Gravity is a part of our system. We can't see gravity. We can only see the effects of it.

— Practical Application —

1.   Let's think again about being out in the wind and your cap blows off. What are the parts of the system?

My head, my cap, and the wind.

2.   Why are they the parts?

They are connected in some way.

3.   How are they connected?

My cap was resting on my head and the wind blew it off.

4.   Are all of the parts of the system visible?

No.

5. Which part is not?

    The wind.

6. How do we know that it is part of the system?

    The wind is what made my cap blow off.

7. So, we can't see the wind, but we can see the effects of it?

    Yes.

8. When your cap blew off, what is the reason that it didn't stay up in the air?

    Gravity pulled it to the ground.

9. Let's review what we know about the parts of a system.

    All of them are connected, but they don't all have to be visible.

ACTIVITIES 6–9: CONNECTIONS

Goal: To find relationships among the activities for force

Skills: Comparing, classifying, explaining, applying generalizations

— Questioning Strategy —

1. Let's see if we can tie together some of the ideas about force that we have learned. What will happen if you stand in an open area, lean over too far, and don't move your feet?

    I will fall over.

2. Will you fall if you lean over and, with one hand, make contact with a wall?

    No, I won't fall over. I can hold myself up.

3. Why won't you fall over if you push on the wall?

    The wall will hold me up.

4. Which force will be greater: will you be moving the wall or will the wall be moving you?

    Neither one. The forces will be equal.

5. How do you know that?

    There is no movement. (The wall's resisting force is holding the person in place.)

6. What if, as you are playing football, the ball is being held upright on the ground by a player. The ball is not moving. What are the forces acting on the ball?

    The player's fingers are holding the ball upright. Gravity is pulling down on the ball.
    The ground is pushing up on the ball.

7. Is the ball exerting force on anything?

    Yes. The ball is resisting the force of the person's fingers.

8. How do you know that?

    If it weren't, the ball would move; it would fall over on its side.

9. Are there any other forces exerted by the ball?

    It is pushing on the ground.

10. If there is no movement, what do we know about all of the forces acting in this system?

    The forces are equal.

11. Imagine that another player runs up and kicks the football. What direction does the football go in relation to the kicker?

Away from the kicker.

12. Why did it do that?

The force exerted on the ball by the kicker's foot was in that direction.

13. Were forces acting on the ball equal as it was kicked?

No.

14. How do you know that?

The ball moved.

15. We know the kicker exerted force on the ball. Did he/she do any work?

Yes.

16. What evidence do we have that work was done?

The kicker exerted a force and the ball moved a certain distance.

17. Imagine what the path of the football would look like after it was kicked off the ground. Describe it.

It would curve up then curve down to the ground.

18. We already know that the kicker's force made the football go up. What force made it go to the ground in the curved path?

The force of gravity slowly pulled it down toward the ground.

UNIT 3—STATES OF MATTER

Background Information

Matter can exist in the form of a solid, liquid, or gas. All matter is composed of small particles. A solid has a shape of its own.

- The molecules of a **solid** are close together and can move in place, but they can't move away from other molecules.

- The molecules of a **liquid** can move more freely than the molecules in a solid. They can slide and roll over one another or flow like BBs poured from a container. A liquid doesn't have a shape of its own. It takes the shape of its container.

- The molecules in a **gas** can move more freely than the molecules in a solid or a liquid. They can move very far apart and bounce against each other, causing vibrations. A gas takes the shape of its container.

Molecules in a solid

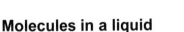

Molecules in a liquid

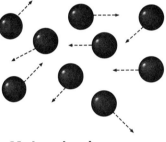

Molecules in a gas

Molecules in all three states of matter vibrate. The molecules of a solid vibrate in place. Liquids and gases are classified as fluids. Their molecules vibrate as they move.

When heat is added to a solid, liquid, or gas, the molecules vibrate faster. When heat is taken away, the vibration of molecules slows down. So, when heat is taken away from a liquid, the liquid may turn into a solid depending on how much cold is added. When an ice cube tray full of water is placed into a freezer, in a short while the water has turned into a solid, ice. Changing from one state of matter to another is called a **phase change**.

The activities in this unit demonstrate different types of phase changes. Activity 12 shows how a gas can be changed to a liquid. Students usually have difficulty with the concept outlined in the Practical Application section. When water is poured into a drinking glass and ice is added, condensation forms on the outside of the glass. When students are asked where they think the water drops on the outside of the glass come from, they usually respond, "They come from the water inside the glass." This is a misconception.

In response, you might say, "Let's see if we can figure this out. Let's wipe the water drops off the outside of the glass, then add some food coloring and more ice cubes to the water in the glass." When the condensation appears again, ask a student to wipe off the condensation to see what color it is. Then ask where they think the water is coming from.

Unit 3–NATIONAL SCIENCE EDUCATION STANDARDS

- *Unifying Concepts and Processes:* Students should develop understanding and abilities with regard tp systems, order and organization; evidence, models, and explanation; and constancy, change, and measurement.

- *Science as Inquiry*—Content Standard A: Students should develop the necessary skills to do scientific inquiry and develop an understanding about scientific inquiry.

- *Physical Science*—Content Standard B: Students should develop an understanding of the properties of objects and materials, and of properties and changes of properties in matter.

- *History and Nature of Science*—Content Standard G: Students should develop an understanding of the nature of science.

ACTIVITY 10: CHANGE OF STATE – ICE CUBE MELT

Goal: To understand that a solid can be changed to a liquid by adding heat

Skills: Observing, describing, supporting inferences with observations, identifying variables, measuring, generalizing

Materials: For each pair of students:
- 2 paper towels
- 2 to 3 ice cubes
- Hand lens (magnifying glass)
- Small plastic zip-top freezer bag
- Small vial, or other liquid measuring device, marked in milliliters

Preparation: Assemble the materials and put them in a place that is easily accessible.

Preparation Time: 5 minutes

Lesson Time: 20–25 minutes

— Procedure and Questioning Strategy —

Ask the students to form pairs. Distribute ice cubes, paper towels, and a hand lens to each pair. Have the students put their ice cubes on their paper towels.

1. Substances can take three forms or states: a solid, a liquid, or a gas. These are known as the three states of matter. Which of the states is the ice in? Is the ice a solid, a liquid, or a gas?

    A solid.

2. How do you know?

    The ice has a shape of its own.

3. Take about 5 minutes to observe your ice with the hand lens. Write as many observations as you can in the 5 minutes. Remember that an observation is something you find out by using one of your five senses. Write only observations, not inferences.

4. Let's share our observations to find out how many different ones were found.

    (Students will make a variety of observations. Among them should be: the ice feels cold; it has small cracks in its surface; it's more transparent on the sides and more white in the middle; we heard it crackle when we moved our ears close to it; it made our fingers and the paper towel wet; after a while there was liquid on the top of the ice; the ice got smaller.)

5. Some of you noticed that the ice got smaller. What do you think caused that?

The ice melted.

6. What do we mean when we say "melt"?

Something changes from a solid to a liquid.

7. What caused the ice to melt?

The air temperature in the room was warmer than the ice.

8. So we added warmth or heat to the ice and that made it begin to change from a solid to a liquid?

Yes.

Distribute plastic bags and vials, or other measuring devices, to pairs. Give these directions:

– Put your ice cubes in the plastic bag, squeeze out most of the air, then zip up the bag.
– Put the bag down and don't touch it until I say "Begin."

Wait until each pair is ready.

– We're going to see who can change their ice to a liquid the fastest.
– With your partner, decide how you're going to melt your ice.
– Since we are going to measure how much liquid you have after 5 minutes, you'll probably want to decide how to melt the ice without putting a hole in the bag.
– When I say "Begin," you will have 5 minutes to do whatever you decide to do to melt the cubes.
– You may not leave your seats.
– When I say "Stop," open your plastic bag and pour whatever liquid you have into your vial. See how many milliliters you have.
– "Begin!"

After you have said "Stop" and the students have poured the liquid from their bags into vials, let the students share how much liquid they have.

9. What are some of the methods you used to melt the ice?

Possibilities are: put the bag under an armpit; sat on the bag; blew on the bag; broke the ice into small pieces; rubbed the bag vigorously; held the bag in our hands.

10. We already learned that the addition of heat to ice caused it to melt. Tell us the reason that your method melted the ice.

Possibilities are: added body heat; added hot air; broke the ice to have more surface area to warm and melt; created friction that produced heat.

11. Summarize what we have found out about how to change a solid to a liquid.

A solid can be changed to a liquid by adding heat.

— Practical Application —

1. **What happens to an ice cube when you put it into a warm liquid?**
   It melts. It gets smaller.

2. **What is the reason for this?**
   The liquid is warmer than the ice.

3. **So is heat added or taken away from the ice?**
   Heat is added to the ice.

4. **Is heat added or taken away from the liquid?**
   It is taken away from it.

5. **How do you know?**
   The liquid gets colder.

6. **What other substances melt when you add heat?**
   Ice cream, chocolate, candle wax, etc.

7. **What happens when you put water in the freezer?**
   After a while it becomes ice, a solid.

8. **Have you added or taken away heat from the water?**
   Taken away heat.

9. **What took away the heat?**
   The cold in the freezer.

10. **What happens to the heat taken away from the food in a refrigerator or freezer?**
    It goes into the air of the refrigerator or freezer and makes the air warmer.

11. **How does the air in the refrigerator or freezer get cool again?**
    When the temperature in the refrigerator/freezer gets warm enough, the refrigerator/freezer motor starts up to cool the air.

12. **Summarize how we can change a liquid to a solid.**
    A liquid is changed to a solid by taking away heat.

■ ACTIVITY 11: CHANGE OF STATE – DISSOLVING SELTZER TABLET ■

Goal: To understand that a chemical change can cause a change in the state of matter

Skills: Predicting, observing, describing, comparing, supporting inferences with observations

Materials: 8- or 12-oz. glass soda bottle
Balloon
Water
Seltzer tablets

Preparation: Assemble the materials where all students can see them.

Preparation Time: 2 minutes

Lesson Time: 15–20 minutes

— Procedure and Questioning Strategy —

While you are setting up this activity, explain to the students what you are doing. Put about 2 inches of water into the soda bottle. Break up one seltzer tablet and put the pieces in the balloon. Carefully fit the neck of the balloon over the neck of the bottle so none of the seltzer pieces goes into the bottle. Hold up the bottle.

1. What states of matter are in this system?

   A solid (the bottle, balloon, pieces of seltzer tablet); a liquid (water); and a gas (air in the bottle and balloon).

2. What do you predict will happen when I lift the balloon up and let the seltzer tablet fall into the water?

Let the students share their predictions.

3. Let's try it. Observe carefully.

Lift the balloon so the pieces of tablet fall into the water.

4. Describe what happened.

   The pieces of seltzer tablet fell into the water.
   The water got lots of bubbles in it.
   Then the balloon stood straight up and grew larger.

Continue watching the system until the tablet pieces have dissolved.

5. Do you see any of the solid seltzer pieces now?

   No.

6. What do you think happened to them?

    They dissolved in the water.

7. What happened as the pieces of tablet dissolved?

    Air bubbles bounced around in the water and up into the air in the bottle.

8. As the tablet pieces dissolved in the water a gas was produced—carbon dioxide. What do you think caused the balloon to blow up?

    The air in the bottle, plus the gas produced, needed more space to expand.

9. What happened when the *solid* seltzer tablet reacted with the *liquid* water?

    A *gas* was produced.

Put one seltzer tablet into a cup almost filled with water. Let students feel the gas bubbles bouncing off their hands.

— Practical Application —

1. What do you predict will happen if we try the same experiment again with *two* seltzer tablets and the same amount of water?

Let the students share predictions for a few moments.

2. Let's try it.

Wash out the bottle and do the experiment again with two tablets.

3. Compare the size of this balloon with the size of the balloon in the last experiment.

    (The balloon should blow up bigger and faster.)

4. What other changes in the experiment can we try to see whether they will have an effect on the size of the balloon?

    Students may suggest a different-sized bottle, more seltzer tablets, a change in the amount of water, or using hot water or ice water.

Try changing as many of these variables as time permits, comparing results after each experiment. Discuss which variables made a difference in the results of the experiments.

▬ ACTIVITY 12: CONDENSATION – CHANGING GASES TO LIQUIDS ▬

Goal: To understand that a gas can be changed to a liquid by lowering the temperature of the gas

Skills: Observing, describing, comparing, explaining

Materials: Heat source (e.g., a portable electric burner or an electric coffeemaker)
Saucepan (two pans if you use an electric burner; one pan if you use a coffeemaker)
Water
Ice
Pot holder or oven mitt
Drinking glass

Preparation: 1. Partially fill a saucepan with water and heat it on the electric burner until it boils, or brew a partial pot of hot water with the coffeemaker.
2. Put ice in another saucepan.

Preparation Time: 3 minutes

Lesson Time: 15–20 minutes

— Procedure and Questioning Strategy —

1. Observe what happens when I hold this saucepan with ice in it over the boiling water.

Use the pot holder or mitt to hold the saucepan containing ice several inches above the boiling water. Be careful of hot steam!

2. What do you see happening?

   Steam is rising from the boiling water. Drops of water are collecting on the bottom of the saucepan that has ice in it. The drops of water are falling back into the boiling water.

3. What is making the steam?

   The boiling water is moving so rapidly that some of the water is evaporating into the air.

4. Compare the temperature of the air under the saucepan I'm holding to the temperature of the saucepan itself.

   The air under the saucepan is much warmer than the saucepan. The saucepan has ice in it that is making it cold.

Explain to students that steam or vapor is moisture in the air.

5. What do you think happens to the hot steam, or vapor, rising above the boiling water when it hits the cold saucepan?

   It gets colder.

6. What happens to the steam when it gets colder?

   It changes into drops of water.

7. This is called CONDENSATION. When the gas (air) becomes cold as it hits the saucepan, the vapor (moisture in the air) condenses or forms drops.

CONDENSATION occurs when a gas is changed to a liquid by lowering the temperature of the gas.

8. What happened when the drops of water on the saucepan got larger?

   They fell into the boiling water.

9. How is this like rain in the water cycle?

   The sun evaporates some of the water on the earth. The warm water vapor in the air rises until it reaches a place in the atmosphere cold enough to make it condense in clouds. When the water drops in the clouds become large and heavy enough, they fall as raindrops.

— Practical Application —

Put water in the drinking glass and add ice. Have a student hold the glass.

1. Describe how the glass feels.

   It's cold. It's getting wet on the outside of the glass.

2. Where do you think the water on the outside of the glass is coming from?

   (A common misconception is that the liquid in a glass comes through the glass.)

3. Compare the temperature of the glass with the temperature of the air in the room.

   The glass is much colder than the air in the room.

4. What have we learned happens when warm air hits something cold?

   The vapor or moisture in the air condenses (forms drops on the cold surface).

5. So where are the water drops on the outside of the glass coming from?

   They are coming from the moisture in the air.

6. What is the reason we sometimes see condensation on windows in the wintertime?

   There is warm air on the inside of the window and cold air on the outside. The moisture in the warm air condenses on the window.

7. What would cause condensation to appear on windows in the summertime?

Air conditioning that makes the air inside a lot colder than the hot summer air outside.

8. Fog is condensation in the air. What do you think causes fog?

When warm, moist air moves over colder land, the moisture in the air condenses to make fog.

9. What do you think would need to happen for fog to form if the land were warm and moist?

Colder air would have to move over the warmer, moist land.

10. Let's summarize what we know about condensation.

When something cool meets something warm and moist, the moisture in the air condenses.

ACTIVITY 13: MAKING A GAS

Goal: To observe that a gas can be made from a solid and a liquid
To understand that carbon dioxide can put out a flame

Skills: Observing, classifying, comparing, describing, explaining

Materials: Medium-sized jar
Baking soda
White vinegar
Measuring spoons or tablespoon
Matches
Piece of cardboard (e.g., from a shirt package or the back of a paper tablet)
Candle 1" to 2" tall (so you don't have to hold the trough up high)
Aluminum pie tin

Preparation: None

Preparation Time: None

Lesson Time: 10–15 minutes

— Procedure and Questioning Strategy —

Hold up the baking soda.

1. **How would you describe the state of matter of baking soda?**

    It's a solid in the form of powder.

2. **How do you know it's a solid?**

    It's not a liquid or a gas. It's little pieces, or particles, of a larger solid.

3. **How do you make a powder?**

    By crushing or grinding a larger solid until pieces of it become small enough to make a powder.

Hold up the white vinegar.

4. **In what state of matter is the vinegar?**

    It's a liquid.

Explain to the students what you are doing. Put about 6 tablespoons of vinegar in the jar. Add about 2 tablespoons of baking soda.

5. **What did you observe?**

    When the baking soda fell into the vinegar, the liquid turned cloudy and fizzed.

6. I am going to hold a lighted match over the jar. What do you think will happen?

Light the match and hold it in the middle of the jar opening.

7. What happened?

> The flame went out.

8. What does a flame need to burn?

> Oxygen.

9. Was there oxygen at the mouth of the jar where I was holding the match?

> No.

10. How do you know?

> The flame went out.

11. The gas that was made when the baking soda and vinegar mixed was carbon dioxide. What have we found out about carbon dioxide?

> It stops a flame from burning.

— Practical Application —

Rinse out the jar to make another jarful of carbon dioxide. Fold the cardboard lengthwise. Light the candle, let wax drip in the center of the pie tin, and set the lighted candle in the melted wax.

1. Let's make some more carbon dioxide and try something else.

Make the carbon dioxide; then hold the folded cardboard like an inclined trough from the jar to the candle. <u>Do not hold the cardboard too close to the candle</u>. Pour the carbon dioxide gas, not the liquid, down the trough.

2. What happened?

> The carbon dioxide put out the flame.

3. What does this tell us about the weight of carbon dioxide?

> It is heavier than the air in the room.

4. How do you know that?

> It went down the trough. If it weren't heavier than the air in the room, it would have gone out or up into the air, not down the trough.

5. What do you think it did to the air around the candle that was keeping the flame burning?

> It pushed it out of the way.

6. How did it put out the flame?

> When the carbon dioxide pushed the air around the flame out of the way, the flame couldn't get any more oxygen from the air, so it went out.

ACTIVITIES 10–13: CONNECTIONS

Goal: To find relationships among the activities involving states of matter

Skills: Describing, comparing, reasoning, applying generalizations, predicting, confirming predictions with observations

— Questioning Strategy —

1. What do you predict will happen if we leave a glass with ice cubes in it on the table in this room for a few minutes?

    Condensation will form on the outside of the glass.

2. Why will that happen?

    The ice will make the glass cold; then the moisture in the warm air in the room will condense on the outside of the cold glass.

3. Yes, the moisture in the warm air will condense on the cold glass. How will the ice make the glass cold: by adding heat to or taking heat away from the glass?

    It will take heat away from the glass.

4. What will happen if we leave the glass with the ice cubes in it on the table for about two hours?

    The ice cubes will get smaller and smaller.
    The ice cubes will melt.

5. Is ice a solid or a liquid?

    A solid.

6. What state of matter will it become after two hours?

    A liquid.

7. At the end of the two hours, how do you think the temperature of the water in the glass and the temperature of the air in the room will compare?

    The water will probably be cooler than the air in the room.

8. How will the water temperature compare with the temperature of the original ice cubes?

    The water will be warmer.

9. Then will heat have been added to or taken away from the ice?

    Added.

10. What will have added the heat?

    The warmer air in the room.

11. So, heat will be added to the water. When will the heat stop being added?

When the water becomes the same temperature as the room.

12. What do you think would happen to the temperature of the water in the glass if we left it on the table overnight?

It would be the same as the air in the room.

TRY IT! Use the thermometer to measure the temperature of the water. The activity can easily be extended by measuring the temperature of the water every 30 minutes and graphing the temperatures.

13. What was similar about the activity we did with the seltzer tablet and water and the activity with the vinegar and baking soda?

Both produced a gas (carbon dioxide).

In both activities, a solid and a liquid were combined to make a gas.

UNIT 4—MASS, VOLUME, AND DENSITY

Background Information

Density is the compactness of the material that makes up an object. It is the relationship between an object's **mass** and its **volume**. Many steps need to be taken in order for students to understand this relationship.

First, students need to be able to work with hands-on materials as they are guided to come up with the characteristics of weight and mass. After this, they can compare these characteristics and describe the difference between weight and mass.

The next step is to build the concept of volume, again with hands-on materials, until students can come up with a description of the characteristics of volume. These characteristics can be compared with the characteristics of mass. Then the relationship between mass and volume can be developed. The characteristics of weight, mass, volume, and density are described in the following paragraphs.

When you weigh yourself on a bathroom scale (a spring scale), you are measuring the amount of gravitational pull on your body, measured in pounds of force. **Weight** is generally defined as the measure of force (pull) of gravity on the mass of a person or object. The pull of gravity is measured on a spring scale. The units of measure generally used to measure the pull of gravity are ounces and pounds or grams and kilograms. See the examples of spring scales illustrated in figure A.

figure A

Mass is the amount of matter, or material, that is in an object. Children may find the concept of mass easier to understand if it's defined as the amount of "stuff" in an object. If the box illustrated below (figure B) contained cotton balls, the mass would be the amount of material in the box, the cotton balls, and the air that takes up the rest of the space in the box.

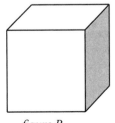

figure B

Mass is measured on a balance (figure C), a scale that balances the mass of an object with standard units of measure like grams, ounces, or pounds. One such balance is shown in figure C. The objects to be measured are on the tray on the left side; on the tray at the right are gram masses which are added one at a time until both trays balance.

figure C

Another example of a balance is found in most doctors' offices. When you go to the doctor and step on the scale, it is generally thought that weight is being measured. Is this really true? Let's think about it. As you're standing on the scale, the nurse moves brass masses until the scale balances your body with the masses. It is your mass that is actually measured rather than your weight. Everything that is included in your body is being balanced with standard units of measure, masses.

The mass of an object doesn't change unless matter is added to it or taken away from it. In comparison, weight can change depending on where it is measured. The farther an object moves from the center of the earth, the less it weighs. When the space shuttle is orbiting Earth, it has less gravitational pull on it and would weigh less than it would if it were on the surface of Earth. Its mass would be the same as it would be on Earth because it still has the same amount of material in it.

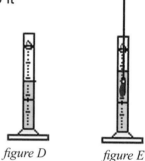

figure D   *figure E*

Now let's think about **volume**. Volume is a measure of the amount of space an object occupies. For example, if you have a regular shaped object, like a box full of cotton balls, its volume can be found by measuring its length, width and height, then multiplying the length x width x height of the box. The result would be in cubic units; for example, cubic inches, cubic feet, cubic centimeters, or cubic meters. If the box of cotton balls measured 10 cm x 10 cm x 10 cm, its volume would be 1,000 cubic centimeters which would represent the amount of space it takes up.

If an object is an unusual shape (e.g., a fishing sinker), its volume can be measured by liquid displacement. A graduated cylinder (figure D) marked with milliliters (ml) can be used for this purpose. A certain amount of water could be poured into the cylinder, maybe 50 ml, then the sinker could be lowered into the cylinder so it is below the surface of the water (figure E). The amount of milliliters that the water rises would be the amount of volume, the amount of space, that the sinker takes up. So if the water rises from the 50 ml mark to the 70 ml mark, the sinker would have a volume of 20 ml. This translates to 20 cubic centimeters because 1 ml of displaced liquid is equal to 1 cubic centimeter.

Now that we have the volume of the sinker, we could measure its mass by placing it on a balance scale and adding gram masses until the scale balances. If the sinker's mass measured 60 grams, we could figure out its **density**, the amount of mass in each cubic centimeter. The mass of the sinker, 60 grams, divided by the volume, 20 cm^3, would give the sinker a density of 3 grams in each cubic centimeter of the sinker.

Density can be thought of as the compactness of an object. If you were to hold the box of cotton balls in one hand and a sinker in the other, which do you think would be made up of material that is more compact? We can figure out the average density of the box of cotton balls so that we can compare its density with that of the sinker. When we measured the volume of the box of cotton balls, it was 1,000 cubic centimeters. Let's say that the mass of the box of cotton balls is actually 75 grams when measured on a balance. So its mass, 75 grams, divided by its volume of 1,000 cm^3, would give us a density of .075 grams per cubic centimeter. When you compare the mass of one cm^3 of sinker, 3 grams, with the mass of one cm^3 of the cotton ball box, .075 grams, you know that the sinker has much more mass compressed into one cm^3 than does the box of cotton balls. When we find out how much mass is in each cubic unit of an object, we can compare one object with another object to find out which one is more dense.

A chart that displays the characteristics of weight, mass, volume, and density is shown on the next page and can be used as a teacher reference.

Unit 4–NATIONAL SCIENCE EDUCATION STANDARDS

- *Unifying Concepts and Processes:* Students should develop understanding and abilities with regard to systems, order and organization; evidence, models, and explanation; constancy, change, and measurement; and form and function.

- *Science as Inquiry*—Content Standard A: Students should develop the necessary skills to do scientific inquiry and develop an understanding about scientific inquiry.

- *Physical Science*—Content Standard B: Students should develop an understanding of the properties of objects and materials, and properties and changes of properties in matter.

- *History and Nature of Science*—Content Standard G: Students should develop an understanding of the nature of science and of science as a human endeavor.

	WEIGHT	MASS	VOLUME	DENSITY
What does it measure?	A measure of the amount of gravitational pull on the mass of an object	A measure of the amount of matter (material or stuff) in an object	A measure of the amount of space that an object takes up	A measure of the amount of mass in a certain amount of volume
How is it measured?	On a spring scale	On a balance (scale) In units of mass (ounces or pounds, or grams and kilograms)	Length X width X height or by water displacement (1 ml = 1 cm^3) In cubic units like cubic inches or cubic centimeters (cm^3)	Density = mass divided by volume, $D = \dfrac{M}{V}$ The amount of pounds in a cubic inch, or grams in a cubic centimeter
Is it a consistent measure?	No, weight changes depending on where it's measured, on Earth, out in space, etc.	Yes. The mass of an object does not change wherever it's measured because an object is measured against a standard unit of measure (masses) like pounds or grams. The gravitational pull on both sides of the balance is always the same, and the standard mass measured against remains the same.	Yes. The volume, the amount of space an object takes up, does not change wherever it is measured.	Yes. The mass or volume of an object does not vary, so the density remains constant wherever it is measured.

ACTIVITY 14: POPULATION DENSITY

Goal: To understand that population density is the number of people in a given area; that population density increases as more people are added to an area and decreases as people move out of an area

Skills: Observing, classifying, inferring, generalizing

Materials: Piece of chalk

Preparation: Draw a large circle, about 6 feet in diameter, on the floor.

Preparation Time: 1 minute

Lesson Time: 15–20 minutes

— Procedure and Questioning Strategy —

1. What shape did I draw on the floor?

    A circle.

2. The edge, or boundary, of the circle outlines the area the circle takes up. What is the boundary of the circle?

    The mark made by the chalk.

Ask five students to stand in the circle spaced well apart.

3. How many people are in the circle?

    Five.

4. If we define population as the number of people in a certain area, what is the population of the circle?

    Five.

5. What will happen to the population of the circle if we add five more people?

    The population will get larger.

Ask five more students to join those already in the circle.

6. What happens when you add more people to the same size area?

    The area gets more crowded.

7. The number of people in a certain area is called POPULATION DENSITY. When was the population density of the circle greatest?

    When there were ten people in it.

Ask the students in the circle to return to their seats.

8. What is the population of our classroom?

    (The total number of students plus the teacher.)

9. What are the boundaries of our classroom?

    The walls with doors and windows.

10. If seven people leave the room, will our room be more or less crowded?

    Less crowded.

11. What will happen to the population density of our room if seven people leave the room?

    It will be less.

12. Why will it be less?

    There will be less people in the same area.

13. How would you define population density?

    It is the number of people in a particular area.

— Practical Application —

1. We can define a town by the amount of area the town takes up. How do you know when you are driving into a certain town?

    There is usually a sign on the road that tells the name of the town.

2. What does the placement of the sign tell us?

    Where the town begins.

3. Can this be thought of as a boundary of the town?

    Yes.

4. How can you tell the area that a town takes up?

    It is the space that is inside the town's boundaries.

5. What do we mean when we say that the population of a particular town is 125,000?

    There are 125,000 people in that town.

6. If another 1,000 people move into that town, what will happen to its population density?

    It will be greater.

7. Why will it become greater?

    There will be more people in the same area. It will be more crowded.

ACTIVITY 15: SQUASHED COTTON

Goal: To understand the concepts of mass, volume, and density

Skills: Observing, inferring, comparing

Materials: Two transparent drinking cups
               Bag of cotton balls
               Fresh bread

Preparation: With a marking pen, write "1" on the first cup and "2" on the second cup.

Preparation Time: 2 minutes

Lesson Time: 20–30 minutes

— Procedure and Questioning Strategy —

Put the numbered drinking cups and bag of cotton balls on a table where all students can see them. Hold up two cotton balls for closer student observation.

1. I have a cotton ball in each hand. What do you notice about them?

    They're soft, white, light. They can be squashed (compressed).

2. How does the amount of cotton in each compare?

    It looks like it is the same.

3. We call the amount of material in an object its *mass*. So how does the mass of the two cotton balls compare?

    It's the same.

4. We're going to put the same number of cotton balls into each of the cups.

Have two students come up to the table. Ask them to count out loud as they put cotton balls into both cups until they are "full" (i.e., they have the same number of cotton balls in each cup.)

5. What do we know about the mass of the cotton in each cup?

    It's the same.

Press the cotton down in the first cup so it is compact.

6. How does the mass of the cotton in the two cups compare?

    It's the same.

7. How do we know?

> We still have the same number of cotton balls. We've just squashed them down in the first cup. We've made them more compact.

8. When we make something more compact, we say that it is more DENSE. How do the densities of the cotton in the two cups compare?

> The density of the cotton in cup 1 is greater.

9. Why is it greater?

> It is more compact.

10. What else is different about the cotton in the two cups?

> The cotton in cup 1 takes up less space than the cotton in cup 2 (it has less area).

11. The amount of space a substance takes up is called its VOLUME. Compare two cups of cotton. Is there a difference in volume?

> The volume in the second cup is greater.

12. Why is it greater?

> It takes up more space.

13. Who can describe the density in terms of mass and volume?

> When two substances have the same mass, but one has less volume, then it is more dense.

— Practical Application —

Fluff up the cotton balls that had been squashed down in cup 1 so both cups appear to have the same volume of cotton.

1. Now let's look at the cups again. Is there a difference in volume?

> They're the same. (The cups are full.)

Put several more cotton balls into the first cup. Squash them down in the cup so both cups look full again.

2. Now, how does the volume of the cotton in the cups compare?

> They're the same.

3. Which one is more dense?

> The first one.

4. How do we know?

> We can see that the cotton is more compact.

5. How does the mass of the cotton in the two cups compare?

    There is more mass in the first cup.

6. Now describe the density again in terms of the mass and the volume (the amount of space taken up).

    When two substances take up the same space, but the mass of one is greater, then it is more dense.

Give each student a half slice of fresh bread. Have them squash it with their hand.

7. How does the density of the bread compare now to before you squashed it?

    It is more dense.

8. Explain why it is more dense.

    The mass is the same, but the volume is less, so it is more dense.

9. Now imagine that someone at home takes some cream and whips it. Which is more dense, the regular cream or the whipped cream?

    The regular cream.

10. How do you know?

    The amount (mass) of cream is the same but the whipped cream now has a larger volume, so the whipped cream is less dense.

ACTIVITY 16: THE DENSITY OF OIL AND WATER

Goal: To apply the concept of density
To understand the principle that less dense substances float on more dense substances

Skills: Observing, comparing, inferring, predicting

Materials: **Balance**
Two small, transparent vials of equal volume
Cooking oil
Water

Preparation: None

Preparation Time: None

Lesson Time: 15–20 minutes

— Procedure and Questioning Strategy —

Hold up the two vials for the students to see.

1. What do you notice about the containers?

> They are the same size. They hold the same amount. They have the same mass.

2. How can we see if they really have the same mass?

> We can put them on the balance.

Put the vials on the balance to confirm that their masses are the same.

3. Are the masses the same?

> Yes.

4. How do we know?

> Both sides of the scale are balanced.

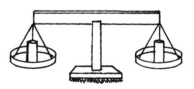

Take the vials off the balance and fill one vial with water and the other with oil.

5. Which side of the balance will go down now?

> (Many students predict that the oil side will go down.)

Put the vials on the balance.

6. What did we see here?

> The water side went down.

7. What does that tell us?

    The water has more mass than the oil.

8. But what do we know about the volumes of the water and the oil?

    The volumes are the same.

9. What does that tell us about the density of water compared to oil?

    Water is more dense than oil.

10. Why do you suppose so many of us predicted that the oil side would go down?

    (Many students will intuitively respond that oil is thicker than water and should be more dense.)

This is a good time to remind students how important it is to rely on observation rather than intuition in studying science. You may choose to make a statement like the following: "This is a good reminder for us. When we study science and develop our thinking, we must rely on our observations and not on our feelings."

11. Now I'm going to pour the water into the container with the oil. What do you think will happen?

    (Some students predict the oil will float on the water; others that the water will float on the oil. Some may suggest that they will mix.)

12. What did you observe?

    The water sank to the bottom and the oil is floating on it.

13. Why do you think the water sank to the bottom?

    The water is more dense than the oil.

14. Let's try to make a generalization that relates density to flotation.

    Less dense substances float on more dense substances.

— Practical Application —

1. We have heard about oil spills and we see people trying to scoop the oil off the water. Why is the oil on top of the water?

    It is less dense than the water.

2. What do you think would happen if heavy globs of crude oil were spilled on the water?

    They would be more dense than water, they would sink to the bottom, and we wouldn't be able to clean them up.

ACTIVITY 17: WAVE MACHINES

Goal: To apply the concept that less dense liquids float on liquids that have greater density

Skills: Observing, comparing, classifying, inferring, generalizing, hypothesizing

Materials: Transparent glass or plastic bottle, 16 oz. or smaller, with tightly fitting cap
Mineral oil
Water
A few drops of blue food coloring
White glue
Bottle of Italian salad dressing that separates

Preparation: 1. Pour water into the bottle until it is about half full.
2. Add mineral oil until the bottle is filled to about one inch below the top of the bottle. (The bottle should have equal amounts of water and mineral oil. BE SURE TO LEAVE ABOUT AN INCH OF SPACE AT THE TOP OF THE BOTTLE TO GIVE EXPANSION ROOM FOR LIQUID.
3. Add a few drops of blue food coloring.
4. Spread glue on the inner sides of the cap.
5. Screw on the cap tightly.

Preparation Time: 4 minutes

Lesson Time: 10–15 minutes

— Procedure and Questioning Strategy —

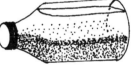

Hold the bottle horizontally so all students can see it.

1. What do you observe about the liquid in this bottle?

The liquid on the bottom is blue and the liquid on the top is almost clear.

2. Which liquid do you think is more dense?

The blue liquid on the bottom.

3. What reason can you give us for that?

Less dense liquids float on liquids of greater density.

4. There are three liquids in the bottle: mineral oil, water, and food coloring. Which liquid do you think is floating on the top?

The mineral oil.

5. What is your reason?

The mineral oil is less dense than water.

6. If the mineral oil is on the top, then the food coloring must have mixed with the water.

What does this tell us about the densities of water and food coloring?

> They are more dense than oil.

7. How do you know that?

> If they weren't more dense, they would both be floating on top of the oil.

Still holding the bottle horizontally, gently raise one end of the bottle, lowering the other end, then raise the other end, moving the ends of the bottle up and down like a seesaw.

8. What do you notice about the liquid in the bottle?

> The blue liquid looks like ocean waves. It's like a wave machine.

Give all students a chance to see the "waves."

9. What do you predict will happen if we shake the bottle?

> The liquids will mix up.

Try it.

10. What do you predict will happen if we set the bottle on the table for a few minutes?

> The liquids will separate with the mineral oil on top.

Try it and discuss the results.

— Practical Application —

Show the bottle of Italian salad dressing to the students.

1. What happens when you shake up Italian salad dressing?

> The liquids in the dressing mix together.

2. What happens when you set the dressing on the table for a few minutes?

> The liquids separate.

3. How many different liquids appear to be in the dressing?

> Two.

4. Oil, vinegar, and water are usually used to make Italian dressing. Which liquid do you think floats on top?

> The oil.

5. Then which liquids are on the bottom?

> The vinegar and water.

6. What do you know about vinegar and water?

> They are more dense than oil.

ACTIVITY 18: COLORFUL LAYERED LIQUIDS

Goal: To apply the concept of density to different liquids

Skills: Observing, comparing, classifying, predicting, inferring, generalizing

Materials: 4 small transparent vials or bottles with lids, such as small
prescription bottles or something similar in size
4 liquids of different densities, enough of each liquid to almost fill a vial: clear
corn syrup, water, salad or cooking oil, liquid glycerine (found in drug stores)
Tall, skinny bottle or graduated cylinder
Food coloring: red, green, and blue

Preparation: Prepare this lesson where the students cannot see what is put into each vial.
1. Fill each vial, leaving a small amount of space at the top, as follows:
first vial – water with a few drops of green food coloring
second vial – salad or cooking oil
third vial – clear corn syrup with blue food coloring
fourth vial – liquid glycerine with red food coloring
2. Put a cap on each vial.
3. Shake each vial until the food coloring mixes well with the liquid.

Preparation Time: 5 minutes

Lesson Time: 15–20 minutes

— Procedure and Questioning Strategy —

Pass the four vials around so students can observe the action of each liquid. Have them turn each vial upside down and watch the air bubble in the vial move to the other end of the vial.

1. Which of these liquids do you think is the most dense?

    The blue one.

2. Why does that liquid appear to be the most dense?

    The bubble of air in the bottle travels the slowest.

3. Of the other three liquids, which liquid seems to be the most dense?

    Answers vary.

Continue questioning until students decide on an order of the liquids, from least dense to most dense. Write their lists of predictions on the board. For example:

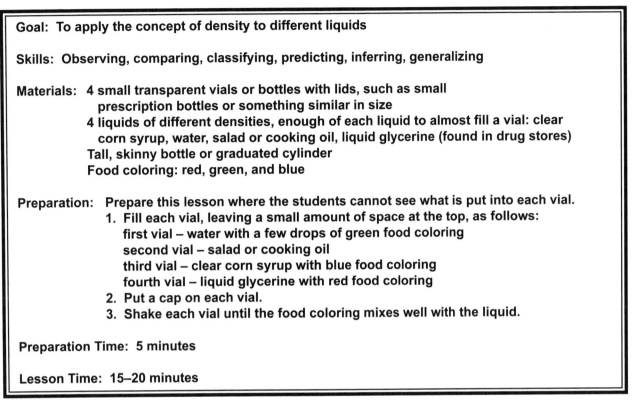

Green	Clear	Clear	LEAST DENSE
Clear	Green	Green	
Red	Blue	Red	
Blue	Red	Blue	MOST DENSE

4. How could we test our lists of predictions?

    Pour them into a container to see which liquids float on other liquids.

Choose one list of predictions to test first. First, pour the liquid predicted to be the **least** dense into the bottle or cylinder. Continue pouring liquids, from predicted least dense to most dense. Pour the second, third, and fourth liquids down the side of the bottle or cylinder. Liquids will layer with the most dense on the bottom and the least dense on the top. The result is a colorful layering of liquids.

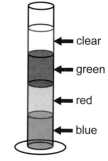

5. Which list of predictions was the most accurate?

    The third list shown above.

6. The blue liquid is colored corn syrup; the red is colored liquid glycerine; the green is colored water. What do you think the least dense liquid is?

    It could be oil.

7. What is your reason for that?

    We have found that oil floats on water.

8. Yes, you're right. It is oil.

ACTIVITY 19: FLOATING AND SINKING – ICE, ALCOHOL, AND WATER

Goal: **To form conclusions by isolating variables**
To apply the principle that less dense substances float on more dense substances

Skills: **Observing, inferring, predicting**

Materials: **Two transparent drinking cups**
Rubbing alcohol
Tray of ice cubes
Water

Preparation: **Out of students' view, fill one of the cups about 2/3 full of water and fill the second cup with the same amount of alcohol.**

Preparation Time: 2 minutes

Lesson Time: 15–20 minutes

— Procedure and Questioning Strategy —

1. Look at the two cups on the table. What do you see here?
   (Students usually say two cups of water.)

Hold up an ice cube.

2. I am going to put this ice cube in the cup. What do you think will happen?
   The water level will go up. The ice will melt. The water will get cold. The ice will float.

Put the ice cube in the water.

3. What did you observe?
   The water level went up. The ice floats. The ice is melting.

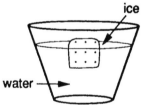

4. Now I am going to try it again with the other cup. What will happen this time?
   (Predictions are usually similar.)

Put the ice in the cup of rubbing alcohol.

5. What did you observe this time?
   The ice sank to the bottom.

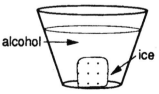

6. What possible conclusions can we make from these observations?

    The two cubes of ice are different. The two liquids are different.

7. How can we check the first conclusion (that the two cubes of ice are different)?

    We can switch the ice cubes in the cups, and if the cubes do what they just did, we know it isn't the ice. (Students may suggest other tests, such as taking additional cubes from the tray and trying them.)

Switch the ice cubes from one cup to the other.

8. What happened?

    The ice still floated in the first cup and sank in the second.

9. What does that indicate to us?

    It isn't the ice.

10. What must we conclude then?

    The liquids must not be the same.

11. How could we test that?

    We could smell them. We could feel them for thickness and texture.
    We could taste them. (Caution the students about tasting unknown substances.)

12. Go ahead and smell them, but it's a good idea to take a small sniff first to make sure that what you are smelling doesn't burn your nose. How do they smell?

    The second one smells strong (the smell of rubbing alcohol).

Identify the liquid as rubbing alcohol.

13. Now what do we know about alcohol and water?

    Ice floats on water but sinks in alcohol.

— Practical Application —

1. Let's compare the density of ice, alcohol, and water.

    Ice is less dense than water, but it is more dense than alcohol.

2. How do we know?

    The ice floated on the water but sank in the alcohol.

3. What do we know about the density of water compared to alcohol?

    Water is more dense than alcohol.

ACTIVITIES 14–19: CONNECTIONS

Goal: To find relationships between the activities for mass, volume, and density

Skills: Observing, gathering data, comparing, classifying, predicting, supporting inferences with observation, explaining, generalizing

(Additional activities are included here for mass, volume, and density since they seem to be difficult concepts for students. It is suggested that you do as many as time permits.)

Materials: Small box or plastic container with lid
Cotton balls
Large container for water (transparent if possible)
Water
Objects to test for sinking and floating. For instance:
    metal jar lid with holes poked in top
    metal nut or bolt
    plastic spoon
    popsicle stick
    Ping-Pong® ball
    piece of tree bark
    paper clip
    rubber band
    pencil
Beach or builder's sand
Small container for sand
Large nut, bolt, or other small, heavy object
Ping-Pong® ball

— Procedure and Questioning Strategy —

1. Let's review what we've learned from our last activities. What is mass?

    The amount of material in something.

Put cotton balls in the box or plastic container until it is full.

2. What makes up the mass inside the box?

    The cotton balls.

3. What will happen to the mass if we add more cotton balls?

    There will be more mass.

Add more cotton balls to the box.

4. What happened to the volume of the box?

    It stayed the same.

5. How do you know?

    It still takes up the same amount of space inside it.

6. What happened to the density of the cotton balls?

    It became more dense.

7. Tell us why you think that.

    There was more material in the same amount of space.

8. Compare population density with the density of cotton balls in the box.

    When more people are added to a certain area, or space, the population density increases just like when you add more cotton balls to the box.

Put about 6–8 inches of water in the large container. Put it where all of the students can see it. Distribute, among the students, the objects you have gathered for sinking and floating. Ask each student who has an object to describe it, compare its density with the density of water, predict whether it will sink or float, then test it in the container of water. Have students try putting their objects in the water in different ways—horizontally, vertically, upside down, right side up—to see if the way they put them in makes a difference.

9. Some of the objects we tested did sink or float as predicted; some didn't. Why do you think that some of the objects you thought seemed more dense than water (like the metal jar lid) floated?

    The jar lid floats because the water does not come up through the holes in the lid, and because the metal in the lid is spread out over a rather large area.

10. What was inside the jar lid when it was upside down or right side up?

    Air.

11. Since air was part of the system that was floating, what did that do to the density of the jar lid?

    It made it less dense.

12. Think about the metal nut (or bolt) that sank. Compare that with the metal jar lid that floated. What other reason can you think of that helped the metal jar lid float?

    The metal in the jar lid, or mass of the lid, was more thinly spread out over a larger area than the metal in the nut.
    The nut (or bolt) did not have a place to hold air like the jar lid.

13. Many huge ships are made of metal. Compare the density of the metal in the ship with the density of water. Which do you think is more dense?

    The metal in the ship.

14. So, how do these ships float?

> They have lots of air in them, so the whole system—the ship and the air inside it—is less dense than water.

15. What happens when more cargo or people are added to the ship?

> The ship floats lower in the water.

16. What does that tell us about its density?

> It gets more dense as cargo or people are added.

17. Does the ship's mass and volume change?

> The ship's volume doesn't change, but there is more mass.

Fill the smaller container about 2/3 full of beach or builder's sand. Hand the large nut or bolt and the Ping-Pong® ball to one of the students.

18. Tell us the differences between these two objects.

> The nut (or bolt) is smaller than the ball.
> The nut is heavier than the ball.
> The ball has air enclosed in it.

19. If I put the Ping-Pong® ball under the sand and the nut (or bolt) on top of the sand and shake the container back and forth, what do you think will happen?

Ask a few of the students for predictions and reasons, then try it. Move the container back and forth horizontally many times.

20. What happened?

> The Ping-Pong® ball rose to the surface of the sand.
> The nut (or bolt) sank under the surface.

21. How can we explain that?

> The Ping-Pong® ball has air inside and is less dense than the sand, so it came up and floated on top of the sand.
> The nut (or bolt) is much more dense than the sand, so it sank in the sand.

22. Car tires are very difficult to dispose of. They aren't burned because of the pollution it would cause. Sometimes tires have been buried in the ground, but they soon end up on the surface of the ground. Why do you think that happens?

> Tires have air in them. When the air is counted as part of the tires, they are less dense than soil, so they rise to the surface of the ground.

UNIT 5—AIR PRESSURE AND THE PRESSURE OF THE ATMOSPHERE

Background Information

Air is made up of gas molecules which, having no forces to hold them together, flow freely to occupy space. As air molecules flow freely, they collide with each other and with objects in their paths. There is more space between molecules of air than there is between molecules of a liquid or a solid, so air can be compressed, either by pushing the molecules closer together or by adding more air.

Let's think about what happens as you add air to your car tires. Visualize molecules of air as tiny Ping-Pong® balls that are in constant motion, continually bouncing off each other and the inner sides of the tire. As the molecules collide and bounce off the inner surface of the tire, they exert a pushing force. The amount of pushing force on one square unit of area is called **pressure**. The number of pounds of force exerted on each square on the inner sides of the tire is called **psi, pounds of pressure per square inch**. As you inflate your tire, you add more molecules of air. As more molecules are added, the air inside the tire becomes more compressed and more dense. The compressed molecules of air collide more often with each other and the inside of the tire wall. As a result, the air pressure gauge shows an increase in pressure. If car tires hold 30 pounds per square inch of air, there is 30 pounds of force exerted on every square inch of the inner surface of the tire.

A common misconception is that air can "suck." Let's illustrate what happens with an eyedropper like the one in figure A. It has air in it.

figure A

figure B

figure C

When the eyedropper is placed into water and the bulb is squeezed (figure B) and then let go, the water rises in the eyedropper. Why does the water rise in the dropper if it's not sucked up? The air in the dropper has less pressure than the water, so water is *pushed* up into the dropper, compressing the air in the top part of the dropper as it rises (figure C).

This concept is demonstrated in Activity 24. When the candle flame burns inside the bottle, it depletes the oxygen in the air, lowering the air pressure (and the density of the air molecules) inside the bottle. The higher pressure exerted by the water causes the water to rise in the bottle. So the greater air pressure exerted on the water pushes the water up into the bottle.

Let's think about what happens when you use a suction cup. When a suction cup is pushed up against a smooth surface like a window, most of the air inside the cup is pushed out. This leaves a low pressure area inside the cup. The pressure of the air that is exerted on the outside of the cup is then higher than the pressure inside the cup, so the suction cup is held against the window. If air is allowed to get into the suction cup, the air inside and outside the cup equalizes and the suction cup drops off the window. The same principle applies when you use a plunger.

The density of the earth's atmosphere varies with altitude. Visualize a huge pile of cotton balls. The cotton balls at the bottom of the pile would be more compressed and would have greater density than the cotton balls closer to the top of the pile. Molecules of air are similar; they are denser in the layers of air closer to the earth and then thin out as their altitude increases. Eventually, the atmosphere thins out so there are very few molecules of air in outer space.

If you stood on the earth at sea level, you would feel more pressure from the air than you would if you stood on a high mountain top. It would take more effort to breathe on the mountain top because there are fewer molecules of air in each breath you take.

Unit 5–NATIONAL SCIENCE EDUCATION STANDARDS

- *Unifying Concepts and Processes:* Students should develop understanding and abilities with regard to systems, order, and organization; evidence, models, and explanation; constancy, change, and measurement; and evolution and equilibrium.

- *Science as Inquiry*—Content Standard A: Students should develop the necessary skills to do scientific inquiry and develop an understanding about scientific inquiry.

- *Physical Science*—Content Standard B: Students should develop an understanding of the properties of objects and materials; position and motion of objects; properties and changes of properties in matter; and motions and forces.

- *Earth and Space Science*—Content Standard D: Students should develop an understanding of the structure of the earth system.

- *History and Nature of Science*—Content Standard G: Students should develop an understanding of the nature of science and of science as a human endeavor.

ACTIVITY 20: AIR PRESSURE

Goal: To understand that air exerts pressure
To understand that air exerts the same pressure in all directions

Skills: Observing, comparing, explaining, hypothesizing, generalizing

Materials: Two round balloons of different sizes
Marking pen

Preparation: None

Preparation Time: None

Lesson Time: 15–20 minutes

— Procedure and Questioning Strategy —

1. Everyone wave your hands back and forth in front of your face. What do you feel?
    Air.

2. Now wave them up and down in front of your face. What do you feel?
    Air.

3. How did the amount of air you felt "back and forth" compare with the amount you felt "up and down"?
    It felt the same.

4. What does this tell us about the air around us?
    Air is all around us.

5. Now watch as I blow up this balloon.

Blow up one of the balloons and tie off the end.

6. What did you observe?
    You put air in the balloon. The balloon got bigger.

7. What made the balloon get bigger?
    The air.

8. What did the air I blew into the balloon do to the pressure inside the balloon?
    It increased the pressure.

9.   Make a generalization about air.

    Air exerts pressure.

10.   Describe the shape of the balloon.

    It's round.

11.   Now watch as I blow up the other balloon.

Blow up the second balloon and tie off the end.

12.   What did you observe?

    You put air in this balloon too.
    This balloon is round too.
    You increased the pressure inside the balloon.
    This balloon is smaller (or larger) than the first one.

You may choose to introduce the term SYMMETRIC to the students at this point if you wish. Point the ends of the two balloons toward the students, indicating that they are symmetric (balanced, or the same, in all directions).

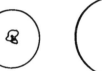

13.   We said the balloons are round. What does the round shape tell us about the pressure of the air inside the balloons?

    It's pushing on all the sides equally.

14.   What would happen if the air didn't push on all the sides equally?

    They wouldn't be round. They would be "caved in" on one side or the other.

15.   Make a generalization about the direction of air pressure.

    Air pressure is the same in all directions.

— Practical Application —

1.   Hold your arm out in front of you. What do you feel?

    Nothing.

2.   But what is all around us?

    Air.

3.   What does the fact that we feel nothing tell us about the air pressure?

    It is the same in all directions.

4.   Suppose the pressure were greater above our arm than below it. What would we feel?

    We would feel the air pushing our arm down.

5. What if the pressure were greater on our left side?

   Our arm would be pushed to the right.

6. Is the pressure of the air always the same in all directions?

   No.

7. When is it not?

   When it's windy outside.

8. What does the fact that it's windy tell us?

   That the air pressure is greater in one direction than another.

9. Where is the pressure greatest?

   Wherever the wind is coming from.

ACTIVITY 21: THE PRESSURE OF THE ATMOSPHERE

Goal: **To understand that our atmosphere exerts pressure**

Skills: **Observing, inferring, hypothesizing, supporting inferences with observation**

Materials: **Large plastic drinking cup, 12 oz.**
Large plastic food storage bag
Rubber bands large enough to fit around the rim of the cup
Bathroom plunger

Preparation: None

Preparation Time: None

Lesson Time: 15–20 minutes

— Procedure and Questioning Strategy —

Have the students wave their hands back and forth and up and down in front of their faces.

1. What do you feel?

    Wind; it feels cool; it tickles; a fan; air.

2. Where does this air come from?

    It's all around us.

If they don't know the term, tell them that the air that is all around us is the ATMOSPHERE. Display the cup for the students.

3. What is in the cup?

    Nothing; it's empty; air.

4. How do we know?

    Air is all around us, so there must be some in the cup.

5. Now watch as I put the plastic bag in the cup.

Put the bag in the cup, fold the edges of the open end over the rim of the cup, and wrap the rubber bands around the mouth as shown in the drawing.

6. What has happened to most of the air in the cup?

    It was pushed out by the bag when you put the bag into the cup.

7. Now let me have (choose a student) come up and pull the bag out of the cup.

8.   What happened?

> The bag is hard to pull out.

Take the rubber bands off.

9.   Now try it.

Have the student pull the bag out.

10.   What happened?

> It came out easily.

11.   Why wouldn't the bag come out the first time?

> Air was holding it in the cup.

12.   How did the air do that?

> Since we pushed the air out of the cup by putting the bag in, the air pressure above the bag was greater than the air pressure below the bag (between the bag and cup), so we couldn't get the bag out.

13.   How do we know it was the air and not the cup that held the bag in?

> The cup was still there when we were able to pull the bag out.

14.   What was the difference between the two times?

> The first time the rubber band was around the rim of the cup and the second time it wasn't.

15.   What did the rubber band do?

> When it was around the rim of the cup, it kept the air around the outside of the bag from getting back into the cup. After the rubber band was removed, air could get back into the cup.

16.   What did letting the air back in do?

> It allowed the air pressure above and below the bag to be the same. Then we were able to get the bag out.

17.   So, where did the air pressure that held the bag in the cup come from?

> The atmosphere. It's the air that's all around us.

— Practical Application —

Show the students the bathroom plunger. Put some small pieces of paper around the rim of the plunger. Push the plunger down—or have a student push it down—on a smooth surface, such as the floor or a table top.

1. **What did you observe?**

   The papers flew away when you pushed the plunger down.

2. **Why do you suppose they flew away?**

   Air was pushed out from under the plunger and the air blew the papers away.

Now pull the plunger up—or have the student pull it up. If the student can't pull the plunger up, have him/her lift it from the side.

3. **What did you observe?**

   It was hard for you to pull the plunger up. It made a noise like air "sucking."

4. **Why was the plunger hard to pull up?**

   The pressure on the outside of the plunger was greater than the pressure on the inside (underneath).

5. **Why was the pressure greater on the outside?**

   When we pushed the plunger down, the air from the inside was pushed out.

6. **How do we know?**

   We saw the pieces of paper blow away.

7. **What was the noise we heard as we pulled up the plunger?**

   It was the air going back into (underneath) the plunger.

8. **If we put pieces of paper on the table near the plunger as the plunger is pulled up, what do you predict will happen to the papers?**

Try it.

9. **What happened?**

   The papers stayed on the table. Some papers moved a little.

10. **Why do you think the papers weren't "sucked" into the plunger?**

    The air pressure in the room wasn't great enough to push the papers into the plunger.

11. **Sometimes a plastic garbage bag gets kind of "stuck" in the trash can. Why might this be the case?**

    When we put the trash bag in the can, we push the air out from underneath it (between the bag and the can). Then the air pressure from above the bag is greater than the air pressure underneath it and it is hard to get out.

12. **What can we do to get the bag out?**

    Lift the edge of the bag off the side of the can. This would let some air in between the bag and the can and the bag would be easier to get out.

ACTIVITY 22: THE CUP AND THE CARD

Goal: To apply the principle that the pressure of the atmosphere is the same in all directions

Skills: Observing, predicting, confirming inferences with observation, hypothesizing

Materials: Transparent drinking cup
Five or six 5" x 8" index cards
Water

Preparation: None

Preparation Time: None

Lesson Time: 15–20 minutes

— Procedure and Questioning Strategy —

Have the students watch you as you fill the drinking cup with water. Put the card over the opening of the cup and invert it with your hand holding the card as shown in the drawing.

1. What will happen when I take my hand away from the card?

    (They usually predict that the card will fall and the water will spill.)

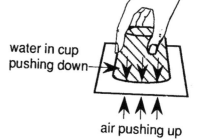

water in cup pushing down

air pushing up

Remove your hand.

2. What do you observe?

    The card stayed under the cup. The card didn't fall down.

3. Let's try to explain why the card didn't fall down. What do we remember about the pressure of the air?

    It's the same in all directions. There is as much air pressure pushing up as there is pushing down.

4. Now let's look at the pressures on the card. What pressure wants to push the card away from the cup?

    The weight of the water.

5. And what pressure wants to hold the card against the cup?

    Air pressure.

6. And what is the direction of the air pressure that is holding the card on the cup?

    Up.

7. How do we know it's air pressure?

> It has to be air pressure. Other than air, there is nothing underneath the card.

8. What do we know about the air pressure compared to the weight of the water?

> The air pressure is greater.

9. What would happen if the weight of the water were greater than the air pressure?

> The card would fall down.

— Practical Application —

1. What do you think will happen to the card if I turn the card and cup on its side and take my hand away?

> It will stay against the cup.

2. Why do you think so?

> Since the air pressure is the same in all directions, the amount that it pushes sideways should be the same as the amount it pushes up. So it should still hold the card on the cup.

Take your hand away to confirm that the card stays on the cup.

3. Do you have to keep your hand on the card as you turn the card and cup sideways?

> No.

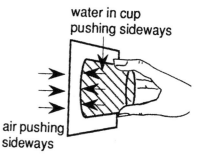

water in cup pushing sideways

air pushing sideways

Turn the card and cup sideways without holding the card on the cup to confirm that the card remains against the cup as it is turned.

4. Why not?

> The air pressure is the same in all directions, and it doesn't change whether or not the cup and the card are moving.

5. Now suppose that I take some of the water out of the cup and put the card under it. What will happen to the card?

> It should stay on the cup.

water in cup pushing down

air pushing up

6. Why?

> Since the weight of the water will be less, the air pressure should hold the card on the cup more easily than before.

Remove your hand to confirm that the card stays against the cup.

7. Suppose I turn the cup sideways with only a small amount of water in it. What will happen to the card?

> It will remain against the cup just as before. The pressure sideways is the same as the pressure up and down, so it should work just as well as when the cup was upside down.

Turn the cup sideways and remove your hand to confirm that the card stays against the cup.

8. How much water do you think we can remove before the card will fall?

> (Answers will vary.)

9. Let's try it.

Experiment with various amounts of water in the cup. Since the card will get wet, you may want to use several different cards. You should be able to remove nearly all the water before the card will fall.

10. Now suppose that we put no water in the cup. What will happen to the card?

> It will fall.

Try this to confirm that the card falls.

11. Why did it fall?

> There is no water in the cup, so air is the only pressure on the card. The air pressure above the card is the same as the air pressure under the card.

12. What makes the card fall?

> Gravity.

ACTIVITY 23: THE BURNING CANDLE

Goal: To understand that a flame needs oxygen in order to burn

Skills: Observing, inferring, predicting, generalizing

Materials: Bottle, at least three times taller and twice as wide as the candle
Metal pie pan
Matches
Candle, at least 3 inches tall

Preparation: 1. Light the candle and let the wax drippings fall on the center of the pie pan.
2. Set the candle on the melted wax, making sure it is secure.
3. Light the candle (if it is not still lit).

Preparation Time: 2 minutes

Lesson Time: 15–20 minutes

— Procedure and Questioning Strategy —

Draw the diagram to the right on the board. Explain to students that the air around us is made up of about 78% nitrogen, 21% oxygen, and 1% other gases. Oxygen is the part of air that we need to live and the part of air that is needed for something to burn.

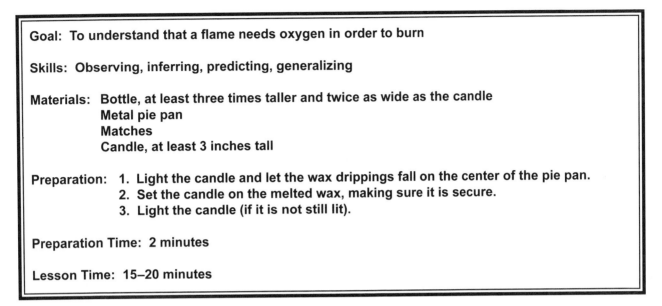

1. What do you predict will happen if we put this bottle over the burning candle?

    The flame will go out.

2. What will cause the flame to go out?

    It will use up the oxygen in the air.

Select one student to watch a clock and see how long it takes for the flame to go out. Put the bottle over the candle.

3. What did you observe?

    The flame burned for a while and then went out.

4. How long did it take to go out, (student's name)?

    (Answers vary from a few seconds to about 15.)

5. What do you think happened to the oxygen in the bottle?

    It was used up by the burning candle.

6. If the oxygen was used up, what do you think happened to the amount of air in the bottle?

    It became less, maybe about 20% less, than the amount of oxygen in the air.

Take the bottle off the candle and quickly put the open end of the bottle down on the table.

7. How can we test the air in the bottle to see if the oxygen was used up?

    Light the candle again and put the bottle back on the candle.

8. Do you think that any oxygen may have gone back into the bottle when I took it off the candle and put it on the table?

    Maybe a little bit.

9. About how long do you think the candle will burn under the bottle this time?

    Less than it burned the first time.

Have a student time the flame when you put the bottle back on the candle.

10. How long did it take this time?

    (Varied answers—much less time than in the first experiment.)

11. So, what do we know from this experiment?

    That there was much less oxygen in the bottle after the first experiment.

12. Let's review. What does a flame need in order to burn?

    Oxygen.

13. What caused the amount of oxygen in the air of the bottle to be reduced?

    The flame.

— Practical Application —

1. If a person's clothes are on fire, a fireman will roll the person up in something like a heavy blanket or rug. Why do you think that is done?

    To put out the fire.

2. How does it put the fire out?

    Rolling the person in something heavy cuts off the supply of oxygen so the flames go out.

3. Baking soda will not burn and is thrown on a grease fire in the kitchen to put the fire out. How do you think baking soda puts out the fire?

    It covers the fire so the flames cannot get oxygen to keep burning. It cuts off the oxygen supply.

4. Would water do the same thing as baking soda?

    No, it would spread a grease fire because grease would simply float to the top of the water and continue burning.

ACTIVITY 24: THE RISING WATER

Goal: To understand that a difference in the air pressure can cause water to move

Skills: Observing, inferring, predicting, generalizing

Materials: Bottle, at least three times taller and twice as wide as the candle
Candle, at least 3 inches tall
Metal pie pan with bumpy bottom so the water can move into the bottle
Matches
Water
Food coloring
For each student:
Paper cup
Straw

Preparation: 1. Light the candle and let the wax drippings fall on the center of the pie pan.
2. Set the candle on the melted wax.
3. Light the candle (if it is not still lit).

Preparation Time: 2 minutes

Lesson Time: 20–25 minutes

— Procedure and Questioning Strategy —

Fill the pie pan half full of colored water. Explain to the students what you are doing.

1. What do you predict will happen if I put this bottle over the candle with the water in the pie pan?

    The flame will go out.

2. What else could happen?

    The flame could burn longer than in our first experiment.

3. What reason do you have for that?

    The flame will use up the oxygen in the air and then take oxygen from the water.
    (This is a common misconception.)

Place the bottle over the candle.

4. Describe what you saw in the order that it happened.

    The candle went out. The colored water rose in the bottle.

5. What is the reason that the candle went out?

    The flame used up most of the oxygen in the bottle.

6. If the flame used up most of the oxygen in the bottle, what do you think happened to the air pressure inside the jar?

> It was reduced by about the same amount.

7. When the oxygen was being used up, and before the water rose in the bottle, where was the air pressure greater, inside or outside the bottle?

> Outside the bottle.

8. What is the reason it was greater outside the bottle?

> The atmosphere is outside the bottle and we used up the oxygen inside.

9. Then what caused the water to rise in the bottle?

> The air pressure on the water outside the jar was greater than the air pressure inside the jar, so the greater air pressure *pushed* the water up into the jar until the pressures were equal.

DIFFERENCE IN AIR PRESSURE – When there is a difference in air pressure, a high and a low pressure area, the higher pressure area moves into the area with lower pressure until the pressures are equal.

— Practical Application —

Distribute a cup, partially filled with water, and a straw to each student. Ask the students to drink some water through the straw and then relate drinking through a straw with what they learned in the last experiment.

1. How is drinking through a straw similar to what happened in our last experiment?

> When you drink through a straw, the water rises in the straw. In the experiment, water rose in the bottle.

2. What decreased the air pressure in the bottle?

> Most of the oxygen was used up by the flame.

3. What do you think is the reason the water rises in the straw?

> You create a lower pressure area inside the top of the straw, then the greater air pressure on the liquid pushes the liquid up the straw and into your mouth.

ACTIVITY 25: PRESSURE – FORCE AND AREA

Goal: To understand that pressure is the amount of force that pushes or pulls on a certain area

Skills: Observing, inferring, comparing, supporting inferences with observations

Materials: For each student:
2 sheets of 8 1/2" by 11" notebook paper
A pencil
A pair of shoes with narrow heels (such as women's high heels)

Preparation: None

Preparation Time: None

Lesson Time: 20–30 minutes

— Procedure and Questioning Strategy —

Have the students work in pairs. Direct one student from each pair to stand with both feet on the notebook paper and have the second student trace around his/her shoes. Reverse the roles. Then have the first student stand on one foot on the second piece of notebook paper and have their partner trace around one shoe. Reverse the roles again. Finally, have each student shade in the area of both shoes and of one shoe. They should each have two pieces of paper that appear as follows:

AREA OF TWO SHOES   AREA OF ONE SHOE

1.   Now let's study what we've done. What do you each have in your hands?

The area of two feet together and the area of one foot. (Technically, it is the area of their shoe soles. The area of their feet is slightly less.)

2.   And what do we mean by area in these drawings?

It is the size (or amount) of the shaded portion on the paper.

3.   How does the area of your two feet compare to the area of your one foot?

It is twice as large for two feet.

4. Now, let's think about the amount of force that the earth exerts on us. What do we call that? (Refer to Activity 8, "Earth Pull," if they are uncertain.)

> The force of gravity.

5. And how do we measure the force of gravity?

> With a scale. It is our weight.

6. Now, let's compare the force of gravity on us when we are standing on both feet compared to when we stand on one foot. How does it compare?

> It is the same.

7. How do you know?

> We weigh the same whether we're standing on one foot or on both feet.

Students may have some difficulty with this concept. You can further demonstrate this idea by having several student volunteers tell their weight and then stand on one foot. As they are standing on one foot, ask them again how much they weigh, reinforcing the idea that their weight doesn't change whether they stand on one foot or two.

8. What was the difference when we stood on one foot compared to two feet?

> Our weight was "spread out" over a larger area when we stood on two feet.

9. Which is "harder" on the floor?

> Standing on one foot. Our weight is sort of "more dense" when we stand on one foot.

10. I'm going to introduce a new term called PRESSURE. Now, think about it. In which case did we exert more pressure on the floor—when we stood on one foot or two?

> When we stood on one foot.

If students are unable to react intuitively to your question, go ahead and tell them what pressure means. PRESSURE is the amount of force that is exerted on a certain area.

11. Now observe what I am doing.

Walk across the floor with a normal stride then tiptoe across the floor. Have the students do the same thing.

12. Now let's compare walking normally to walking on our tiptoes. How did they compare?

> It was harder on our tiptoes. It felt like we were pressing down harder when we were on our tiptoes.

13. How did the forces compare for the two trips?

> The forces we exerted on the floor were the same.

14. **How do we know?**

> The force of gravity on us was the same both times. Our weight was the same.

15. **How do the pressures compare?**

> The pressure was greater when we were on our tiptoes.

16. **How do we know?**

> It felt greater.

17. **Why was it greater?**

> The force was "concentrated" in a smaller area. The force was "spread out" when we weren't tiptoeing.

— Practical Application —

1. Imagine that you fall asleep in a chair sitting up, and let's compare that to sleeping in your bed. In which case is the pull of gravity on you greater?

> In neither case. It is the same.

2. How about the pressure?

> You exert more pressure (on the chair) sitting up than you do (on the bed) lying down.

3. Why?

> Your weight is concentrated over a smaller area when you are sitting up and spread out over more area when you are lying down.

4. Now, let's think about a tough one. I have a friend who weighs a bit more than I weigh. Would it ever be possible for me to exert more pressure on the floor than he/she does?

> Yes.

5. How might that happen?

> Female: If I wore a shoe with a narrow heel, like a high heel.
> Male: If I walked on my tiptoes.

You may demonstrate this by walking in high heels if you are a woman or by walking on your tiptoes if you are a man.

6. Elephants have very large flat soles on their feet. Why do you suppose they have such large soles?

> Elephants are very heavy. If they didn't have large soles to distribute their weight, they would sink into the ground and it would be hard for them to walk.

7. Why does a sharp knife cut better than a dull knife?

> A sharp blade allows the weight of the knife to be concentrated, so it exerts more pressure on the material and, as a result, cuts it more easily.

ACTIVITY 26: THE CARTESIAN DIVER SUBMARINES

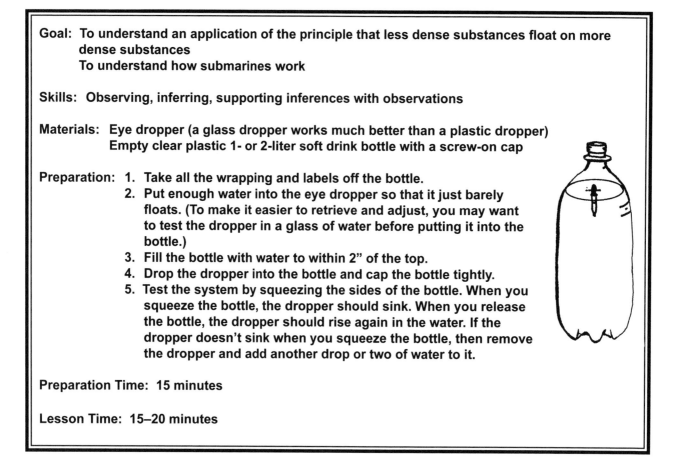

Goal: To understand an application of the principle that less dense substances float on more dense substances

To understand how submarines work

Skills: Observing, inferring, supporting inferences with observations

Materials: Eye dropper (a glass dropper works much better than a plastic dropper)

Empty clear plastic 1- or 2-liter soft drink bottle with a screw-on cap

Preparation:
1. Take all the wrapping and labels off the bottle.
2. Put enough water into the eye dropper so that it just barely floats. (To make it easier to retrieve and adjust, you may want to test the dropper in a glass of water before putting it into the bottle.)
3. Fill the bottle with water to within 2" of the top.
4. Drop the dropper into the bottle and cap the bottle tightly.
5. Test the system by squeezing the sides of the bottle. When you squeeze the bottle, the dropper should sink. When you release the bottle, the dropper should rise again in the water. If the dropper doesn't sink when you squeeze the bottle, then remove the dropper and add another drop or two of water to it.

Preparation Time: 15 minutes

Lesson Time: 15–20 minutes

— Procedure and Questioning Strategy —

1. We are going to define the system, in this case, as the *dropper*, the *water in the dropper,* and the *air in the dropper.* What do you observe about the system?

> The system is floating.
> The air is above the water in the system.
> There is a hole in the bottom of the dropper.

2. What do we know about the density of the system?

> It is less dense than water.

3. How do we know?

> It is floating.

Now squeeze the sides of the bottle and make the dropper sink to the bottom.

4. What do we know now about the density of the system?

> It is more dense than water.

5. How do we know?

> It sank.

6. Now let's figure out how the density changed. What happened when we squeezed the bottle?

> The pressure on the inside of the bottle increased.

7. And what did that do?

> The increased pressure made more water move up into the dropper.

8. How can we determine if that is true?

> We can look at the dropper and see if the water level goes up when we squeeze the bottle.

Have the students observe the water level in the dropper to confirm that it goes up (additional water goes into the dropper) when the bottle is squeezed.

9. What did you see?

> The water level went up.

10. What did that do to the system?

> It increased its mass since the amount of water in the system became greater.

11. And what did increasing the mass of the system do?

> It increased the density and the system sank.

— Practical Application —

1. Let's compare the system to a submarine. What do we know must be true about a submarine if it sinks?

> It is more dense than water.

2. We saw how we made our system sink. Compare our system to a submarine and explain how a submarine crew must make it sink.

> They must somehow get water into the submarine to increase its mass, which will increase its density, so it will sink.

Ask if any student can explain how a submarine is first made to sink and is later made to float. If no one can, explain that submarines have tanks into which water is pumped to increase the mass and therefore the density. It is exactly like the dropper, except we **squeezed the bottle** to get more water into the dropper while submarines **pump** the water in.

3. How do they get the submarine to float again?

    They pump compressed air into the tanks. The compressed air fills the tanks, pushing the water out.

4. How does that compare to our system?

    We let the water back out when we stopped squeezing. They pump in air to fill the tanks and push the water out.

ACTIVITIES 20–26: CONNECTIONS

Goal: To understand the relationships between pressure and the movement of air

Skills: Comparing, explaining, hypothesizing, supporting hypotheses with observations

— Questioning Strategy —

1. Let's review what we know about force and pressure. How are force and pressure related?

   Pressure is the amount of force on a certain area.

2. So, what is air pressure?

   The amount of force or "push" of the air on a certain area.

3. Let's continue with what we know about air and air pressure. Let's list as many things as we can.

   Air is all around us.
   Air pressure is normally the same in all directions.
   If the pressure is greater in one direction than another, some kind of movement results.
   Air is composed of oxygen and other gases.

4. Let's look now at some examples. What did we observe which told us that the pressure of the air is the same in all directions?

   The balloons were symmetric.
   In the activity with the cup and the card, it didn't matter if you held the cup upside down or sideways. The card stayed on the cup both ways.
   When we sit here, we don't feel the air pushing on us.

5. What did we learn that told us things move when air pressures are different?

   The wind blows when the air pressure is greater in one direction than another.
   The water went up into the bottle when the candle went out.

6. How was the pressure changed when the candle was burning?

   The candle used up the oxygen in the bottle. When the oxygen was used up, the pressure was lowered.

7. How do we know the pressure was lowered?

   The water went up into the bottle.

8. Why do you think the water went up into the bottle?

   The atmospheric pressure on the water outside the bottle was greater than the pressure on the inside of the bottle, so the water went up inside the bottle until the pressures were equal.

9. We said that the air is about 1/5 oxygen. Suppose now that air were 1/2 oxygen instead. What do you think would have happened in the experiment?

    The water would have gone farther up into the bottle.

10. Why do you think so?

    Since more of the air is oxygen, more would have been used, so the pressure would have been lowered farther and the water would have gone farther up into the bottle.

11. Now let's look at another application of air pressure. Let's look again at the system (the dropper, the water in it, and the air in it). What did that activity have to do with air pressure?

    When we squeezed the bottle we changed the air pressure, which then changed the density of the system.

12. Let's review again how we did that. How does the mass of the system when it is floating compare to the mass when it is on the bottom?

    The mass is greater when it's on the bottom.

13. How do we know?

    More water went into the system when we squeezed the bottle.

14. How did squeezing do that?

    Squeezing increased the air pressure outside the system which forced water into the dropper.

15. What about the mass of the air in the system?

    It's the same. All we did was make the air more compact ("squeezed it up").

16. How do we know?

    No air got in or out.

17. How could we tell if some air got in or out?

    We would see a bubble.

18. What about the volume of the system?

    It is the same. (The volume of the dropper stays the same.)

19. So, explain how that affects the density.

    There was more mass in the same amount of volume so the density was increased. Because the system was more dense, it sank.

20. Compare this to our experience with the oil and water in Activity 16. (Remind students about what happened in Activity 16.)

    It was the same in Activity 16. The water had more mass than oil in the same amount of volume, so it was more dense than the oil.

UNIT 6— HEAT, EXPANSION, AND THE MOVEMENT OF MOLECULES

Background Information

Air is all around us. It is part of the atmosphere that encircles Earth. Gases make up the atmosphere, most of which are in the first 30 miles, approximately 19 miles above the surface of Earth. Earth's gravity holds the atmosphere in place around Earth. The molecules that make up air are energized by the warm rays of sunlight and are sent into continual motion. The hotter the molecules become, the faster they move and the farther apart they become depending on how much space they have in which to move.

If the heated molecules of air are limited by the amount of space they can occupy, the amount of pressure they exert increases. The increasing number of collisions they have with a surface also increases the amount of pressure. Pressure is the amount of force exerted on one square unit of area.

Let's think about the tires we mentioned in the introduction to air pressure in the previous unit. We increased the pressure in the tires by adding more molecules of air to the tires. If we add heat to the air in the tires, this also increases the pressure exerted on each square inch of the inside of the tires.

How could heat be added? Rub your hands together. How do they feel? Are they warmer than before you rubbed them together? The friction caused by rubbing makes them warmer. When you drive a car, the friction of the car tires rubbing on the road also causes the tires to heat, which in turn, heats the molecules of air in the tires. So if you were to measure the amount of pressure in your tires before you started driving many miles, then measure it again when you stopped driving, the pressure in the tires would show an increase.

Imagine what the molecules of air look like in a cool tire. They may be moving around rather slowly, bumping into each other and into the inner sides of the tire. Imagine what these molecules look like as they heat up, moving faster and faster, colliding more often with the insides of the tire, exerting more and more pressure on each square inch of the tire. The tire represents a closed system. No air molecules are entering or leaving the system. There is a certain amount of space available for the molecules to occupy.

When air is heated in an open system, like the air in the outside atmosphere, the air molecules can move far apart. Since they are farther apart, they have more space to move freely. The mass of the air becomes less dense and exerts less pressure because the molecules have fewer collisions with each other. When compared with cold air, the heated molecules exert much less pressure. The molecules of cold air are much closer together, are more dense, and so exert more pressure than the less dense warm air molecules.

To relate this difference in pressure with weather, imagine that a mass of cold air called a **cold front** is sweeping in a southeastern direction from the state of Washington (in the northwest United States) toward a mass of heated air. What do you think would happen?

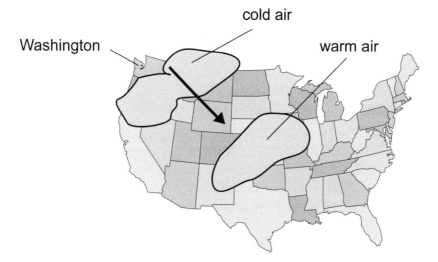

Cold fronts move faster than warm fronts because the air in a cold front is colder and heavier, and it exerts more pressure than the air in a warm front. A cold front can push lighter, warmer air out of its way. The warm air usually rises quickly as the cooler air moves in to occupy its space. The cold front moving from Washington would push the warmer air in the Midwest out of the way, and the temperature in the midwestern states would drop as the cold front moved through.

Unit 6–NATIONAL SCIENCE EDUCATION STANDARDS

- *Unifying Concepts and Processes:* Students should develop understanding and abilities with regard to systems, order, and organization; evidence, models, and explanation; and constancy, change, and measurement.

- *Science as Inquiry*—Content Standard A: Students should develop the necessary skills to do scientific inquiry and develop an understanding about scientific inquiry.

- *Physical Science*—Content Standard B: Students should develop an understanding of the properties of objects and materials; light, heat, electricity, and magnetism; properties and changes of properties in matter; and motions and forces.

- *Earth and Space Science*—Content Standard D: Students should develop an understanding of the structure of the earth system.

- *History and Nature of Science*—Content Standard G: Students should develop an understanding of the nature of science and of science as a human endeavor.

■ ACTIVITY 27: EXPANDING AIR WITH HEAT – THE RISING BALLOON ■

Goal: To understand that heat makes air expand

Skills: Observing, inferring, comparing, generalizing, identifying irrelevant information

Materials: Two identical glass bottles with small opening (like a ketchup bottle)
                 Two round balloons of the same size
                 Source of hot water (such as a coffee pot, tea kettle, or pan of water on a hot plate)

Preparation: Heat the water. (If you use a coffee pot, fill it about 2/3 full.)

Preparation Time: 5 minutes

Lesson Time: 20–30 minutes

— Procedure and Questioning Strategy —

Display the two bottles.

1. What do you notice about the bottles?

   (Among their answers may be: they're the same size; they probably weigh the same amount; they're the same height; they would hold the same amount of liquid; they have writing on them.)

2. What is in the bottles?

   Air.

Display the two balloons.

3. Now look at the balloons. Do they seem to be the same size?

   Yes.

Put a balloon over the mouth of each bottle.

4. What do we know about the amount of air in each system?

   It's the same.

5. How do we know?

   The bottles are the same size and the balloons are the same size.

Put one of the balloon-covered bottles into the pot of hot water, wait for the balloon to pop up, and take the bottle out of the pot. Place it beside the unheated bottle and balloon.

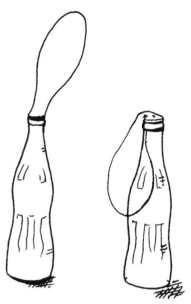

6. What comparisons can we make between these two systems?

> The balloon is sticking up in one but not the other.
> One is hot and the other isn't.

7. Is there more air in the system with the balloon sticking up?

> No.

8. How do we know?

> The bottles and balloons are the same size and we put the balloons on the bottles, so no air could get in or get out. The amount of air must be the same.

9. What will happen to the expanded balloon if we lay the bottle on its side—will the balloon stick up or will it stick out sideways?

> It will stick out sideways.

10. Let's try it.

Lay the bottle on its side to confirm that the balloon sticks out sideways.

11. Let's explain why the balloon got bigger.

> The air in the system expanded.

12. How do we know the reason is that the air expands and not that "hot air rises"?

> If the reason were that "hot air rises," the balloon would stick *up* rather than *sideways* when the bottle is on its side.

13. Make a generalization about heating air.

> Heat makes air expand.

— Practical Application —

1. After driving many miles at highway speeds, your neighbor stops at a service station to check the air pressure in his/her car tires. Assuming the tires don't leak, how will the pressure then compare to the pressure before he/she started the trip?

> It will be higher.

2. Why will it be higher?

> As the tires roll over the road, friction makes them heat up. The heated air in the tires makes them want to expand, which increases pressure in the tires.

3. Suppose you're out camping. You're hungry and decide to heat a can of pork and beans in the campfire. If you don't open the can or poke a hole in the top, what will happen?

    The can will burst.

4. Why will it burst?

    Heating the contents of the can makes the pork and beans want to expand. The can tries to prevent them from expanding. When the can is no longer able to prevent them from expanding, the can bursts.

5. What could you do to prevent this?

    Poke a hole in the can so some of the contents can escape.

6. Now compare the can to the balloon. The can would burst, but we saw that the balloon didn't. Why not?

    The balloon is made of rubber and the rubber will stretch as the air expands. The metal in the can will expand a little but won't stretch, so it will burst as the pork and beans expand.

7. Could we ever make the balloon burst?

    Yes, if we were to heat it sufficiently so that it expanded enough, it would burst. We didn't heat it that much.

8. Now, let's think about cars that are left outdoors in the hot summer sun with all the windows rolled up. Occasionally a window in a car will burst. Relate this to what we've already discussed and explain why the window bursts.

    The sun's energy heats the air inside the car and, as a result, the air tries to expand. If the windows can't withstand the pressure, they will burst, just as the can of pork and beans bursts.

9. What do people usually do to keep the windows from breaking?

    They open one or more windows slightly or open the air vents.

10. How does this help?

    It allows the expanding air to escape so the pressure of the air inside the car does not increase.

▬▬ ACTIVITY 28: HEAT AND THE MOVEMENT OF MOLECULES ▬▬

Goal: To understand that heat makes molecules move faster and move away from each other

Skills: Observing, comparing, inferring, generalizing, using models

Materials: The soft-drink bottles, balloons, and hot water from Activity 27, "Expanding Air With Heat"
The drawing on page 103
For each group of three students:
  5–6 marbles or Ping-Pong® balls
  2' long piece of thick rope

Preparation: 1. Make a transparency from the drawing on page 103.
2. Prepare the bottles, balloons, and water as in Activity 27.
3. Put the marbles/balls into bags for each group of students.

You may need to do this activity as a demonstration. If so, you need one set of marbles/balls and one piece of rope. You can use the surface of the overhead projector so the students can see the shadows of the marbles/balls on the screen.

Preparation Time: 30 minutes

Lesson Time: 20–30 minutes

— Procedure and Questioning Strategy —

Put one of the bottles into the hot water until the balloon pops up, then display the two bottles as in Activity 27. Tell students that the *system* in each case is the bottle, the balloon, and the air trapped inside.

1.   Now we want to try to figure out what is happening to the air inside each of the systems. Let's look at this transparency that represents the bottles and balloons (systems).

Display the transparency for the students.

2.   Look at the transparency. What observations can we make?
> The drawings look like the bottles and balloons.
> There are dots in each drawing. There are little curved lines (parentheses) around the dots.

3.   What do you suppose the dots and parentheses represent?
> The dots are air molecules. The parentheses represent their movement.
> The two sets of parentheses mean they're moving faster than those with only one set.

4. Which system does drawing B represent?

    The heated one.

5. Compare the molecules in system A to those in system B.

    There are the same number of molecules in A as in B. There are only a few air molecules in the balloon for system A, but there are several in the balloon for system B.

6. You said the total number of air molecules in each system is the same. What does this tell us?

    The amount of air in each system is the same.

7. Make another comparison.

    The air molecules in B (the heated system) are moving faster than those in A.

8. Make a generalization about heat and the movement of molecules.

    Heat makes molecules move faster.

9. Make another comparison.

    The air molecules in B are farther apart than in A.

Hold the bottles and balloons up for the students again.

10. Look again at the bottles and balloons. What do you observe that tells you that the molecules are farther apart in the heated one?

    The balloon has expanded and is sticking up.

11. Make a generalization about heat and the spacing of molecules.

    Heat makes molecules move away from each other.

12. Let's try to figure out *why* the molecules move away from each other. We're going to imagine that the marbles you see here are the air molecules and the rope is the inside surface of the bottle and balloon.

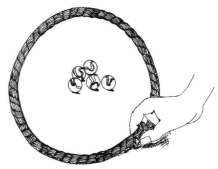

Each group of three students needs a level surface. Give them the marbles/balls and rope. Have them form a circle with the rope and group the marbles/balls closely together inside. Have one student hold the ends of the rope, the second be the observer, and the third be the shooter. Have the shooter snap one of the marbles/balls into the group. If you choose to demonstrate the activity, use the overhead projector top as the suface.

13. What did you observe?

> The marbles/balls bounced against each other and moved away from each other.

Have students group the marbles/balls again and snap the shooter into the group with greater force than the first time.

14. What did you observe this time?

> The marbles moved away from each other faster and they hit the rope harder.

15. Now let's relate the marbles/balls to the air molecules. Why do you suppose heat makes them move away from each other?

> Heat makes them move faster, and when they move faster, they collide with each other and bounce away from each other.

16. Let's relate the marbles/balls hitting the rope to the air molecules in system B.

> When the molecules move faster and away from each other, they also hit the sides of the bottle and the balloon. When they hit the balloon, this causes the balloon to expand and rise.

— Practical Application —

1. Think about the car tire that has been heated because it has been driven on the road. What conclusions can we make about the air molecules in the tire?

> They are moving faster than before the car was driven.

You may want to repeat the activity with the marbles/balls and the rope at this point.

2. What did the marbles do to the rope when they hit it?

> They pushed the rope outward a little.

3. Let's relate the marbles bumping each other and pushing on the rope to the molecules in the car tire. What happens to the molecules as a result of their faster movement?

> They bump into each other when they're heated. They also bump the sides of the tire. More bumping on the tire results in more pressure.

4. Think about the pork and beans that burst in the fire. Explain, using what we know about heat and the movement of molecules, why the can bursts.

> When the pork and beans molecules get heated they move faster and bump into each other and into the sides of the can. When there are so many bumps that the can is no longer able to withstand the pressure, it bursts.

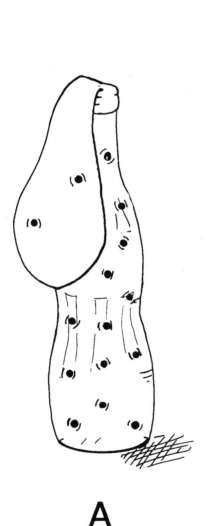

A

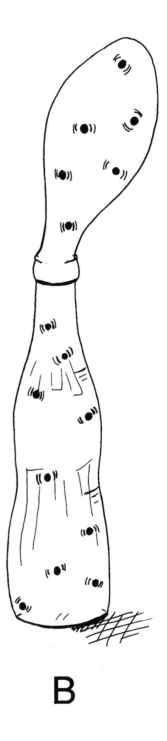

B

ACTIVITY 29: THE EGG IN THE BOTTLE

Goal: To understand that a difference in air pressure can cause movement of an object

Skills: Observing, inferring, predicting, hypothesizing, generalizing

Materials: 32-oz. bottle (An apple juice bottle works well.)
2 hard-boiled eggs, one with shell removed (Use a large egg with a larger-mouthed
  bottle or a small egg with a smaller-mouthed bottle.)
Three 4" squares of newspaper, crumpled
Matches
Paper towels
Cotton ball
Sponge
Balloon, blown up
Golf ball

Preparation: Place the egg on top of the bottle.

Preparation Time: 1 minute

Lesson Time: 15–20 minutes

— Procedure and Questioning Strategy —

Show students the two hard-boiled eggs, one with a shell and one without. Ask them to compare how the eggs feel (particularly their textures and flexibility). Show students that the peeled egg will not go into the bottle without being crushed.

1. How do you think we could get the egg into the bottle without crushing it?

    By reducing the air pressure inside the bottle.

2. How could we do that?

    By taking some of the oxygen out of the bottle.

Light the paper, put it in the bottle, then put the egg on top immediately with the smaller end of the egg pointed down.

3. Describe what happened in the order that it happened.

    The egg bobbed up and down on top of the bottle. The flame went out. The egg popped into the bottle.

4. What do you think made the egg bob up and down?

    The heated air inside the bottle was rising and escaping through the neck of the bottle around the egg.

5. What made the flame go out?

The flame used up most of the oxygen in the bottle.

6. When the flame went out, where was the pressure greatest—inside or outside the bottle?

> Outside the bottle.

7. What made the egg move into the bottle?

> Making the air pressure inside the bottle less than the air pressure outside the bottle. The higher air pressure outside the bottle pushed the egg into the bottle.

8. How can we get the egg out of the bottle?

> By making the air pressure inside the bottle greater than the air pressure outside the bottle.

9. How can we do that?

> By blowing air into the bottle.

Gently rinse the ashes out of the bottle with cool water (making sure the egg remains inside) and let the bottle drain until it is no longer dripping. Wipe the neck of the bottle with a paper towel. Invert the bottle, cover the neck of the bottle with your mouth, and blow into the bottle. Move your mouth away quickly as you feel the egg coming through the neck of the bottle.

10. What forced the egg out of the bottle?

> The greater air pressure inside the bottle pushed it out.

— Practical Application —

1. Why do you think we used a peeled egg for this experiment?

> If the eggshell were on the egg, the egg wouldn't be flexible enough to change its shape as it went through the neck of the bottle.

2. What do you think would happen if an egg in its shell were used for this experiment?

> It might break the shell.

Try it! Repeat the experiment with the unpeeled hard-boiled egg.

Pass around soft and hard objects for the students to feel: a cotton ball, a sponge, a blown-up balloon, a golf ball, and an eggshell.

3. Why aren't things that are soft—like a cotton ball, sponge, or balloon—crushed by the air around them?

> There is usually more air inside softer things than there is in harder objects, and the pressure of the air inside a soft object is equal to the pressure outside it. Softer things are usually more flexible than harder things.

ACTIVITY 30: THE COLLAPSED CAN

Goal: To apply the principle that air exerts pressure
To apply the principle that heat makes air expand

Skills: Observing, inferring, supporting inferences with observation, predicting, hypothesizing

Materials: Empty gallon metal can
Strong heat source (such as a hot plate)
Hot pads or thick leather gloves
Water

Preparation: Wash out the can thoroughly with water.

Preparation Time: 5 minutes

Lesson Time: 20–30 minutes

— Procedure and Questioning Strategy —

Have the students watch as you do the following activity. Put about two inches of water in the bottom of the can. Heat the can on the hot plate WITH THE CAP OFF until the water is boiling vigorously. (This takes a few minutes so you need to plan another activity for these minutes.) Then remove the can from the hot plate and quickly put the cap on tightly. SAFETY TIP: Be sure you use the gloves or hot pads when handling the can. It will be VERY HOT!

1. Let's make some observations. Describe in order what I did.

      You put some water into the can. You put the can on the hot plate. When we saw steam coming out of the can, you took it off the hot plate and put the cap on it.

2. What do you observe now?

      The can is collapsing. The sides are caving in. It is making noise.

3. Let's try to explain why the can collapses. First, how did the air pressure inside the can compare to the air pressure outside the can *before* the can was heated?

      The pressures were the same.

4. How do we know?

      The cap was off and the temperatures inside and out were the same.

5. What did heating the can do to the air inside the can?

      Heating forced some of the air out of the can. (The boiling water in the can helped force some of the air out.)

6. Let's compare this activity to the balloons and bottles and try to figure out why heating the can forced some of the air out. Why do you suppose the air went out of the can?

> Heating the air made it expand. When it expanded some of it escaped, just like the air escaping from a car on a hot day as we discussed in Activity 27.

7. We saw that the balloon expanded when the bottle was heated, but the can didn't expand when it was heated. Why was there a difference?

> The air was allowed to escape from the can because the cap was off, but in the balloons and bottles activities, the balloon was over the mouth of the bottle which prevented the air from escaping from the system. (The balloons and bottles were *closed* systems, but the can was an *open* system.)

8. What happened to the pressure inside the can when the air was allowed to escape?

> The pressure was reduced.

9. Why did the can collapse?

> The pressure inside the can was less than the pressure outside the can, so the sides of the can were pushed in and it collapsed.

10. If I take the cap off the can, will air rush in or will it rush out?

> It will rush in.

Have the students watch carefully as you remove the cap. No danger exists in removing the cap. You will hear a slight "whoosh" as air rushes into the can.

11. What did you observe?

> We heard the sound of air rushing into the can. (The sides of the can also bulge out slightly, but this is hard to see unless the students are watching closely.)

12. What would have happened if I'd left the cover off the can when I took it off the hot plate?

> The can wouldn't have collapsed.

13. Why not?

> The pressures inside and out would have become equal again as the can cooled, so it wouldn't have collapsed.

— Practical Application —

1. What could we do to get the can to expand back to where it was?

> Heat it again.

2. With the cap off or on?

> On.

3. Why?

> If we heat it with the cap off, hot air will escape and the pressure inside the can won't build up.

Put the cap on tightly, put the can back on the hot plate, and heat it again vigorously. When the can gets back to approximately its original shape, remove it from the hot plate. SAFETY TIP: Be sure to remove the can from the hot plate as soon as it is back to its approximate original shape. Extra heating at this point could make it burst. Again, use the hot pads or gloves when handling the can.

4. Let's explain why the can expanded back to its original shape.

> Heating the air in the can made the air want to expand. As it expanded, it exerted pressure on the sides of the can and pushed them back out.

5. Let's think about the air molecules when we *first* heated the can. What happened to them?

> Heating made them move faster. They bounced into each other and into the sides of the can. Some of them bounced out.

6. What did that do?

> It reduced the pressure inside the can so the pressure inside the can was less than on the outside, and the can collapsed.

7. What happened when we heated the can again with the cap on?

> The molecules moved faster and bumped into the sides of the can. The bumping increased the pressure, so the can expanded again.

8. What will happen when the can cools again?

> If we leave the cap on, the can will collapse. If we take the cap off, it will stay "normal."

ACTIVITIES 27–30: CONNECTIONS

> **Goal: To understand the relationships between heat, pressure, and the movement of molecules**
>
> **Skills: Comparing, explaining, supporting explanations with observations**

— Questioning Strategy —

1. Let's review for a moment. What generalizations have we found in this set of activities?

> Heat makes molecules move faster.
> Heat makes molecules bump into each other.
> Heat makes materials expand.

2. What does expand mean?

> The molecules in the materials move away from each other.

3. Why do you think they move away from each other?

> They bump, and when they bump they bounce away from each other.

4. Let's make some comparisons between the egg and the bottle and the crushed can. In what ways were they alike?

> We heated the inside of the bottle with the burning paper, and we also heated the inside of the can with the hot plate. Air escaped from the bottle and air escaped from the can. Because the air escaped, the pressure inside each was lower than the pressure outside. The pressure outside pushed the egg into the bottle, and the pressure outside pushed the sides of the can in.

5. Let's think a bit farther. How do we know the air was escaping from each?

> We saw the egg bob up and down, and we saw the steam coming out of the can.

6. Let's think about what happened in terms of the molecules of air. What happened to them when the bottle and can were heated?

> The molecules started moving faster because they were heated. They bounced around. Some of them bounced out of the jar and some of them bounced out of the can. Because there were fewer molecules inside the jar and inside the can (than there were on the outside), the pressure inside was reduced.

7. What was the critical difference between the egg and bottle activity and the crushed can activity?

> In the egg and bottle activity, the pressure was lowered both by heating and by using some of the oxygen, but in the crushed can activity, the pressure was lowered by heating alone.

8. In the egg and bottle activity, how do we know the pressure was lowered by using some of the oxygen?

> We burned the paper and the burning used oxygen, which lowered the pressure. We saw this same thing happen in Activity 24, "The Rising Water." (You may need to prompt them to relate the burning and oxygen consumption in this activity to the burning and oxygen consumption in Activity 24.)

9. Now let's compare getting the egg out of the bottle to the can expanding again. How were they alike?

> In both cases we increased the pressure on the inside. The increased pressure pushed the egg out of the bottle and the increased pressure pushed the sides of the can back out.

10. How were they different?

> We increased the pressure inside the bottle by putting more air into it (we blew in it, putting more molecules into it). We increased the pressure inside the can by heating the air (making the molecules move faster).

UNIT 7—TRANSFER OF HEAT

Background Information

Heat tends to move from warmer to cooler objects. When objects close to one another have different temperatures, those that are warmer become cooler and those that are cooler become warmer until objects in the same area reach the same temperature. There are three reasons that cause this equalization of temperature—**convection, radiation,** and **conduction.**

As mentioned in the introduction to the States of Matter activities, the molecules of a liquid can move from their places, rolling over and under each other. Molecules in warmer or hot water move faster and farther apart than do the molecules in cooler or colder water.

Think about what happens to warm water when it is poured into an ice cube tray and placed in a freezer. At first, the warm molecules of water are moving rather freely. As the molecules cool, they slow down and get closer together, becoming more densely packed until they turn into ice. Then the molecules just vibrate in place.

Now, imagine that it is summertime. The sun's rays are warm. If you dove into the pond, it would feel warm near the surface and cooler as you reached the bottom of the pond. Why do you think that happens?

The heat from the sun warms the water so the water close to the surface is less dense than the cooler water closer to the bottom of the pond. What do you think would happen if a stream of warm water entered the colder water near the bottom of the pond? The water would rise to the warmer water near the surface of the pond. The movement of warm water from a cool to a warm area is called **convection**. The same thing happens to warm air. Warm air moves upward until it floats on more dense cooler air. Convection is the transfer of heat by a heated substance moving in a current through a fluid, either liquid or gas.

Another way to transfer heat is by **conduction.** Have you ever touched a metal spoon as it rests in a metal saucepan sitting on a hot burner? The spoon feels hot. The heat from the burner is transferred to the saucepan, then to the spoon from the part of the spoon in contact with the hot saucepan. The heat travels up the spoon. When your hand comes in contact with the hot spoon, it feels hot. The transfer of heat, moving from the burner to the pan, through the spoon, and to your hand, is called *conduction.* Metals conduct the transfer of heat very well. In conduction, heat energy is transferred from one particle to another. The molecules of metal in the spoon vibrate the fastest where they touch the hot saucepan. Hot molecules of metal vibrate fast and bump into nearby molecules, making them move faster. The faster the molecules vibrate, the hotter they get. The heat energy is transferred from vibrating molecule to vibrating molecule moving the heat up the spoon. The molecules of metal don't move up the spoon. The molecules pass heat energy from molecule to molecule.

Air is a poor conductor of heat energy, so materials that have more spaces for air within them, like wood and Styrofoam™, are good insulators because they contain air. Many cooking utensils have wooden handles; disposable cups for hot coffee are made of Styrofoam™.

The third way in which heat energy is transferred is through **radiation**. Imagine that you've walked out of an air conditioned room and are standing outside in the summer sun. You can feel the heat of the sun's rays quickly warming you. Radiant energy from the sun travels in waves. It is different from the transfer of heat by convection or conduction because the radiant energy from the sun travels in waves rather than by passing heat energy by moving molecules. Radiant energy is not heat. It changes into heat as it is absorbed by materials that are rough and dark in color. Smooth, light-colored materials reflect most of the radiant energy that hits them and do not become very hot. A fire, stove burner, and light bulb are other sources of radiant energy.

Buildings, cars, and clothes that are light in color keep cooler in the summer because they reflect most of the radiant energy from the sun. Darker colored objects absorb more rays and so become warmer.

Unit 7–NATIONAL SCIENCE EDUCATION STANDARDS

- *Unifying Concepts and Processes:* Students should develop understanding and abilities with regard to systems, order, and organization; evidence, models, and explanation; constancy, change, and measurement; evolution and equilibrium; and form and function.

- *Science as Inquiry*—Content Standard A: Students should develop the necessary skills to do scientific inquiry and develop an understanding about scientific inquiry.

- *Physical Science*—Content Standard B: Students should develop an understanding of the properties of objects and materials; position and motion; light, heat, electricity, and magnetism; properties and changes of properties in matter; and transfer of energy.

- *History and Nature of Science*—Content Standard G: Students should develop an understanding of the nature of science and of science as a human endeavor.

◼◼◼ ACTIVITY 31: HEAT – THE DENSITY OF HOT AND COLD WATER ◼◼◼

Goal: To understand that hot water is less dense than cold water

Skills: Observing, inferring, confirming inferences with observation, hypothesizing

Materials: Four 1-quart jars (such as mayonnaise jars)
Food coloring
Hot water (use a coffee maker or heat water in a pan on a burner)
Cold tap water
Tray of ice cubes
Two pieces of cardboard, 6" square (such as cardboard from writing tablets)
Rubber gloves (like for dishwashing)
Paper towels

Preparation: None

Preparation Time: None

Lesson Time: 15–20 minutes

— **Procedure and Questioning Strategy** —

Display all the materials.

1. Now everyone, watch what I am doing here.

Drop 4 to 5 ice cubes into one of the jars and fill it with cold tap water to slightly below the rim.

2. What do you observe?

    You have a jar filled with cold water.

3. How do you know the water is cold?

    You filled it from the cold tap and put ice in it.

Put a few drops of food coloring in a second jar and fill it with the hot water.

4. Now what do you observe?

    You have a jar of hot water. The water is colored.

Put on the rubber gloves, cover the mouth of the jar with one of the cardboard pieces, invert the jar, and place it carefully over the mouth of the jar of cold water.

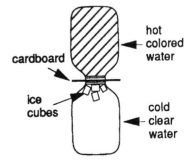

5. Now we want to try to pull the card out from between the two jars.

You can play this up as "high drama." (Students often believe that this can't be done.) Hold the jars steady so they don't slide back and forth over each other. Have a student pull the card out from between the two jars firmly and steadily. Don't have him/her "yank" the card out. You should only spill a small amount of water in accomplishing this.

6. Now what do you observe?

> The jar of hot colored water is sitting upside down on the jar of cold water. The colored water and the clear water are only mixing a little bit. The colored water is mostly floating on the top of the clear water. The ice cubes went to the top of the hot colored water.

7. Now let's think about this. Why do you suppose the hot water is floating on the cold water?

> The hot water is less dense than the cold water.

If students are unable to respond, remind them about their experience with the oil and water as well as with the ice, alcohol, and water.

8. How do we know?

> Less dense substances float on more dense substances, and the hot water is floating on the cold water so it must be less dense.

9. What do we know about ice, based on what we observe here?

> Ice is less dense than both cold and hot water.

10. How do we know?

> It went up and floated on the hot water.

11. Now, what do you suppose would happen if the hot water were on the bottom and the cold water were on top?

Have them hypothesize.

12.   Let's try it.

Fill the third jar with hot water. Put food coloring into the fourth jar, fill it with cold tap water and ice, cover its mouth with the second cardboard square, then invert it and place it over the jar of hot water.

ice
cubes

cold
colored
water

cardboard

hot
clear
water

13. Now watch carefully.

Again, have the student pull the cardboard from between the two jars firmly and steadily.

14. What do you observe this time?

The water in the two jars is mixing quickly. The cold water is moving down into the hot water and pushing it up. The ice cubes are staying at the top of the cold water.

15. **Why do you suppose this is happening?**

    The cold water is more dense than the hot water so it won't float on the hot water. It sinks to the bottom. The ice cubes are the least dense so they stay at the top.

16. **Now let's look again at our first two jars. Will the colored and clear waters ever mix in them?**

    Yes.

17. **When will this happen?**

    When the temperatures become the same.

18. **What will that do?**

    When the temperatures become the same, the densities will be the same, and the colored and clear waters will mix.

Leave the two jars as they are for several hours or overnight. Discuss the results later or the next day.

— Practical Application —

1. **Imagine that you are out swimming in a lake (or ocean). Where would you expect the water to be warmer, at the top or down several feet?**

    The water will be warmer at the top.

2. **Why do you think that will be the case?**

    Warm water is less dense than cold water, so it floats to the top.

3. **You're out fishing for a particular kind of fish and you know that it likes to live in cold water. Would you keep your hook near the surface of the water to catch this fish or would you dangle it near the bottom?**

    Near the bottom.

4. **Why do you think dangling the hook near the bottom will work the best?**

    The water is colder near the bottom, so this is where this fish is most likely to be.

5. **Let's think about the water heater in our homes. Where would we expect to find the hottest water in the water heater?**

    At the top.

6. **Why do you think so?**

    Hot water is less dense than cold water, so the hot water will rise to the top of the water heater and the colder water will sink to the bottom.

ACTIVITY 32: HEAT TRANSFER – CONVECTION

Goal: To understand convection as a method of transferring heat in substances

Skills: Observing, inferring, comparing, confirming inferences with observations

Materials: Large transparent container (such as a very large pickle jar or a fish bowl)
Baby food jar
Food coloring
Piece of aluminum foil (to cover the mouth of the baby food jar)
Rubber band
Hot water (use a coffee maker or heat water in a pan on a burner)
Tray of ice cubes
The drawing on page 119
Thread
Scissors
Light bulb and socket (such as a mechanic's lamp or a table lamp)

Preparation: 1. Fill the large jar or bowl 2/3 full of cold water and put several ice cubes in it.
2. Cut out the spiral on page 119. Attach it to the thread with a stapler.

Preparation Time: 5 minutes

Lesson Time: 15–20 minutes

— Procedure and Questioning Strategy —

Place the container of cold water in front of the students.

1. What do you observe here?

    (Students will make a variety of observations. Among them may be: there is jar of water; you can see through the jar; the jar is nearly full; the water is cold.)

2. How do you know that the water is cold?

    It has ice in it.

3. Now watch what I do and observe carefully.

Drop 3–4 drops of food coloring into the baby food jar, fill it with hot water, cover it with the aluminum foil, and bind the foil to the jar with the rubber band.

4. What do we have here?

    A little jar of water. The water is colored. The water is hot.

5. How do we know that the water is hot?

    You poured it out of the pot/pan that had been heating the water.

You may want to have them confirm that the water is hot by having a student hold his/her hand near the jar so he/she can feel the heat.

6.   Now watch.

Put the baby food jar of hot water into the large jar of cold water. Poke a small hole in the aluminum foil with the point of a pencil.

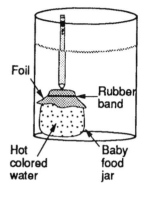

7.   What do you observe?

> You poked a hole in the aluminum foil. A little stream of colored water is moving up to the top of the jar/bowl. The colored water is sort of floating on the top of the cold water.

8.   What is the difference between the little stream of water and the water in the jar/bowl?

> The little stream is hot and colored and the water in the jar/bowl is cold and clear.

9.   Why does the little stream of water go up to the top of the cold water?

> It is less dense.

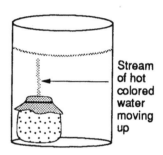

10.   How does this compare to the movement of the water in our last activity (Activity 31)?

> In this activity, the warm water floated on the cold water. In Activity 31, the cold water sank down into the warm water and pushed the warm water up.

11.   This movement of warm water, because it is less dense than cold water, is called CONVECTION.

CONVECTION is the transfer of heat as a result of the particles (molecules) of the warm substance actually moving from one place to another.

— Practical Application —

Turn on the lamp and wait a moment for the bulb to get hot. Display the spiral for the students, holding it over the naked bulb.

1.   What do you observe?

> The spiral is beginning to rotate.

2.   Now let's try to figure out why it rotates. What is the light bulb doing?

> It is heating the air above it.

3. Now let's think carefully back to what we did with the hot and cold water. How do you suppose the warm air above the bulb compares to the cooler air around it?

    It is less dense.

4. How do we know?

    The hot water was less dense than the cold water, so the warm air should be less dense than the cooler air.

5. Because it is less dense, what does the warm air do?

    It floats on the cooler air and moves upward, like the water did.

6. So, why did the spiral rotate?

    The warm air moving upward from the light bulb made it rotate.

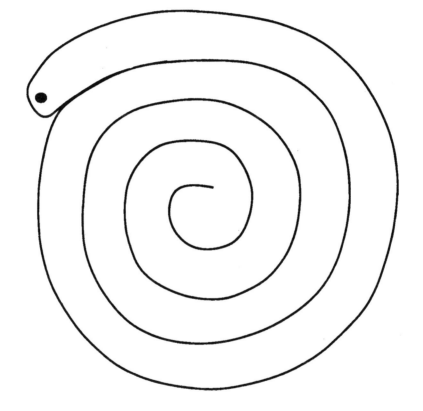

▬▬▬▬ ACTIVITY 33: HEAT TRANSFER – CONDUCTION ▬▬▬▬

> **Goal:** To understand how heat is transferred through the process of conduction
>
> **Skills:** Observing, inferring, comparing, confirming inferences with observations
>
> **Materials:**   Transparent heatproof container
>   Source of heat, such as a burner or hot plate
>   Long metal object, such as a pair of all-metal tongs
>   Water
>
> **Preparation:** Heat the water in the container on the hot plate.
>
> **Preparation Time:** 5 minutes
>
> **Lesson Time:** 15–20 minutes

— Procedure and Questioning Strategy —

Hold up the tongs for all students to see and ask two or three students to feel the handles. Now display the container with the hot water in it, then put the tongs inside.

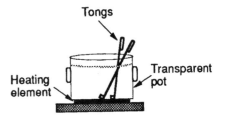

1. Some of you felt the tongs as we were all getting ready for science. What did you feel, (student's name)?

    They were hard. …smooth. …cold.

Direct the next questions to other students.

2. What do you observe about the container?

    (Among their observations will be: there is water in the container; the tongs are in the container; the container and water are hot.)

3. Now, (student's name), feel the top of the tongs. How do they feel this time?

    They are still hard. …smooth. They are warm.

4. How does the temperature of the handle of the tongs now compare to the temperature when you felt them the first time, (student's name)?

    They are warmer now.

5. Let's everyone make some other comparisons. In addition to the tongs being warmer now, what other differences are there?

(They will make a variety of comparisons. In the process, prompt them to make the following: the tongs are in the pot with the hot water now and they weren't before; the tongs are touching the bottom of the container now; the container is touching the burner/hot plate.)

6. **What is the source of the heat?**

    The burner/hot plate.

7. **Where did the heat go?**

    To the container.

8. **Then where?**

    To the bottom of the tongs.

9. **And finally to where?**

    Up the tongs to the handle.

10. **Let's compare this process of heating to what we did in Activities 31 and 32. What is the difference?**

    In those activities the hot water particles (molecules) actually moved from one place to another. Here the tongs got hot, but the molecules in the tongs didn't really move to a different location.

11. **How do you know?**

    The tongs didn't change their shape or "run" like water runs.

12. **What are the molecules in the tongs doing?**

    They are moving faster. As they bump each other, they move faster part of the way up the tongs. Gradually, the faster movement works its way to the top of the tongs.

13. **Does anyone know what we call this process that heated the tongs?**

    (Assuming that no one knows the term, identify it as CONDUCTION.)

CONDUCTION is the process of transferring heat where objects are in contact with one another and the particles of the heated substance don't move from one place to another.

— Practical Application —

1. **Let's think of some examples of conduction that we see in our daily lives.**

    (They will give a variety of answers. Among them can be: a pan on the burner of a stove; your feet on a hot sidewalk in the summer.)

.

2. What do these examples have in common?

> The object that is being heated is in contact with the object that is heating it.
> The particles of the heated object don't move from one place to another.

Hold your hand above the warm container.

3. My hand is getting warm. Is it being heated by conduction?

> No.

4. Why not?

> Your hand is not touching the container.

ACTIVITY 34: HEAT TRANSFER – RADIATION

Goal: To understand radiation as a method of heat transfer

Skills: Observing, comparing, generalizing

Materials: Source of hot water, such as a coffee maker or a burner with a pan
The drawing on page 126
For each group of four students:
A plastic drinking cup
Hot water

Preparation: 1. Heat the water so that it is quite warm, but not so hot the students can
burn themselves.
2. Place empty drinking cups in (or near) groups so that all four students
can hold their hands over and near the cups.
3. Make a transparency from the drawing on page 126.

Preparation Time: 2 minutes

Lesson Time: 10–15 minutes

— Procedure and Questioning Strategy —

1. To begin today, everyone rub your hands together as fast and hard as you can. Keep rubbing them together.

Wait a few seconds as they vigorously rub their hands together. Go around the room and pour hot water into the drinking cups as they are rubbing their hands together.

2. What do you feel or observe?

Our hands are getting very hot.

3. Now hold your hands up very near your cheeks, but DO NOT TOUCH THEM. What do you feel now?

We feel warmth on our cheeks.

4. Where is the heat coming from?

Our hands.

5. Now hold your hands near the sides and above the drinking cups but do not touch them. What do you feel?

Heat.

6.   Where is the heat coming from?

   The hot water.

7.   Now let's compare our two examples. What do they have in common?

   We felt warmth both times. It came from our hands in the first case and from the water in the second case.

8.   What else do they have in common?

   We weren't touching anything in either case. We were just up close.

9.   Is the heat we felt the result of conduction?

   No.

10.   Why not?

   Objects are touching each other when they're heated by conduction.

11.   Was the heat we felt the result of convection?

   No.

12.   Why not?

   No material (molecules) moved from one place to another.

13.   Now look at the transparency.

Display the transparency for them.

14.   What do you observe in the transparency?

   People are sitting by the fire. They are holding their hands up. There are waves coming from the fire.

15.   What do you suppose the people are doing?

   Warming their hands.

16.   What do you suppose the waves are?

   Heat waves.

17.   The transparency shows people getting warm by an open fire. Do you think that heat waves come off of other objects, such as the cup of hot water?

   Yes.

18.   Why do you think so?

We held our hands near the cup and we felt heat, just like the people in the transparency are holding their hands up and are feeling heat.

19. So, what kinds of objects do you think send off heat waves?

Any hot object.

20. This is another way that heat is transferred. It is called RADIATION.

RADIATION is a method of transferring heat by sending the heat energy out in waves from the warm object.

21. Let's form a definition of radiation.

It is sending off heat waves from any warm object.

— Practical Application —

1. Let's think about some objects that radiate heat. What are some examples?

The burner on a stove.
A candle.
A fireplace.
A pan of hot water.
A cup of hot chocolate.
A cup of coffee.
A portable heater.
Hot pavement or sand that has soaked up heat from the sun (you can often see the heat waves rising).

Be sure to warn the students not to hold their hands too near hot objects, such as the burner on a stove, a candle, a hot pan, a steam heat register, a light bulb, or a wood-burning stove.

2. What is another very important source that radiates heat for all of us?

(Prompt students to say "the sun.")

3. Once we get past our atmosphere, is there any air between us and the sun?

No.

At this point you may want to tell the students that a VACUUM is space that contains no matter.

4. What does that tell us about radiation?

It doesn't need anything to pass through. It will pass through a vacuum.

ACTIVITY 35: HEAT AND INSULATION

Goal: To understand that the loss of heat can be prevented by using insulation

Skills: Observing, inferring, generalizing

Materials: Plastic funnel (to make filling the soft drink cans easier)
　　　　　　Pitcher of hot water, not boiling (from the tap or use a heat
　　　　　　　source)
　　　　　　For each pair of students:
　　　　　　　A soft drink can (For consistent results, be sure all cans are
　　　　　　　the same brand.)
　　　　　　　A school science thermometer (or fever thermometer if no
　　　　　　　other type is available)
　　　　　　For one-third of the groups:
　　　　　　　Paper towels
　　　　　　　Tape or rubber bands
　　　　　　For another third of the groups:
　　　　　　　Styrofoam™ insulators for the soft drink cans

Preparation: 1. Fill the pitcher with hot water from the tap, pan, or pot.
　　　　　　　2. Distribute the paper towels with tape or rubber bands
　　　　　　　　and the Styrofoam™ insulators to the groups that are
　　　　　　　　supposed to get them. Give a thermometer to each group.

Preparation Time: 5 minutes

Lesson Time: 20–30 minutes

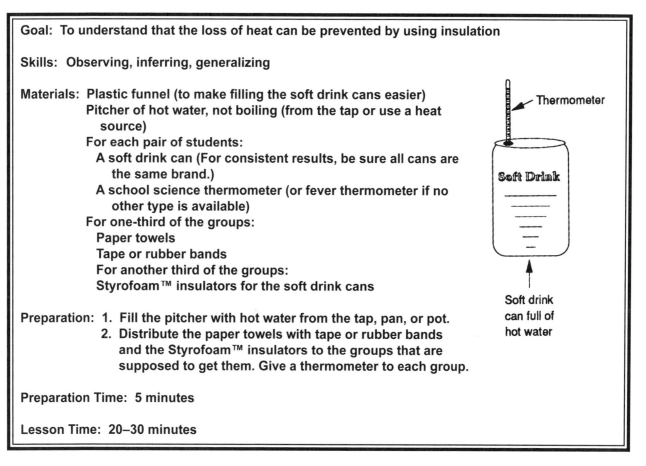

Thermometer

Soft Drink

Soft drink
can full of
hot water

— Procedure and Questioning Strategy —

1. We have been studying how heat is transferred using conduction, convection, and radiation. Today we're going to investigate what kinds of things best keep heat from escaping. For the third of you who have the paper towel, fold the towel in thirds, wrap it around your can, and fasten it with the tape or a rubber band. For the third of you with the Styrofoam™ container, put the can in it.

Give students a minute to wrap the towels around their cans and to put their cans into the Styrofoam™ containers.

2. I'm going to come around and fill your cans with hot water. As soon as I do, put the thermometer in the can, read it, time yourself for 2 minutes, then read it again. Continue to read the thermometer every 2 minutes until you have 5 readings. Write the temperature down each time. Both of you read the thermometer to be sure you're accurate.

Go around the room filling each group's can with hot water. Monitor the students to be certain that they are reading their thermometers and recording their data accurately. As you monitor their progress, prepare a chart on the chalkboard that appears as follows:

	No Insulation				Paper Insulation				Styrofoam™			
Group →	1	2	3	...	1	2	3	...	1	2	3	...
Reading 1												
2												
3												
4												
5												

After all the groups have recorded their data, begin.

3. Now, let's look at the chart. What kinds of patterns do we see there?

Our readings kept getting smaller.

4. Why did they get smaller?

The water in the cans was cooling off. The temperature was getting lower.

5. What other patterns do you see?

The cans that didn't have any wrapping on them cooled off the fastest.

6. How do you know?

The temperatures for those groups dropped the fastest.

7. What does this tell us about the escaping heat?

The heat escaped the fastest from the cans without anything on them.

8. What else do you observe?

The temperature didn't drop very much for the cans in the Styrofoam™ covers.

9. What does that tell us?

Styrofoam™ is good for keeping heat from escaping.

10. How good is paper?

It is better than nothing, but not as good as Styrofoam™.

11. How do you know?

The temperature didn't go down as fast as it did when there was no insulation, but it went down faster than when the Styrofoam™ was used.

12. We say Styrofoam™ is a good INSULATOR. Now let's state a definition of an insulator.

An insulator is a material that prevents heat from passing through it easily.

AN INSULATOR is a material that doesn't readily conduct heat energy.

— Practical Application —

1. When we go outdoors when it's cold, what do we always put on?

A jacket, coat, or sweater.

2. Why do we put on a jacket or coat?

It keeps us warm.

3. How does it do that?

It prevents the heat from escaping from our bodies.

4. So what would we call the jacket or coat?

An insulator.

5. Where else do we find insulators?

(Prompt them to suggest the insulation in their homes.)

If you have time, or if you want to extend this activity, you can examine the effects of insulation on cold water as well. In this case, simply put cold water in the cans and record the temperature increases. Then conduct the questioning sequence as above and note that insulation works for both warm and cold materials.

ACTIVITIES 31–35: CONNECTIONS

Goal: To understand the relationships between convection, conduction, and radiation

Skills: Comparing, explaining, inferring, supporting inferences with observation

---

— Questioning Strategy —

1. Let's think about conduction, convection, and radiation and make some comparisons. What are some of the ways that all three are alike?

   They are all ways that heat moves from one place to another. We have common experiences with all three.

2. Now let's think about differences. How is radiation different from conduction and convection?

   Radiation doesn't need any matter to travel through, but conduction and convection do.

3. What is an example which shows that radiation doesn't need matter to travel through?

   We get radiation from the sun. The sun's radiation travels through space to get here. There is no matter in space. It is a vacuum. (Technically, there is no such thing as a vacuum because all space as we know it contains some matter. But for all intents and purposes, space is a vacuum.)

4. How are conduction and convection different?

   With convection the molecules of the heated substance actually move from one place to another, but with conduction, they don't.

5. What evidence did we have which shows that?

   The little stream of warm, colored water actually moved to the top of the cold water. This was a convection current. With the tongs, the molecules bumped each other, but they didn't actually move from one place to another.

6. How do we know the molecules of the tongs didn't move from one place to another?

   The tongs stayed the same as they were to start with.

7. What would have happened to the tongs if the molecules in them had moved from one place to another?

   Their shape would have changed. They would have begun to melt like an ice cube.

8. Now let's see how insulation affects conduction, convection, and radiation. What does insulation do?

   It keeps heat from passing through it.

9. Give me a common example of a substance that is a good insulator.

   Styrofoam™, wood, leather, cloth (focus on the Styrofoam™).

10. Would you say the molecules of the Styrofoam™ are close together or are not close together?

    Probably not close together.

11. Why do you think so?

    Styrofoam™ is not very dense. A large piece (large volume) doesn't weigh very much (small mass).

12. Let's make a generalization about insulators.

    Insulators in general tend to have low densities.

13. How about glass? Is it a good insulator?

    No, not very.

14. How do we know?

    We use glass for cookware. This means it must conduct heat. If it didn't conduct heat, we wouldn't cook with it.

15. Which do you think conducts heat better, glass or metal?

    Metal.

16. How do we know?

    Hot liquids cool off faster in a metal cup than they do in a glass cup, and warm liquids warm up faster in a metal cup than they do in a glass cup.

You can easily test this idea by putting hot water into both a metal cup and a glass cup, putting a thermometer in each, and recording the changes in temperature for each. This would also be a good way to extend Activity 35.

UNIT 8—FLIGHT AND AERODYNAMICS

Background Information

In the unit on Air Pressure, we found that air can exert pressure on objects and exposed surfaces of water. When you add air to a tire, the pressure exerted by the air is the same on all inner parts of the tire. All sides of the tire increase in size equally. This is because air generally exerts the same amount of pressure in all directions. Look at figure A. Think about the system involved when air is blown into the tire.

figure A

The tire, pump, and air create a closed system. Nothing from outside the system can enter the system. In this closed system, the fast-moving air pumped into the tire creates higher pressure in the tire.

Imagine a jet flying though the air (figure B). Think about how this is an example of an open system. Imagine that the jet is moving forward, cutting through the air, separating it. Some air moves over the plane, and some air moves under it.

figure B

Look at the shape of the wings. The top of the wing is curved, and the bottom of the wing is flat. As the air flows over the top of the wing, it has a greater distance to travel than does the air flowing under the wing.

Figure C shows a cross section of the airplane wing.

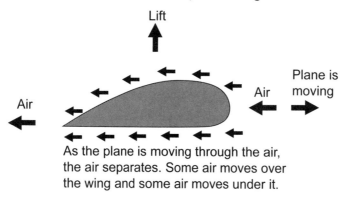

As the plane is moving through the air, the air separates. Some air moves over the wing and some air moves under it.

figure C

As the plane cuts through the air, the shape of the wing causes the air molecules to move faster over the top of the wing. The air molecules flowing over the top are farther apart than the molecules flowing under the wing. When air molecules are farther apart, they are less dense and exert less pressure on the surfaces they pass, like the top of the wing. Molecules under the wing are more dense and exert more pressure. This causes the higher air pressure under the wing to push upward, causing the plane to lift. The amount of lift also depends on the speed of the plane. The faster the plane travels, the more lift is created. The decrease in the amount of pressure exerted on the top surfaces of the wings actually causes the airplane to lift, counteracting the force of gravity that is pulling it in a downward direction.

Bernoulli's principle explains this phenomenon. The faster that air (or any fluid) flows over a surface, the less force it exerts on the surfaces it passes. When lift and the pull of gravity are equal, the plane can fly horizontally. A plane climbs upward until it reaches a certain altitude, then it can level off and continue flying at a constant altitude.

Bernoulli's principle also applies in a tornado system. The circular, whirling winds of a violent tornado can reach up to 500 mph (800 kilometers per hour). Because these winds are moving so fast, they exert less pressure on the air inside the tornado, causing a low pressure to develop inside the tornado. The decrease in pressure on the inside of the tornado causes the higher pressure outside the whirling winds to push objects that are in the tornado's path upward into the low-pressure area in the center of the tornado. Other examples of the effects of the Bernoulli principle are included in the lessons in this unit.

Unit 8–NATIONAL SCIENCE EDUCATION STANDARDS

- *Unifying Concepts and Processes:* Students should develop understanding and abilities with regard to systems, order, and organization; evidence, models, and explanation; constancy, change, and measurement; evolution and equilibrium; and form and function.

- *Science as Inquiry*—Content Standard A: Students should develop the necessary skills to do scientific inquiry and develop an understanding about scientific inquiry.

- *Physical Science*—Content Standard B: Students should develop an understanding of the properties of objects and materials; position and motion of objects; properties and changes of properties in matter; and motions and forces.

- *Earth and Space Science*—Content Standard D: Students should develop an understanding of the structure of the earth system.

- *History and Nature of Science*—Content Standard G: Students should develop an understanding of the nature of science and of science as a human endeavor.

ACTIVITY 36: SPEED AND FORCE OF AIR

Goal: To understand Bernoulli's principle which says the faster that air flows over a surface, the less force it exerts on the surface

Skills: Observing, inferring, comparing, generalizing, supporting inferences with observations, explaining

Materials: A sheet of 8 1/2" x 11" paper for each student

Preparation: 1. Divide the students into pairs. One member will perform the activity while the second observes (then have them switch roles).
2. Have the students fold and tear their pieces of paper in half "widthwise."
3. Tell the students to take their two pieces of paper and hold them parallel to each other about one to two inches apart (see drawing below).

Preparation Time: 1 minute

Lesson Time: 15–20 minutes

— Procedure and Questioning Strategy —

1. We are going to blow between the two pieces of paper. What will happen to them?

   They usually predict that the papers will fly apart at the bottom.

Ask the first member of each pair to blow between the papers and tell the second member to make several careful observations. Tell them to switch roles and repeat the activity using their own paper.

2. What did you observe?

   The papers came together at the bottom. They made noise. They fluttered. If you blow harder, they come together harder. They move back apart when you stop blowing. The harder you blow, the more they flutter.

3. Let's make an inference about the force on each of the papers. Was the force greater between the papers pushing out or on the outside of the papers pushing in?

   On the outside pushing in.

4. How do we know?

   The papers moved inward.

5. What would have happened if the force between the papers had been greater?

   The papers would have moved apart.

6. Where was the speed of the air greater—between or on the outside of the papers?

   Between the papers.

7. How do we know?

> That's where we blew.

8. Now let's try this. Take one of the papers and hold it just below your bottom lip. What will happen when we blow over the paper?

> Answers will vary.

Have the first member of each pair blow over the paper while the second makes observations. Switch roles and repeat.

9. What did you observe this time?

> The paper came up. The paper fluttered.
> The harder you blew, the more the paper seemed to come up.

10. Let's make an inference about the force on the paper. Was the force greater on the top pushing down or on the bottom pushing up?

> On the bottom pushing up.

11. How do we know?

> The paper went up.

12. Where was the air moving faster—over the top of the paper or underneath the paper?

> Over the top.

13. Compare the activity with the two papers to the activity with the single paper. What kind of pattern do we see?

> In both cases where the speed of the air over the surface of the paper was greater, the force it exerted on the paper was less.

14. Think about the two papers again. What things could we change about the papers without affecting the experiment?

> Whether or not they have writing on them, whether or not they are lined, whether or not they have holes along the edges, what color they are—none of these affect the experiment.

— Practical Application —

1. You're standing in a shower that has a shower curtain. As you're showering, what does the curtain tend to do?

> It comes in toward you.

2. Explain why it comes in.

> Some of the air inside the shower moves with the water, so the speed of the air inside is greater than the speed outside. As a result, the force is less inside and the shower curtain is pushed in.

ACTIVITY 37: THE BALL AND THE FUNNEL

Goal: To understand Bernoulli's principle, which says the faster that air flows over a surface, the less force it exerts on the surface

Skills: Observing, inferring, predicting, generalizing, hypothesizing, explaining, supporting inferences with observations

Materials: Small transparent glass or plastic funnel
Ping-Pong® ball

Preparation: None

Preparation Time: None

Lesson Time: 15–20 minutes

— Procedure and Questioning Strategy —

1. I am going to put the Ping-Pong® ball into the mouth of the funnel and blow through the neck of the funnel. As soon as I start blowing, I am going to take my finger away from the ball. What will happen to the ball?

   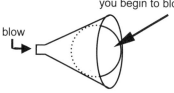

   Students usually predict that the ball will fly out or drop down. Some may predict that it will remain in the funnel.

Blow, or have a student blow, through the neck of the funnel.
SAFETY TIP: Clean the neck of the funnel with soap and water or alcohol, and rinse thoroughly, if you have more than one student demonstrate the activity.

2. What did you see? (Ask for several observations.)

   The ball stayed in the funnel.
   It rotated.
   We could hear a sound.
   The ball bounced around in the funnel.

3. I want (select a student) to hold his/her finger in front of the ball without touching it. Then I want him/her to hold a finger inside the rim of the funnel as I blow.

   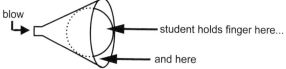

Blow through the funnel and have the student hold his/her finger directly in front of the ball and then just inside the rim of the funnel.

4. Have the student describe for the rest of the class where he/she felt the air moving faster.

    Around the rim of the funnel. Little air movement can be felt directly in front of the ball.

Put a drawing on the chalkboard for reference showing where the fastest air can be felt.

5. Where is the air moving faster—behind the ball (2) or in front of the ball (1)?

    Behind the ball (2).

6. How do we know?

    We blew in there and we felt little air movement in front of the ball (1).

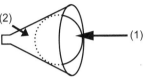

7. Let's make an inference about the force. Where is the force greater—in front of the ball pushing it in (1) or behind the ball pushing it out (2)?

    In front of the ball (1).

8. How do we know?

    The ball stays in the funnel when we blow into it.

9. Relate the speed of the air over the surface of the ball to the force on the ball.

    Where the speed of the air was greater (behind the ball), the force it exerted on the ball was less.

— Practical Application —

1. Think about the ball and the funnel again. What if we held the funnel with the mouth straight down and blew through the neck of the funnel? What would happen to the ball?

    It would still stay in the funnel since the speed over the back of the ball is greater than the speed in front of the ball.

2. Suppose the window in your neighbor's car is somehow broken and he/she covers the open area with a piece of plastic. As you're riding in the car, the plastic sort of bulges. Does it bulge out or does it bulge in?

    It bulges out.

3. Why does it bulge out?

    As the car travels along the road, the air is moving faster on the outside of the car than it is on the inside of the car. Because of this air movement, the force of the air is greater on the inside, and the plastic is *pushed out*.

ACTIVITY 38: THE CARD AND THE SPOOL

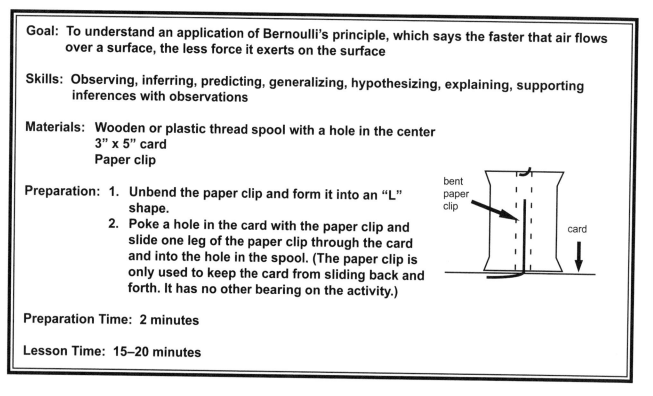

Goal: To understand an application of Bernoulli's principle, which says the faster that air flows over a surface, the less force it exerts on the surface

Skills: Observing, inferring, predicting, generalizing, hypothesizing, explaining, supporting inferences with observations

Materials: Wooden or plastic thread spool with a hole in the center
3" x 5" card
Paper clip

Preparation: 1. Unbend the paper clip and form it into an "L" shape.
2. Poke a hole in the card with the paper clip and slide one leg of the paper clip through the card and into the hole in the spool. (The paper clip is only used to keep the card from sliding back and forth. It has no other bearing on the activity.)

bent paper clip

card

Preparation Time: 2 minutes

Lesson Time: 15–20 minutes

— Procedure and Questioning Strategy —

Hold the spool between your fingers, hold the card under it, and stand so students can observe the activity easily.

1. I am going to blow through the hole in the spool. What will happen to the card?
   (Predictions will vary.)

Blow through the hole, taking your hand away from under the card as soon as you start blowing.

2. What did you observe?
   The card stayed on the spool.
   I heard a noise.
   The card rotated a little.

bent paper clip
air   air
card

3. Why did the card stay next to the spool?
   You were blowing through the hole in the spool, so the speed of the air was increased over the top of the card, which decreased the force on the top of the card.

4. How can we determine if the speed of the air is greater over the top of the card?
   We can feel it.

5. Let's try it.

Blow through the hole in the spool while the student puts his/her finger above the card, then below, without touching the card or spool.

6. What did you feel?

    The air was moving faster over the top of the card than it was below the card.

7. Let's make an inference about the force on the card. Where was the force greater—above the card pushing down or below the card pushing up?

    Below the card pushing up.

8. How do we know?

    The card didn't fall down.

9. What would happen if the force on top were greater?

    The card would fall.

10. How can we compare the behavior of the card to the behavior of the papers in Activity 36 or to the ball in the funnel in Activity 37?

    In each case where the speed of the air over the surface was greater, the force it exerted on the surface was less.

— Practical Application —

1. You are riding in a car with an open window. Your arm is resting on the door and a ribbon is tied to your wrist. What happens to the ribbon?

    It tries to go out the car window.

2. Explain why it tries to go out the window based on our generalization?

    The air is moving faster outside the car (because the car is moving through the air) than it is inside the car, so the force outside the car is less than the force inside the car and the air is *pushed out*.

3. Let's look again at the spool and the card. Suppose we held it like this (the hole parallel to the ground and the card vertical). What would happen to the card?

    It would stay next to the spool because the speed of the air over the card is greater next to the spool (1) than it is behind the card (2).

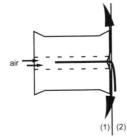

━━ ACTIVITY 39: AIRPLANE WINGS – THE FLIGHT OF AIRPLANES ━━

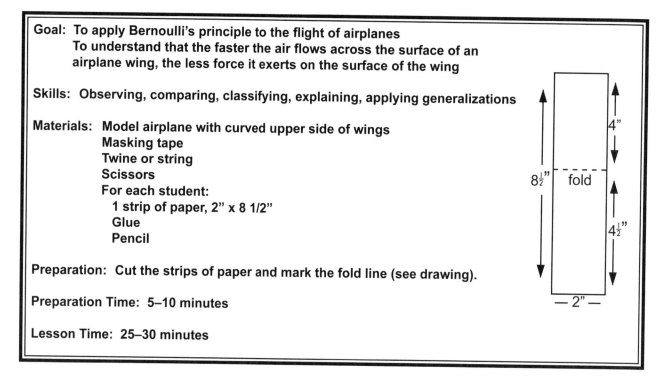

Goal: To apply Bernoulli's principle to the flight of airplanes
To understand that the faster the air flows across the surface of an airplane wing, the less force it exerts on the surface of the wing

Skills: Observing, comparing, classifying, explaining, applying generalizations

Materials: Model airplane with curved upper side of wings
Masking tape
Twine or string
Scissors
For each student:
1 strip of paper, 2" x 8 1/2"
Glue
Pencil

Preparation: Cut the strips of paper and mark the fold line (see drawing).

Preparation Time: 5–10 minutes

Lesson Time: 25–30 minutes

— Procedure and Questioning Strategy —

Drop a pencil, letting it fall to the floor.

1. What caused the pencil to fall to the floor?
   Gravity.

2. Suppose you threw a ball up into the air. What would happen to it?
   It would go up into the air then fall back down.

3. Would a ball always come back down?
   Yes. Unless there were no gravity.

Show the model airplane, demonstrating how it would rise in the air at takeoff.

4. Gravity tugs at an airplane, pulling it down as it takes off from the runway. What does it need to overcome the pull of gravity so it can take off?
   Some force that lifts it up.

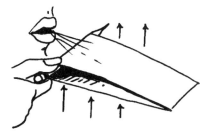

Distribute a strip of paper, glue, and a pencil (if necessary) to each student. They are going to make and test an airfoil as shown in the drawing. Have them:

- Crease the paper on the fold line.
- Glue the ends of the paper together to make the airfoil.
- Hold the airfoil with a pencil placed horizontally in the curved side of the airfoil.
- Hold their lower lips close to the curved fold of the airfoil.
- Blow a fast stream of air over the top of the airfoil as shown in the drawing.

5. What happened to the airfoil?

It lifted up in the air.

6. Where was the fastest-moving air?

Above the airfoil.

7. What do we know about the speed of air and the force it exerts on a surface?

The faster the speed of air, the less force it exerts.

8. So what is the reason the airfoil lifted up?

The higher air pressure under the airfoil lifted it up.

9. Let's see how that works with an airplane.

Show the model airplane. Have the students measure across the top surface of the wing. If it is aerodynamically sound, the top surface of the airplane wing is more curved than the bottom surface.

Draw this diagram about 3 or 4 feet long on the board:

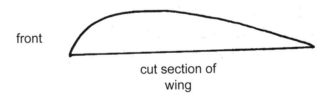

front

cut section of
wing

Demonstrate with the model airplane that the wing of an airplane separates the air as it moves through it. Some of the air flows over the wing and some flows under the wing. The section of air above the wing and the section of air under the wing separates as the front of the wing cuts through the air. Each section of air meets at the back of the wing at the same time.

Ask a student to help you tape a single piece of twine or string along the entire wing outlined on the board. Cut the piece of twine off at the front and back of the wing so that you will have two pieces—one showing the actual length of the top and the other the actual length of the bottom of the wing. Untape the two pieces of string and hold

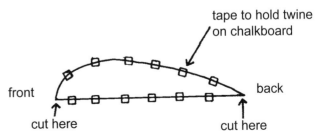

tape to hold twine
on chalkboard

front

back

cut here   cut here

them up so the students can compare their lengths.

10. Which piece of string is longer?

    The piece from the top of the wing.

11. So is the distance farther along the top of the wing or under the wing?

    Along the top of the wing.

12. Think about the air all around us in this room.

Hold the airplane and move it horizontally through the air.

13. What happens to the air as the airplane goes through it?

    It moves over and under the airplane.

14. The wings of the airplane are shaped like the airfoils we just made. Would air move faster on the top surface or the under surface of the wings?

    On the top surface (over) the wings.

15. What reason do you have for saying that?

    The air on the top of the wing has a farther distance to go in the same amount of time.

16. If the air on top of the wing travels faster, then where would the greater force be exerted, on the top surface of the wing or the bottom surface?

    On the bottom surface.

17. How do you know that?

    Because the faster the air flows, the less force it exerts. There would be less force on the top and more force on the bottom of the wing.

— Practical Application —

To demonstrate this more concretely, make another diagram on the floor (like the one drawn on the board) from masking tape. The diagram should be at least 6 feet long so students can walk around it. Have the students walk in pairs, with one student from each pair speeding up to meet the other student in the pair at the back of the wing.

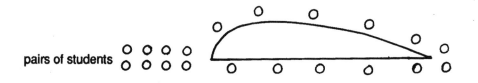

1. Which person in your pair had to move faster to meet at the back of the wing?

    The person walking along the top of the wing.

2. If each of you were molecules of air, would you be closer together when you were moving along the top or the bottom of the wing?

    Moving along the bottom of the wing.

3. If you were closer together along the bottom of the wing, then would you be exerting more or less force on the wing than the "air molecules" on top of the wing?

    More force.

4. What would that do to the airplane wing?

    Lift it up into the air.

ACTIVITY 40: THE FLATTENED CARD

Goal: To apply Bernoulli's principle, which says that increasing the speed of air over a surface decreases the force it exerts on the surface

Skills: Observing, predicting, explaining

Materials: For each pair of students:
5" x 8" card or piece of paper
3" x 5" card or piece of paper
2 drinking straws

Preparation: None

Preparation Time: None

Lesson Time: 15–20 minutes

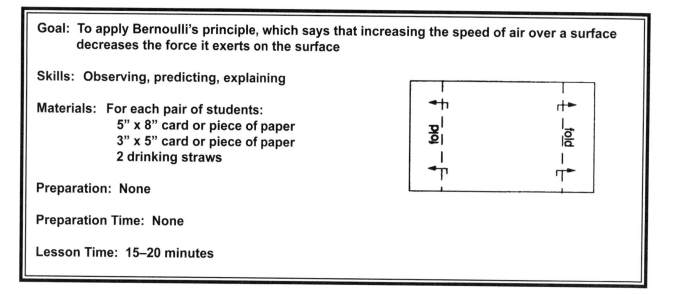

— Procedure and Questioning Strategy —

Pass out the cards and straws to each pair (each student should use his/her own straw). One member of each pair will perform the activity while the other observes. Then have them switch roles. Have the students fold both cards as shown in the drawing above.

1. Look at the large card. When I tell you to do so, slide the straw about a third of the way under the card and blow through the straw. What do you predict will happen to the card?

   (Predictions will vary. Some predict the card will slide away. Others say the card will move down; still others say the card will move up. Some say it will not move.)

Have students blow through the straw under the card.

2. What did you observe?

   The card moved downward.

3. Let's figure out why the card moved downward.

   When we blew under the card, the speed of the air was faster under the card than it was above it, so the force of the air under the card was less, and the force above the card pushed it down.

4. What would happen if we pushed the straw all the way under the card?

   Predictions will vary.

5. Try it.

6. What did you observe?

    The card didn't move.

7. Why didn't the card move?

    Since the straw was all the way under the card, the speed of the air under the card wasn't affected, so the force wasn't affected.

8. Now suppose we change the size of the card and repeat the experiment. What do you think will happen?

    Answers will vary.

Have students do the activity with the 3" x 5" card.

9. What did we observe?

    The card still went down.

10. Why did the card still go down?

    The only thing involved is the speed of the air, so the size of the card doesn't matter.

— Practical Application —

1. Now let's relate this activity to what we saw in our activity with the airplane wing. How do they compare?

    The air moved faster over the airplane wing, and the air moved faster under the card.

2. What effect did this have?

    The faster air over the wing made the airplane go up, and the faster air under the card made the card go down.

ACTIVITY 41: TORNADO IN A BOTTLE

Goal: To apply the principle that faster moving fluids, like air or water, exert less pressure than slower moving fluids

To apply the principle that areas of higher air pressure move into areas of lower pressure

Skills: Observing, predicting, inferring, explaining, generalizing

Materials: 1-liter transparent soda bottle with label removed
Pinch of salt
One drop of liquid dishwashing detergent
Blue food coloring

Preparation:
1. Fill the liter bottle with water to within an inch of the top.
2. Add a drop of liquid dishwashing detergent, a few drops of food coloring, and a pinch of salt.
3. Screw the cap on the bottle tightly.

Preparation Time: 2 minutes

Lesson Time: 15–20 minutes

— Procedure and Questioning Strategy —

Hold the bottle horizontally. Move your hands in a circular motion in one direction as fast as possible for about 30 seconds so the liquid in the bottle whirls around in the bottle. Quickly turn the bottle right side up and show students the "Tornado in the Bottle."

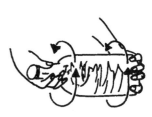

1. What do you see in the bottle?

   It looks like a tornado.

2. It is like a tornado in a bottle. How is it similar?

   It has the shape of a tornado. It has a funnel shape.

3. How is it different from a tornado?

   A tornado is swirling winds; this is swirling water.

4. Where do you think the water is moving the fastest?

   Where it looks like a funnel.

5. What do we know about the pressure exerted by fast-moving air?

   It exerts less pressure than slow-moving air.

6. That is true of any fluid. A fluid is any gas, like air, or any liquid, like water. So what do we know about the pressure exerted by the fast-moving water?

   It exerts less pressure than slower-moving water.

7. In a tornado, the fast-moving air forms a funnel or cone shape. Where do you think the lowest air pressure would be, inside the funnel or outside of it?

   Inside.

8. What do you think causes so much damage to houses, cars, and other property in a tornado? Some objects are even lifted off the ground and up into the tornado (like the house in the *Wizard of Oz*).

   The higher pressure from outside the tornado moves into the lower pressure inside the tornado, pushing almost anything that's in its path up into the tornado.

9. Once in a while a tornado touches down on water. What do you think happens to the water?

   It is pushed up into the middle of the tornado and comes out the top.

10. Yes. That is called a *waterspout*.

— Practical Application —

1. It has been reported that windows of houses have been blown out when tornadoes were nearby. What do you think causes that to happen?

   The tornado creates a low pressure area outside the house, so the higher pressure inside the house pushes the windows out.

2. During tornado warnings, we are told to open some windows in buildings. What effect would this have if a tornado came close to a building?

   It would help let some of the higher air pressure inside the building move outside so the windows would not blow out. The inside and outside pressures would become closer to equal.

ACTIVITY 42: THE ATOMIZER

Goal: To apply the principle that faster moving air exerts less pressure
To apply the principle that areas of higher air pressure move into areas of lower pressure

Skills: Observing, comparing, explaining, predicting, inferring, generalizing

Materials: Cup
Plastic drinking straw
Water
Scissors

Preparation: 1. Pour water into the cup until it is about 1/2" from the rim.
2. Cut two 3" pieces of straw.
3. Hold one piece of straw in the water vertically so that only about 1/2" of straw is above the surface of the water.
4. Hold the other piece of straw horizontally so that its opening is at the edge of the vertical straw opening.

Preparation Time: 2 minutes

Lesson Time: 10–15 minutes

— Procedure and Questioning Strategy —

1. What do you think will happen if I blow hard through the horizontal straw, forcing air over the opening of the vertical straw in the water?

    (Answers will vary.)

2. Is this an open or closed system?

    It is an open system.

3. What do we know about fast moving air in an open system?

    The faster the air, the less pressure it exerts.

4. Where do you think the air will move fastest when I blow over the vertical straw in the water?

    At the top of the vertical straw.

5. Will the air pressure over the top of the vertical straw be increased or decreased when I blow through the horizontal straw?

    It should be decreased because the air being blown over it is moving fast.

Blow hard through the horizontal straw, making certain to position it against the vertical straw as shown in the drawing above, keeping all but about 1/2" of the vertical straw under the surface of the water. A stream of water should spray out. (This may take a little practice.)

6.   What did you see happen?

      Water sprayed out.

7.   What happened before the water sprayed out?

      You blew across the top of the vertical straw.

8.   What do you think happened to the air pressure on top of the vertical straw when I blew across the top of it?

      It reduced the air pressure at the top of the straw.

9.   What do you think happened then to the air inside the top part of the straw that was at normal air pressure?

      It moved up into the lower air pressure area on top of the straw.

10.   How do we know that?

      We know that air in a higher pressure area moves into a lower pressure area. You had made a lower air pressure area on top of the vertical straw when you blew across the straw opening.

11.   If the air inside the top of the vertical straw moved up and out the top of the straw, where did it go?

      It moved into the stream of air you were blowing through the horizontal straw and was blown off to the side.

12.   So what did that leave in the top of the vertical straw?

      Probably nothing if all of the air moved out.

13.   Then how did the water rise in the vertical straw and come out in a spray?

      As the air moved out of the top of the vertical straw, there was less air pressure there than in the air pressing down on the water in the cup. So the higher air pressure on the water in the cup pushed the water up inside the straw. Then the fast moving air over the vertical straw blew the water in a spray.

14.   Let's draw each step of what happened on the board (or on an overhead) so we can see the sequence.

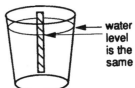

15.   Before I blew through the straw, the water in the cup and in the vertical straw were at the same level.

16.   Describe the pressure of the air at points A, B, and C.

      They were all the same—at room air pressure.

17. What happened to the air pressure above the vertical straw when I blew over it?

It became lower than the normal pressure at B and C.

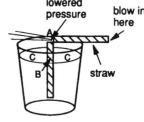

18. Why?

Because faster-moving air has less pressure.

19. In what kind of system does faster-moving air have less pressure?

In an open system.

20. Then what happened to the air pressure at B in the top of the vertical straw?

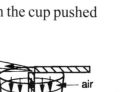

It became lower.

21. Why?

The air moved up in the vertical straw and out into the lower pressure area.

22. What happened next?

The higher (normal) air pressure pushing down on the top of the water in the cup pushed the water up into the vertical straw.

23. Then what happened?

The water at the top of the vertical straw was blown out in the stream of air coming from the horizontal straw.

24. You got it! That took a lot of thinking and you did it!

Let the students try this with their own cups, water, and straws. You might do this part outside. Remind the students to aim their atomizers away from other students.

— Practical Application —

1. This is how a perfume bottle with an atomizer works. What creates the fast moving stream of air in an atomizer?

The bulb has air in it. When you squeeze the bulb, the air rushes over the top of the tube in the perfume.

2. What other kinds of household things can you think of that work like the atomizer?

Window cleaning sprays. A spray gun.

ACTIVITIES 36–42: CONNECTIONS

Goal: To find relationships between the activities for flight and aerodynamics

Skills: Comparing, classifying, explaining, generalizing

Materials: Balloon

— Questioning Strategy —

1. Let's look at similarities among some of the activities we have been doing. Think about the Ping-Pong® ball and the funnel. What were the parts of that system?

    The ball, the funnel, your mouth, the air blown into the funnel, and the air in the room.

2. What happened when we blew through the funnel at the Ping-Pong® ball?

    The ball stayed in the funnel.

3. Where did the air go when it was blown through the funnel?

    Past the ball and out into the room.

4. Was it a closed system or could the air get out of the system?

    Air could get out of the system.

5. If air could get out of the system, we would call it an open system. Where was the fastest-moving air?

    Through the funnel out past the Ping-Pong® ball.

6. What have we learned about fast-moving air?

    It exerts less pressure than slower-moving air.

7. Think about the airfoils we made. When we blew over them, they rose in the air. Why did this happen?

    The faster-moving air was moving over the wings. This air exerted less pressure on top of the wings than the slower-moving air under the wings. The air under the wings had greater pressure and the airfoil lifted up in the air.

8. Was the airfoil system open or closed?

    Open.

9. Think of the card that we folded like a tunnel. We blew through the straw under the card and the card tunnel flattened on the table. Was this a closed or open system?

    It was an open system.

10. Think about the card and the spool. We blew toward the card through the hole in the middle of the spool. What happened to the card?

> It stayed on the bottom of the spool.

11. Think about the atomizers we made. Where was the lesser pressure?

> Where the faster-moving air was going across the vertical straw coming out of the water.

12. In the activities for this section, did faster-moving air always exert less pressure?

> Yes.

Show the students the balloon.

13. What would happen if I blew into this balloon?

> It would blow up.

14. What would be the parts of the system?

> The balloon, your mouth, and the air blown into the balloon.

15. Watch as I blow up the balloon.

Blow it up, then hold the neck of the balloon so the air stays in the balloon.

16. As I blew up the balloon, was the system open or closed?

> Closed.

17. Where was the faster-moving air?

> Going into the balloon.

18. Did it exert more or less pressure on the sides of the balloon than the air in the room?

> More pressure.

19. How do you know that?

> The balloon blew up. More pressure had to be inside the balloon.

20. How is this different from the activities we did where faster-moving air exerted less pressure?

> This is a closed system. The systems were open in the other activities.

21. Let's summarize what we have learned about faster-moving air in open and closed systems.

> Faster-moving air exerts less pressure in open systems and more pressure in closed systems.

UNIT 9—THE SPEED OF FALLING BODIES

Background Information

Imagine that you were to catch a baseball shaken loose from a tree branch about two meters (a little more than 6 1/2 feet) above your head. Do you think it would be safe to catch it? Probably it would be safe because the baseball wouldn't be falling too fast to catch. Would you want to catch the same baseball if it were dropped from the roof of a 16-story building? Why not?

Instinctively, we know that something that starts to fall from a resting position gains speed as it falls. We'd move fast to move away from the point where the baseball would hit after it falls a great distance.

When a baseball or other similar object falls, it gains speed (accelerates) at approximately 10 meters (or 32 feet) every second it falls. For example, if each story of a building were five meters tall, a 16-story building would be approximately 80 meters tall. It would take 4 seconds for the ball to fall 80 meters; it would be traveling at 40 meters per second as it reached the ground and would hit with great force. (See diagram.)

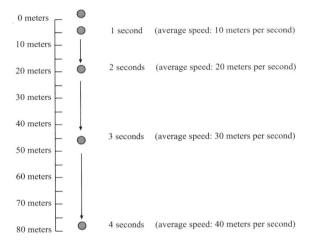

FREE FALL

Do all objects fall with the same increase in speed, the same rate of acceleration due to Earth's gravity? Does the weight, size or shape make a difference?

Earth's gravity causes all objects to accelerate as they fall, although some objects—for example, a piece of notebook paper or a feather—are more buoyant as they fall, which causes them to fall in a path that is not straight. It takes more time for buoyant objects like these to reach the ground.

When any object is in free fall, affected only by gravity, it increases its speed an average of 10 meters per second for each second it falls. Effects of air resistance are not considered. If the feather, the notebook paper, and the baseball were dropped from the same altitude, at the same time, in a vacuum where there is no air resistance, each object would fall in a straight path and reach the ground at the same time. The weight, size, and shape of the objects would make no difference.

Unit 9—NATIONAL SCIENCE EDUCATION STANDARDS

- *Unifying Concepts and Processes*—Students should develop understanding and abilities with regard to systems, order, and organization; evidence, models, and explanation; constancy, change, and measurement; and form and function.

- *Science as Inquiry*—Content Standard A: Students should develop the necessary skills to do scientific inquiry and develop an understanding about scientific inquiry.

- *Physical Science*—Content Standard B: Students should develop an understanding of the properties of objects and materials; position and motion of objects; properties and changes of properties in matter; and motions and forces.

- *History and Nature of Science*—Content Standard G: Students should develop an understanding of the nature of science and of science as a human endeavor.

ACTIVITY 43: FALLING BODIES – DOES WEIGHT MAKE A DIFFERENCE?

Goal: To understand that objects of the same size and shape fall at the same rate of speed even when their weights are different

Skills: Observing, describing, comparing, predicting, summarizing

Materials: 2 small unbreakable plastic containers, with lids, that are the same size (e.g., vitamin or medicine containers, 35-mm film containers, small shampoo bottles)
Sand

Preparation: None

Preparation Time: None

Lesson Time: 15–20 minutes

— Procedure and Questioning Strategy —

Show the students the two empty containers. Pour sand into one container so that it is about 3/4 full. Completely fill the other container with sand. Explain to the students what you are doing. Let one student hold both containers.

1. What is similar about both of these containers?

    They're the same size and shape.

2. What is different about them?

    One is heavier than the other.

    One has more sand in it.

Let other students hold the containers to confirm these observations.

3. What do you predict will happen if these two containers are dropped from the same height at the same time?

    (Students usually answer, "The heavier one will hit the floor first.")

Stand on a sturdy chair or table, or have a student do this, and drop the two containers onto the floor. Have students watch to see if the containers were dropped from the same height at the same time.

container full of sand

container 3/4 full of sand

4. What happened?

    The containers hit the floor at the same time.

5. How do you know that?

   > We saw it.

6. What other evidence do we have?

   > We heard one sound as they hit the floor.

If students don't respond, ask them how many sounds they heard. Drop the containers in the same way a few more times.

7. What does this tell us about the speed of the falling containers?

   > They both fall at the same rate of speed.

8. What could we have concluded if we had heard two sounds?

   > The containers hit the floor at different times.
   > They fell at different rates of speed.

9. Let's take some sand out of the lighter container. Do you think this will make a difference in its speed?

Take sand out of the lighter container until it is about 1/4 full. Repeat the experiment.

10. What happened?

    > They still fell at the same speed.

11. Who can summarize what we have learned about falling objects?

    > Objects that are the same size and shape, but have different weights, fall at the same speed. (All objects, regardless of size or shape, would fall at the same rate of speed if there were no air resistance such as in a vacuum.)

— Practical Application —

With proper supervision, let the students take the containers outdoors and drop them from higher elevations (for example, from the top of stairs, the top of a slide or other types of playground equipment) to observe if there is a difference in the speed at which they fall. Make certain students check the area where they are dropping their objects to be certain it is clear of people.

ACTIVITY 44: FALLING BODIES – DO SIZE, SHAPE, OR WEIGHT MAKE A DIFFERENCE?

Goal: To understand that high density objects fall at about the same rate of speed regardless of size, shape, or weight

Skills: Observing, describing, comparing, predicting, summarizing

Materials: Objects found around the classroom, for example:
Books of differing sizes
Tennis shoe
Box of paper clips, taped shut
Box of ends and pieces of old crayons, taped shut
Containers with sand used in the previous activity

Preparation: Place the objects where all students can see them.

Preparation Time: 1 minute

Lesson Time: 20–25 minutes

— Procedure and Questioning Strategy —

1. Let's review what we learned in the last activity when we tested the rate of speed at which containers fall. What was similar about the containers?

    They were the same size and shape.

2. What was different?

    They were different weights.

3. What did we find out from our experiments?

    The containers hit the floor at the same time when we dropped them from the same height at the same time. The containers fell at the same rate of speed.

4. When we dropped them, did the weights of the containers make a difference in their rates of speed?

    No.

5. Since we know that weight didn't make a difference, let's test some objects that have different weights *and* different sizes. Look at the objects. Which two have the same shape but are different in size and weight?

    The box of crayons and the box of paper clips. Two of the books.

Test the objects mentioned, dropping them from the same height at the same time. The bottoms of the objects need to be the same distance from the floor. Have the students watch to see if the distance appears to be the same.

6. What did you observe?

> The two objects hit the floor at the same time.
> There was one sound as they hit the floor.

7. What does that tell us about their rates of speed?

> They both fell at the same rate.

8. So does size make a difference with the objects we tested?

> No.

9. Let's try objects of differing sizes, weights, and shapes. Which two objects could we try?

> The tennis shoe and the box of crayons (or any two items that fit the description).

Try many combinations of objects.

10. Did the shape of the object make a difference?

> No.

11. What have we found out about falling objects from the previous activity and the activity we just did?

> The objects we tested fell at the same rate of speed even though they were different sizes, shapes and weights.

12. What do you think causes the objects to fall to the ground at the same rate of speed?

> Gravity.

— Practical Application —

Have students suggest other objects in the classroom to test and to compare their rates of speed. If some objects do not fall at the same rate, ask the students to think of reasons for this that they can share during the next activity.

ACTIVITY 45: FALLING BODIES AND AIR RESISTANCE

Goal: To understand that objects with lower density encounter air resistance and fall more slowly than objects with higher density

Skills: Observing, describing, comparing, predicting, explaining, summarizing

Materials: Small book (about the size of a paperback or slightly larger)
Box of ends and pieces of old crayons, taped shut
Sheets of paper, 8 1/2" x 11"
Feather

Preparation: Put the materials on a table where all students can see them.

Preparation Time: 1 minute

Lesson Time: 15–20 minutes

— Procedure and Questioning Strategy —

1. In our last two activities, we dropped objects of differing sizes, shapes, and weights. What did we find out about their rates of speed?

    They fell at the same rate.

For the next two questions, ask several students for their predictions and reasons.

2. What do you think would happen if we dropped a book and a sheet of paper at the same time?

3. What reason do you have for your answer?

4. Watch carefully as I drop the book and paper.

5. What did you observe?

    The book reached the floor first.
    The paper went much slower than the book.

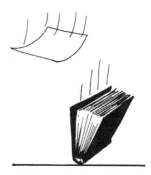

6. What caused both objects to fall to the floor?

    Gravity.

7. What was different about the paths of the book and paper as they fell to the floor?

    The book fell in a straight path.
    The paper floated back and forth as it fell. Its path wasn't straight.

8. What do you think caused the path of the paper to be different from the path of the book?

    Air held the paper up more than it did the book.

9. What do you think is the reason that air had a greater effect on the paper than it did on the book?

> The paper is much lighter in weight.
> The paper's light weight is spread out over a large area.
> The paper is much thinner than the book.

10. What else could we use for this experiment?

> Possibilities are: the box of crayons and a sheet of crumpled paper; the feather and the box of crayons; the feather and a sheet of paper.

Test each of the students' suggestions.

11. What have we found out about the speed of falling objects?

> The more solid, heavier objects fall at about the same speed.
> The lighter objects fall more slowly.
> Air affects lighter objects and makes them fall more slowly.

— Practical Applications —

1. What if we hold the paper under the book and drop them together?

Hold a sheet of 8 1/2" x 11" paper under the book and drop them together (the paper should be larger than the book).

2. What happened?

> They both fell together.

3. What do you think made the difference?

> The book's weight made the paper fall with it.
> Air did not have enough force to hold up the paper with the book on top of it.

4. What if we drop the book with the paper on top of it?

> The paper will fall more slowly than the book.

Try it.

5. Was the paper slower?

> Yes.

6. How do you explain that?

> The air could get between the book and paper and hold the paper up.

7. What if we use a piece of paper smaller than the book?

Try it! Then allow time for students to suggest other objects to test.

ACTIVITY 46: SWINGING PENDULUMS – THE LENGTH

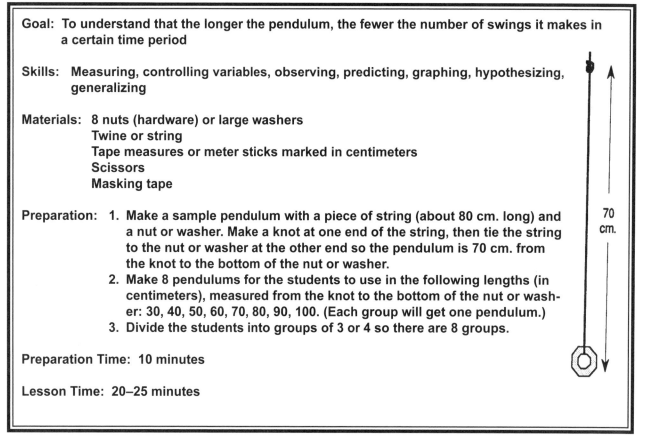

Goal: To understand that the longer the pendulum, the fewer the number of swings it makes in a certain time period

Skills: Measuring, controlling variables, observing, predicting, graphing, hypothesizing, generalizing

Materials: 8 nuts (hardware) or large washers
Twine or string
Tape measures or meter sticks marked in centimeters
Scissors
Masking tape

Preparation: 1. Make a sample pendulum with a piece of string (about 80 cm. long) and a nut or washer. Make a knot at one end of the string, then tie the string to the nut or washer at the other end so the pendulum is 70 cm. from the knot to the bottom of the nut or washer.
2. Make 8 pendulums for the students to use in the following lengths (in centimeters), measured from the knot to the bottom of the nut or washer: 30, 40, 50, 60, 70, 80, 90, 100. (Each group will get one pendulum.)
3. Divide the students into groups of 3 or 4 so there are 8 groups.

Preparation Time: 10 minutes

Lesson Time: 20–25 minutes

70 cm.

— Procedure and Questioning Strategy —

Show the class the pendulum. Hold the pendulum by the knot. With your other hand, bring the nut up so the string is taut and horizontal to the floor. Keep your hand holding the knot steady and let the nut go so it swings back and forth like a pendulum.

1. This is an example of a pendulum. Describe what it is doing.

    It's swinging back and forth.

2. Where have you seen a pendulum?

    In a clock.
    In a metronome (used to time music).

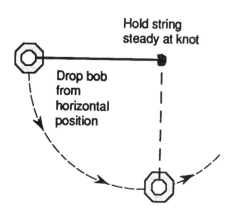

Hold string steady at knot

Drop bob from horizontal position

Explain to the students: Pendulums are usually made up of a long piece of wood or metal with a bob at the bottom (like the pendulum in a grandfather clock). The bob can be made of different kinds of materials and can be of different weights.

3. What takes the place of the long piece of wood or metal in this pendulum?

> The string.

4. What represents the bob?

> The nut (or washer).

Hold up the 70 cm.-long pendulum by the knot. Ask one student to help time the pendulum for 15 seconds, letting you know when to drop the bob and when the 15 seconds are up. Explain that a complete swing of the pendulum is from the beginning side to the other side and back to the beginning side. Ask the rest of the students to count the complete swings of the pendulum.

5. How many complete swings did it make?

> It made 8 complete swings, then it only got to one side for the next swing.

6. How many swings can we say it made?

> 8 1/2 .

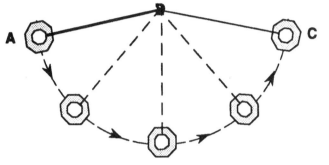

1/2 swing – A to C
1 complete swing – A to C to A

Give each team one of the pendulums and a tape measure or meter stick to measure it. Each member of a team could do a particular part of the experiment:
  – holding the pendulum and dropping the bob.
  – counting the number of pendulum swings in 15 seconds.
  – timing the 15 seconds and saying when to start and stop.
  – recording the number of swings for each trial.

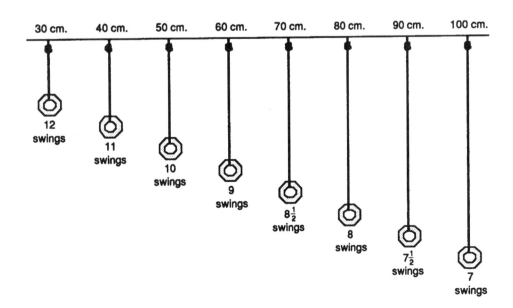

Ask each team to do 5 trials with their pendulum. When the trials are completed, tape the pendulums on the chalkboard in order from shortest to longest and note the length and the number of swings each made in 15 seconds.

7. Compare the shortest pendulum to the longest pendulum. What difference is there in the number of swings every 15 seconds?

    The 30 cm. pendulum made 5 more swings than the 100 cm. pendulum.

8. What generalizations can we make about the pendulums?

    The longer the pendulum, the fewer the number of swings.
    The shorter pendulums make more swings than the longer pendulums.

— Practical Application —

1. About how long do you think a pendulum would be that would make 13 swings in a 15-second time period?

    About 20 cm. long.

2. If you had a pendulum clock that was fast and you wanted to slow it down, would you raise or lower the bob on the pendulum?

    Lower it.

3. What reason would you have for doing that?

    If you lowered the bob, the pendulum would be longer.

4. What would that do?

    The longer the pendulum, the fewer the number of swings. The clock would run slower.

Have each student record the data from the concrete graph shown by the pendulums taped to the chalkboard. Data will be used in the next activity.

SAVE THE PENDULUMS FOR THE NEXT ACTIVITY ON PENDULUMS.

ACTIVITY 47: SWINGING PENDULUMS – THE WEIGHT

Goal: To understand that the weight of the pendulum does not make a difference in the number of swings a pendulum makes in a certain time period

To understand different kinds of variables: experimental, independent, and dependent variables

Skills: Measuring, controlling variables, observing, predicting, graphing, defining variables, generalizing

Materials: The 8 pendulums used in Activity 46
Data gathered from Activity 46
8 additional nuts or large washers
Tape measures or meter sticks marked in centimeters
Masking tape
Copies (one per student) of the pendulum graph at the end of this activity
An overhead transparency of the pendulum graph

Preparation: Divide the students into 8 groups.

Preparation Time: 3 minutes

Lesson Time: 30–40 minutes

— Procedure and Questioning Strategy —

1. What did we find out about pendulums when we tested them?

    The longer the pendulum, the fewer number of swings it makes in 15 seconds (or the shorter the pendulum, the greater the number of swings it makes in 15 seconds).

Hold up the 50 cm. pendulum.

2. This pendulum took 10 complete swings in 15 seconds. What do you think will happen to the weight of the bob if we add another nut (or washer) to the pendulum bob?

    The bob will be twice as heavy.

3. What do you predict will happen to the number of swings the pendulum makes in 15 seconds if we double the weight of the bob?

    (Students usually predict that the number of swings will increase because the additional weight will make it swing faster.)

Thread a nut on the string at the top of each pendulum, letting it drop down on top of the nut already attached to the bottom of the pendulum. Give each team a pendulum and a tape measure or meter stick. Ask them to:
    – measure their pendulum.
    – count the number of pendulum swings in 15 seconds for 5 trials.
    – record the number of complete swings in 15 seconds for each trial.

When trials are completed, tape the pendulums on the chalkboard in order from shortest to longest, noting the length and the number of swings each made in 15 seconds.

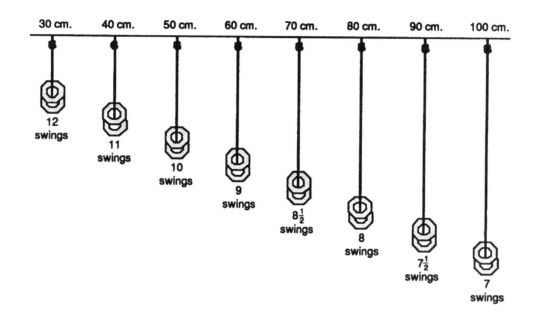

5. Compare the number of swings each pendulum made with the heavier bob with the number of swings it made with the lighter bob. What happened to the number of swings in 15 seconds?

    They stayed the same.

6. So which determines the number of swings—the length of the pendulum or the weight of the bob?

    The length of the pendulum.

7. When we doubled the weight of the bob, did that have an effect on the number of swings?

    No.

8. Let's review. Summarize what we learned about pendulums in this activity.

    The weight of the bob did not make a difference in the number of swings that a pendulum made in 15 seconds.

— Practical Application —

Have the students use copies made from the pendulum graph (provided at the end of this activity) to record the number of swings of each pendulum so that they can see how the concrete graph (the real pendulums taped on the board) relates to a more abstract graph on paper. Use an overhead transparency of the following sample graph to demonstrate possible results of the experiment.

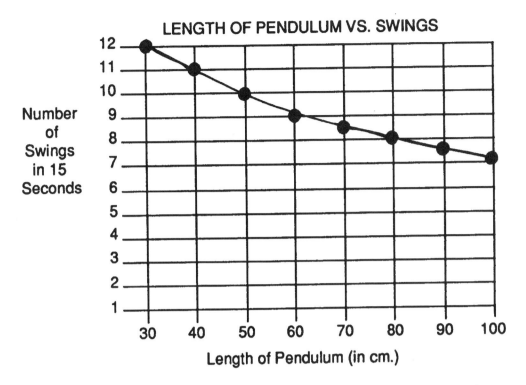

LENGTH OF PENDULUM VS. SWINGS

Number of Swings in 15 Seconds

Length of Pendulum (in cm.)

1. How is this graph similar to the graph made with our pendulums that we have on the chalkboard?

Possible answer: In both graphs it shows that the number of swings gets smaller as the length of the pendulum gets longer.

2. A VARIABLE is something we use or something we do during an experiment. For example, one thing we used for this experiment was string. Since each team used the same string for each pendulum, the string is a CONTROLLED VARIABLE. A controlled variable is something we use or something we do that remains the same throughout different experiments. What other variables did we control besides the string?

The nuts (or washers) used as bobs were the same.
Each pendulum had a knot at the top.
Each team used two nuts (or washers) as a bob.

3. Another type of controlled variable is the way we did the experiment. Each team held the bob so the pendulum was parallel to the floor as each trial was started. In which other ways did we control variables?

We counted the number of swings in 15 seconds.

4. So the amount of time was controlled?

Yes.

5. What is another variable we controlled?

The way we counted the swings and half swings.

6. Another kind of variable is an INDEPENDENT VARIABLE, sometimes called the EXPERIMENTAL VARIABLE. An independent or experimental variable is something we use or a way of doing things that is changed. Usually only one variable is changed at a time; other variables are controlled or not changed. For example, what was different about each team's pendulum?

  The length of the pendulum.

7. What effect did the difference in pendulum length have on the results of our experiment?

  The pendulum length made a difference in the number of swings each pendulum made.

8. The number of swings each pendulum made is called the DEPENDENT VARIABLE. The independent variable (the length of the pendulum) causes changes in the dependent variable. Which data should we identify as the dependent variable?

  The data on the vertical line.

9. What data on the graph—the data on the horizontal line or the vertical line—should we identify as the independent (experimental) variable?

  The data on the horizontal line.

10. Which variable causes changes in the other variable?

  The independent variable causes changes in the dependent variable.

11. Which variable shows the effects of the changes made?

  The dependent variable.

Have students add the following information to their graphs.

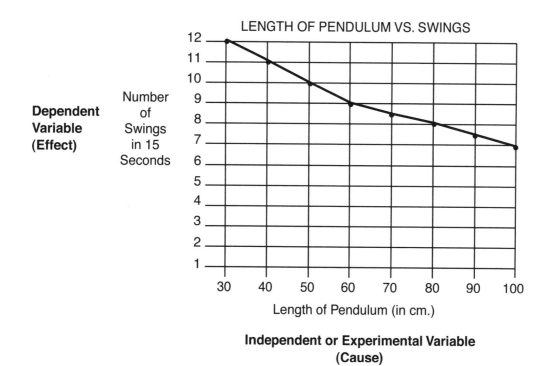

Independent or Experimental Variable
(Cause)

ABSTRACT GRAPH

Use this graph to record information taken from the chalkboard.

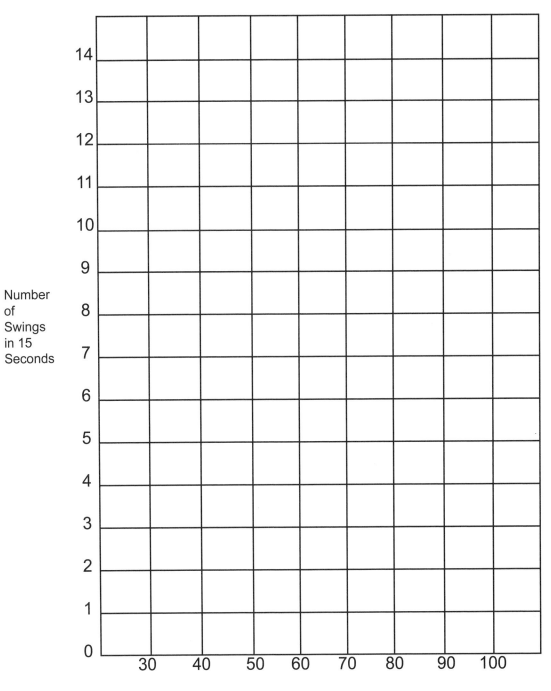

LENGTH OF PENDULUM VS. SWINGS

Number of Swings in 15 Seconds

Length of Pendulum (in cm.)

ACTIVITIES 43–47: CONNECTIONS

Goal: To find relationships among the activities for falling bodies

Skills: Comparing, classifying, explaining, applying generalizations

— Questioning Strategy —

1. Let's think about some of the things we have learned. What happened when we dropped the containers with different amounts of sand in them?

   They fell at the same rate of speed.
   They hit the floor at the same time.

2. What happened when we dropped the tennis shoe, crayons, book, and box of paper clips?

   They fell at the same rate of speed.
   They hit the floor at the same time.

3. Did everything we dropped at the same time fall at the same rate of speed?

   No, the paper and the feather fell at slower rates of speed than the book.

4. What did we decide was the reason that happened?

   Air held up the paper and feather more than it did the book because they were much lighter in weight than the book.

5. What is the reason that objects fall to the ground?

   Gravity pulls them down.

6. Describe the pathways of the objects we dropped.

   Most of the objects fell in a straight path to the floor. Some of the lighter weight objects, like the paper and feather, floated down. Their paths were not straight.

7. When we dropped the pendulums so they would swing, what kind of path did the pendulums take?

   Curved.

8. What forces do you think caused that?

   Gravity pulled the bobs down toward the floor, but the strings and our hands held the bobs so that they couldn't fall to the floor. This kept the bobs swinging back and forth in a curved path.

9. What happened when we changed the weight of the bobs and kept the pendulum lengths the same?

The extra weight did not change the speed of the pendulums. They still make the same number of swings in 15 seconds.

10. What have we already learned about dropping objects at the same time that might have helped us predict that the weight of the bobs would not make a difference?

We learned that objects fall at the same speed unless they are light in weight and the weight is spread out.

11. Imagine there are two swings, exactly the same, on the playground. One person gets on each swing. One person is twice as heavy as the other one. Will their difference in weight make a difference in the speed of their swings?

No.

12. How do you know that?

Weight did not make a difference in the speed of the swings of the pendulums.

UNIT 10—VARIABLES

Background Information

In real life, we often plan, design experiments, and control variables even though we seldom think of what we do in terms of variables. For example, one softball player was having trouble hitting the ball, so she slightly changed the way she held the bat. She kept the same batting stance and swing. Her batting average increased by 25%. As teachers, we try different strategies, many times altering one part of a strategy at a time, to see if the change has an effect on student understanding. Variables are being controlled in both of these examples.

The pendulum activity in the previous unit was planned to model the process of identifying and controlling variables during an experiment. The copter activities in this unit are designed for students to investigate the effects of changing variables.

The first step is for students to identify the variables as part of their experimental design. Variables are the factors that will change during an experiment. If students are studying the effects of different types of activities on heart rate, the type of activity and the heart rate would be the two variables. The type of activity would be the **independent variable** because the activities would be changed to find the effect they have on heart rate. The heart rate would be the **dependent variable** because the heart rate "depends" on the type of activity.

Students could plan the experiment as the next step. For example, the plan could be for each student to run a hundred meters, rest for 10 minutes, then do 20 push-ups. Each student could count and record his or her ending heart rate immediately following each of these activities. The type of activity, the independent variable (the variable that was changed), could be thought of as being the **cause**. The ending heart rate, the dependent variable, would show the **effect** of the change in activity.

The third step could be for each child to follow the plan for the experiment. A class average for heart rate after each activity could be computed, and the data could be compared to find the effects of different activities on heart rate.

If the experiment is planned in this way, are all variables held constant while one variable is changed? There is more than one independent variable. Yes, the type of activity was an independent variable that was changed to find its effect on heart rate. The differences among children are also independent variables that may cause differences in heart rates for each activity.

So how could the experiment be designed to control for differences among students? Could each student graph his or her own data? Could one student perform the three activities? Could students be grouped in pairs with one student performing the activities and the other student recording the data?

Ask your students, "What do you think would be the best way to control all variables except the one being tested?" Have students brainstorm as many ways as possible. Students could be divided into groups to decide on the "best way" and list the reasons for their decisions. Group decisions and reasons for decisions could be shared with the whole class. Students could be invited to give feedback, and final decisions could be made for the design of an experiment or experiments to test their ideas. Students will learn more about the planning and designing process when they listen to feedback on their own designs and to the plans and designs of students in other groups. Allow time for students to try out their experiments, share, compare results, and make generalizations about the effects of different types of activities on heart rate.

Unit 10–NATIONAL SCIENCE EDUCATION STANDARDS

- *Unifying Concepts and Processes:* Students should develop understanding and abilities with regard to systems, order, and organization; evidence, models, and explanation; constancy, change, and measurement; and form and function.

- *Science as Inquiry*—Content Standard A: Students should develop the necessary skills to do scientific inquiry and develop an understanding about scientific inquiry.

- *Physical Science*—Content Standard B: Students should develop an understanding of the properties of objects and materials; position and motion of objects; and motions and forces.

- *Science and Technology*—Content Standard E: Students should develop abilities of technological design.

- *History and Nature of Science*—Content Standard G: Students should develop an understanding of the nature of science and of science as a human endeavor.

ACTIVITY 48: TWIRLING COPTERS!

Goal: To explore the behavior of copters, investigating the effects of variables in experimentation

Skills: Measuring, observing, predicting, identifying and controlling variables, generalizing

Materials: 4" x 6" index cards, one for each student
Rulers marked in centimeters
Scissors
2 boxes of small paper clips, 4 clips for each student

Preparation:

1. Draw the following diagram of a copter on the board (or duplicate the copter pattern found at the end of Activity 49).

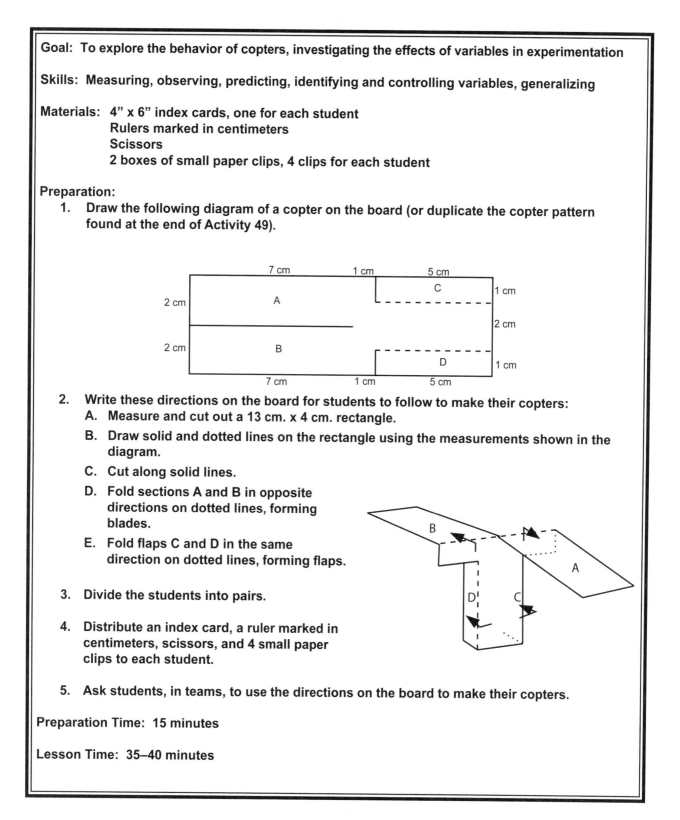

2. Write these directions on the board for students to follow to make their copters:

   A. Measure and cut out a 13 cm. x 4 cm. rectangle.

   B. Draw solid and dotted lines on the rectangle using the measurements shown in the diagram.

   C. Cut along solid lines.

   D. Fold sections A and B in opposite directions on dotted lines, forming blades.

   E. Fold flaps C and D in the same direction on dotted lines, forming flaps.

3. Divide the students into pairs.

4. Distribute an index card, a ruler marked in centimeters, scissors, and 4 small paper clips to each student.

5. Ask students, in teams, to use the directions on the board to make their copters.

Preparation Time: 15 minutes

Lesson Time: 35–40 minutes

— Procedure and Questioning Strategy —

When all the students have finished making their copters, allow time for them to explore the copter's flight for at least 5 minutes. Guide them to observe the copter's flight with no paper clips attached, then with 1, 2, 3, and 4 paper clips attached to see if the number of clips or where they are placed affects the pathway or speed of the copter. Ask students to place paper clips on the body of the copter rather than on the blades (A and B in the drawing).

1. When you experimented with the copter with no paper clips, what did its flight path look like?

    It did not go straight to the floor.

2. What effect did adding clips have on the flight path of the copter?

    It fell in a straighter path.

3. What effect did adding clips have on the speed of the copter?

    It fell faster with clips.

4. What effect did adding clips have on the speed the copter twirled?

    It twirled faster when more clips were added.

5. When you experimented with your copter and watched the ways others experimented with their copters, you probably noticed that there were many different ways to test a copter's flight. What different ways of testing them did you see?

    Some possibilities are: the height from which the copter was dropped; how the copter was set in motion, dropped, tossed up or thrown; where the copter was held as it was released, for instance, just below the blades; where the paper clips were placed on the copter.

Write the different ways of experimentation on the chalkboard.

6. If we were to test one copter against another to see which was faster, which of these ways of testing (or variables) could we control so the test would be most fair?

Remind students that a variable is something used or a way of experimenting that can be varied or controlled (held constant). Students should recognize that they could control all of these variables. Have students decide, as a group, how they would like to control each variable.

7. How could we control the height from which the copters are dropped?

    Everyone could drop their copters from the same height.

Decide how to determine the height. For instance, a piece of string could be strung across the room. Copters could be released with their blades touching the underside of the string.

8. How could we better control how the copters are released—by dropping or throwing them?

    Dropping them would result in a more fair test.

9. How could we control where the copter is held when it is dropped?

    (Decide on a place together.)

10. How could we control where the clips are placed?

    They could be placed either horizontally or vertically on the parts of the copter labeled C and D.

Have the students get into teams of two to test the copters.

11. Each team has two copters. Test your copters by dropping both of them at the same time from the same height. Hold the copters where we decided, as a group, to hold them. Place your paper clips in the positions we decided. Keep a chart on your observations of which copters reached the floor faster and which copters twirled faster.

12. Test your two copters, each with a different number of clips for each test. Do at least 3 trials for each test to be sure of your answers. Fill in your charts as you decide on an answer for each test.

When all teams have finished their tests, discuss their results. Some results may vary depending on how closely the variables were controlled. Discuss the differences in results.

13. Summarize what we found out about the copters when we changed the number of clips.

    Possible answers are: the more clips, the faster the copter fell; the more clips, the faster the copter twirled; the more clips, the straighter the path of the copter.

14. In which direction did your copter twirl—clockwise or counterclockwise?

    (Teams may have different answers. Have students look at a copter that twirled clockwise and one that twirled counterclockwise.)

15. What is the difference between them?

    The blades are folded differently.

Test two copters with the blades folded the same way for confirmation.

Practical Applications are at the end of the next lesson.

═══ ACTIVITY 49: MORE TWIRLING COPTERS! ═══

Goal: To investigate the effects of controlling variables on the flights of copters

Skills: Observing, predicting, controlling variables, generalizing

Materials: The copter diagrams on page 177
1 box of small paper clips, three clips per student

Preparation: 1. Make copies of the copter diagrams on page 177, one for each team.
2. Divide the students into teams of three, with one student on each team collecting the materials needed for the team.
3. Have each student on a team cut out and fold one of the three copters shown on the diagrams so that each team has three different copters.
4. Have students follow the directions under the diagrams to make their copters.

Preparation Time: 10 minutes

Lesson Time: 25–30 minutes

— Procedure and Questioning Strategy —

1. Look at the three copters you have made for your team. How is Copter II different from Copter I?

   It's wider than Copter I.

2. How is Copter III different from Copter I?

   It's longer than Copter I.

3. If we wanted to test these copters fairly, we would need to control all of the other variables since these three copters are different sizes. In addition to the variables we controlled when we tested the other copters, which other variable needs to be controlled?

   The number of clips placed on the copters.

4. How many clips do you think we should use on all of the copters?

   2, 3, or 4 would probably work well.

5. Where should everyone place their clips?

   (Agree on the best placement for everyone.)

6. Which copter do you think will be the fastest?

   (Accept all answers and ask for reasons.)

7. Which copter do you think will be the slowest?

   (Accept all answers and ask for reasons.)

8. Let's test the copters. Your team needs to have three trials for each test:
    Copter I vs. Copter II
    Copter I vs. Copter III
    Copter II vs. Copter III

Make sure you control your variables for fair tests. Keep notes on your observations.

9. Summarize what you observed about the different-sized copters. Relate their sizes with their speeds.

    Possible answers are: the longer copter was the fastest; the wider copter was the slowest.

10. What variable(s) do you think caused the differences in speed?

    The wider blades on the slowest copter kept it up in the air the longest.
    The length of the longer copter could have made it the fastest.

— Practical Applications —

1. How is your copter similar to a helicopter?

    Possible answers are: they both have blades that whirl above the copter; they both land by coming straight down.

2. How is your copter's flight different from a helicopter's flight?

    Possible answer: a helicopter can go up, straight ahead, and turn corners.

3. If you were designing a copter that fell slower than Copter III, how would you design it?

    Usually a shorter copter with wider wings would be slower.

4. Use another piece of paper to design a copter you think would be slower than Copter III, then test it against Copter III.

Discuss results.

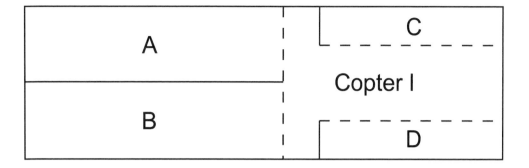

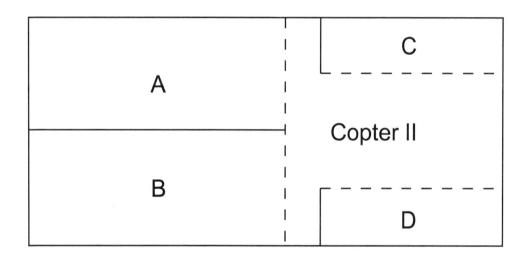

Cut on solid lines, fold on dotted lines.
Fold A and B in opposite directions.
Fold C and D in the same direction.

ACTIVITIES 48–49: CONNECTIONS

Goal: To find relationships between the activities for copters

Skills: Identifying, comparing, and classifying variables

— Questioning Strategy —

1. Let's think about the two activities we did with the copters. When we tested the first copters that we made from index cards, what were some of the variables we controlled? (Remind students that a controlled variable is a way of testing that is kept the same during all test trials.)

   Size of the copters.
   Material used for construction of copters.
   Height from which the copters were dropped.
   How the copters were set in motion (i.e., they were dropped).
   Where the copter was held as it was dropped.
   Placement of the paper clips on the copters.

2. What was the experimental (or independent) variable when we tested these copters? (The experimental variable was the one that was changed during the trials.)

   The number of paper clips placed on the copter.

3. When we made three different-sized copters from paper and tested them with the same number of clips on each copter, what was the experimental variable?

   The size of the copter.

4. What was the dependent variable? (The dependent variable shows the effects of the changes made in the experimental variable. In this activity, it shows the effects of varying the size of the copters.)

   The speed of the copter.

5. What caused the differences in the speed of the copters?

   The different sizes of the copters.

6. Imagine that we made three copters the same size—one from paper, the second from an index card, and the third from cardboard—and tested them with two paper clips on each copter to see which copter was the fastest. What would be the experimental variable?

   The materials the copters were made from.

7. What would be the dependent variable?

The speed of the copters.

8. If they were real copters, which one would you rather be flying in?

The paper copter with the wide wings.

9. What is your reason?

The paper copter would probably be the slowest and have the softest landing.

10. Why do you think that?

The paper copter would be the lightest in weight, so the air under it would hold it up more than it would hold up the heavier copters.

UNIT 11—THE FLIGHT OF ROCKETS

Background Information

The three activities in this unit demonstrate **Newton's Third Law of Motion**: for every action there is an equal and opposite reaction. When a balloon is filled with air, then released, the air that rushes out exerts pressure. It pushes on the air outside the balloon. This push causes the balloon to move forward. The **action** is the released air moving backward. The forward movement of the balloon is the equal and opposite **reaction** (figure A).

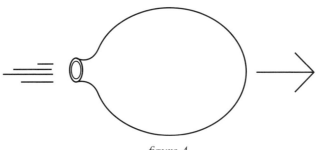

figure A

This action/reaction takes place in a system that contains the balloon, the air inside the balloon, and the air outside the balloon. The force of the air leaving the balloon is equal to the push that moves the balloon forward. If the balloon has a greater amount of air in it before it is released, it will travel faster and farther than the same balloon with a lesser amount of air.

The activities for balloon rockets were designed to model the flight of a rocket. Conventional rockets burn fuel that forms superheated gases. These gases stream from the back of the rocket, exerting tremendous force and propelling the rocket into space. The rocket needs to reach an "escape velocity" of 25,000 mph to escape Earth's gravitational pull and continue into outer space. The heavier an object is, the more force and fuel it needs to reach high speeds. Rockets are designed to be able to carry an adequate amount of fuel and to get rid of unneeded excess weight.

Generally, rockets have three stages. The *Saturn V* rocket (figure B) that launched the *Apollo* spacecrafts and the *Delta II* rocket that ferried the *Mars Climate Orbiter* and the *Mars Surveyor* into space have multiple stages. The first stage is fired and the rocket is launched, thrusting the second and third stages upward until the fuel in the first stage is depleted and the first stage is jettisoned. The second stage is ignited, forcing the third stage to continue to rise. The atmosphere is now thinner, or less dense, so air resistance has lessened. The container for the second stage can be smaller than the container needed for the first stage because it doesn't need to carry as much fuel. Once the rocket reaches a speed of approximately 10,000 mph, the second stage is dropped and the third stage is ignited. Without the weight of the first two stages, this last and smallest stage can reach the required speed of 25,000 mph.

figure B

Figure C is a picture of a space shuttle. Shuttles and rockets are configured differently. A shuttle has four main components: the orbiter, the external tank (the largest part of the vehicle), and two solid rocket boosters. The shuttle lifts off when the three main engines in the tail of the winged orbiter are ignited. Fuel for the engines, liquid hydrogen and liquid oxygen, are supplied from the external tank. Within the next few seconds, the two solid propellant boosters on the sides of the external tank are ignited. Two minutes after lift-off, the rocket boosters separate from the external tank and are dropped into the ocean by parachute. Within 8 or 9 minutes after lift-off, the fuel in the external tank is exhausted and the tank is jettisoned. The shuttle continues to rise until it reaches the altitude where it will orbit the Earth, generally between 200–400 miles above Earth.

figure C

When students have finished the activities in this unit, they could be challenged to figure out a way to model the stages of a space shuttle.

The NASA web site at *http://www.nasa.gov* has a wealth of information, photos, videos, and links to additional web sites about rockets, space shuttles, and space travel.

Unit 11–NATIONAL SCIENCE EDUCATION STANDARDS

- *Unifying Concepts and Processes:* Students should develop understanding and abilities with regard to systems, order, and organization; evidence, models, and explanation; constancy, change, and measurement; and form and function.

- *Science as Inquiry*—Content Standard A: Students should develop the necessary skills to do scientific inquiry and develop an understanding about scientific inquiry.

- *Physical Science*—Content Standard B: Students should develop an understanding of the properties of objects and materials; position and motion of objects; properties and changes of properties in matter; and motions and forces.

- *Science and Technology*—Content Standard E: Students should develop abilities of technological design and develop an understanding about science and technology.

- *History and Nature of Science*—Content Standard G: Students should develop an understanding of the nature of science and of science as a human endeavor.

ACTIVITY 50: ROCKET POWER

Goal: To understand that the action of the air being released from a balloon causes an equal and opposite reaction and the balloon moves forward (This is an example of Newton's Third Law.)

Skills: Observing, classifying, inferring, predicting, measuring, controlling variables, collecting data, graphing, generalizing

Materials: The blank Rocket Power Graph on page 186
The sample Rocket Power Graph on page 185
To demonstrate and for each group of three students:
    Round sturdy balloon (about 18" inflated)
    Twine or fishing line that is long enough to stretch across the room
    Half a drinking straw, paper or plastic
    Pieces of 2"-wide masking tape, 3" to 4" long
    Measuring tape

Preparation:
1. Duplicate the graphs, one for each group (make a transparency of the sample graph if you prefer).
2. Thread the half-straw on the piece of twine.
3. Have two students stretch the twine across the room and hold each end so it's taut.
4. Blow up the balloon and hold the neck closed so the air doesn't escape.
5. Have a student tape the balloon to the straw while you continue to hold the neck of the balloon closed.

Preparation Time: 3 minutes

Lesson Time: 20–25 minutes

— Procedure and Questioning Strategy —

1. What do you predict will happen when I let the balloon go?

    It will travel along the twine.

2. How far do you think it will go?

    (Students usually say the balloon will go about halfway across the room.)

Release the balloon.

3. What happened?

    The balloon went all the way across the room.

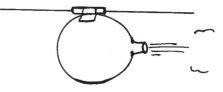

4. What do you think made it do that?

> The air came out of the balloon.

5. Let's call the part of the balloon with the neck the back of the balloon. When the air rushed out of the back of the balloon, in which direction did the balloon go?

> Forward.

6. Compare the direction of the air going out of the balloon with the direction that the balloon moved.

> They were opposite in direction. When the air went out the back, the balloon moved forward.

Remind the students that this activity demonstrates Newton's Third Law: for every action there is an equal and opposite reaction.

7. What stopped the balloon?

> (Student's name)'s hand, or the balloon ran out of air.

8. What might cause the balloon to go a longer or shorter distance?

> How much the balloon was blown up.
> The size of the balloon.

Distribute the materials and the graphs. Ask the students, in groups of three, to assemble and set off their rocket balloons. Each student in a group could have a special job: rocket launcher, measurer of the balloon and the distance it travels along the twine, and recorder. Each group needs to make at least 3 trials, varying the balloon circumference for each trial. For each of the trials, the jobs should be rotated. Data from each trial is to be recorded on the blank graph. When all of the groups have finished their 3 trials and recorded their data, ask the students the following questions.

9. How could you summarize the data you have collected during your three trials?

> The more air in the balloon rocket, the greater the distance it travels.

10. What may have caused some rockets to travel different distances even though they were the same size?

> Possible answers: how tightly the string was held; placement of the straw on the balloon; how the tape was attached to the balloon rocket.

— Practical Application —

1. How is the balloon rocket like a rocket launched into space?

> The balloon rocket and a rocket being launched into space both have air or gas rushing out in one direction and the rocket moving in the other direction.

2. How is the balloon rocket different?

> The balloon rocket moves across the room and a rocket goes up into the air.
> *Air* comes out of the balloon and *gases* from the burning rocket fuel come out of a rocket.

3. What might cause one rocket to take off faster than another?

> The amount of gas that comes out of the rocket.

4. Since there is no air on the Moon, would a rocket work there?

> Yes. The rocket moves forward in *reaction* to the gases coming out of it, not because the gases *push* on the air outside the rocket.

5. The Moon has less gravity and less atmosphere than the Earth. How do you think that would affect a rocket when it takes off?

> It should take off faster since there would be less gravity and atmosphere to slow it down.

ROCKET POWER GRAPH
(Sample)

TRIAL	BALLOON CIRCUMFERENCE (inches around)	DISTANCE TRAVELED (feet)
1	6	15
2	12	30
3	18	45

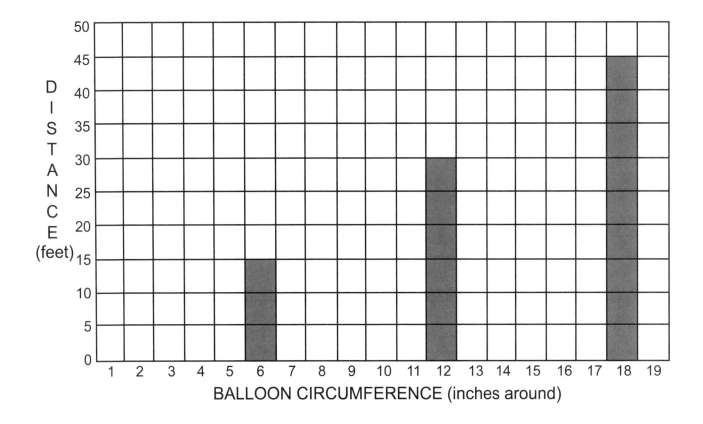

BALLOON CIRCUMFERENCE (inches around)

ROCKET POWER GRAPH
(Sample)

TRIAL	BALLOON CIRCUMFERENCE (inches around)	DISTANCE TRAVELED (feet)

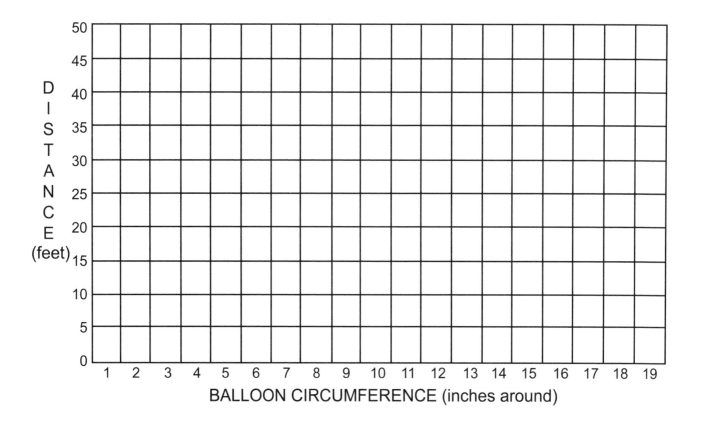

ACTIVITY 51: MORE ROCKET POWER!

Goal: To apply the generalization that the action of the air being released from a balloon causes an equal and opposite reaction, causing the balloon to move diagonally, or upward

Skills: Observing, classifying, inferring, predicting, controlling variables, generalizing

Materials: Round sturdy balloons (about 18" inflated)
Twine or fishing line that is long enough to stretch across the room
2 drinking straws, cut in half
2 pieces of 2"-wide masking tape, 3" to 4" long
Measuring tape

Preparation: 1. Thread one-half of a straw on a long piece of twine.
2. Have two students stretch the twine across the room and hold each end so it's taut.
3. Blow up the balloon and hold the neck closed so the air doesn't escape.
4. Have another student tape the balloon to the straw while you continue to hold the neck of the balloon closed.

Preparation Time: 3 minutes

Lesson Time: 15–20 minutes

— Procedure and Questioning Strategy —

1. What do you think will happen if the twine is held at an angle and the balloon is released?

     Students usually say it will go halfway up the twine.

Lift, or have one of the students lift, one end of the twine to about a 45-degree angle (it may be necessary for you or the student to stand on a chair). Release the balloon.

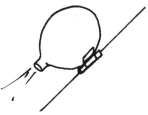

2. How far did the balloon go?

     To the other end of the twine.

Blow up the balloon again and hold the neck closed.

3. How far do you think the balloon will go if the twine is held straight up?

     To the other end of the twine.

Hold, or have one of the students hold, one end of the twine straight up (the twine will need to be shorter for this activity and, again, you or the student may need to stand on a chair).

4. What happened?

   The balloon went to the other end of the twine.

5. How was the movement of this balloon different from the movement of the first balloon?

   This one was slower.

6. What might have caused it to move slower?

   The position of the string. Gravity was pulling on it harder than before.

7. How could we make the second balloon go faster?

   Put more air in it.

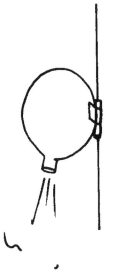

8. How would that make it go faster?

   The more air that comes out the back of the balloon, the faster the balloon will move.

Try it!

— Practical Application —

1. Which balloon launch is more similar to a rocket being launched?

   The straight up position.

2. What is the reason that rockets are usually launched straight up?

   They escape the Earth's gravity more quickly when they point straight up.

ACTIVITY 52: TWO-STAGE BALLOON ROCKETS!

Goal: To understand that the first stage of a two-stage rocket gives the initial thrust, then the thrust of the second stage keeps the rocket in motion

Skills: Observing, inferring, predicting, controlling variables, generalizing

Materials:

> 2 round sturdy balloons (about 18" inflated)
>
> Twine or fishing line long enough to stretch across the room
>
> Paper cups for hot and cold drinks, 8 oz.
>
> 2 pieces of 2"-wide masking tape, 3" to 4" long
>
> Drinking straw, cut in half
>
> Scissors

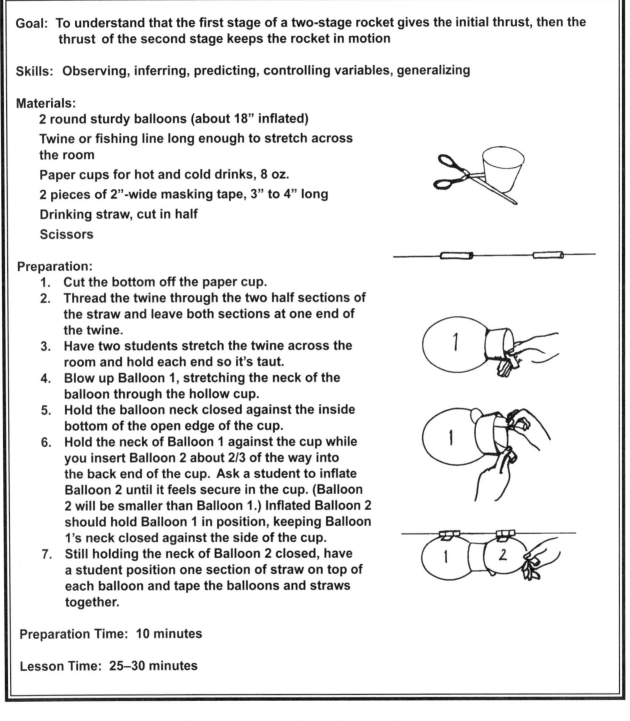

Preparation:

1. Cut the bottom off the paper cup.
2. Thread the twine through the two half sections of the straw and leave both sections at one end of the twine.
3. Have two students stretch the twine across the room and hold each end so it's taut.
4. Blow up Balloon 1, stretching the neck of the balloon through the hollow cup.
5. Hold the balloon neck closed against the inside bottom of the open edge of the cup.
6. Hold the neck of Balloon 1 against the cup while you insert Balloon 2 about 2/3 of the way into the back end of the cup. Ask a student to inflate Balloon 2 until it feels secure in the cup. (Balloon 2 will be smaller than Balloon 1.) Inflated Balloon 2 should hold Balloon 1 in position, keeping Balloon 1's neck closed against the side of the cup.
7. Still holding the neck of Balloon 2 closed, have a student position one section of straw on top of each balloon and tape the balloons and straws together.

Preparation Time: 10 minutes

Lesson Time: 25–30 minutes

— Procedure and Questioning Strategy —

1. What do you predict will happen first when the balloons are released?

> Air will be released from the smaller balloon (the first stage of the rocket) and the balloon rocket will travel along the string.

2. What do you predict will happen next?

> Air will come out of the larger balloon (the second stage of the rocket) and the balloon will keep traveling along the string.

3. Why will the first stage of the rocket balloon need to deflate before the second stage can take over?

> The smaller balloon keeps the mouth of the larger balloon closed.

4. What do you think will happen to the first stage of the balloon rocket when it deflates?

> It will separate from the second stage.

Release the balloons.

5. What happened?

> The first stage gave the first push to the balloon rocket, then it separated from the second stage of the balloon rocket. The second stage then kept the balloon rocket moving forward.

6. What do you think would happen if we used larger balloons and larger cups?

> The balloon rocket would go faster and farther.

7. What reason can you think of for the rocket going faster and farther?

> More air would come out of the balloon, giving the balloon more force to go forward.

8. What do you think might happen if we used fishing line instead of twine?

> The balloon rocket might go faster and farther.

9. For what reason?

> The fishing line isn't as thick as twine and it's smoother, so it wouldn't catch on the straw.

— Practical Application —

1. Why do rockets have stages?

> To reduce weight.

2. How would a two-stage rocket reduce the rocket's weight?

> When the first stage separated and dropped off, the rest of the rocket would be lighter in weight.

3. How would this affect the rocket's flight?

> It would be able to go faster and farther with less weight.

4. How would this affect the rocket's use of fuel?

It would need less fuel.

5. How would having two stages help the rocket escape the pull of Earth's gravity?

A two-stage rocket would have more push, or thrust, than a one-stage rocket, so it would be able to escape Earth's gravity more easily.

ACTIVITIES 50–52: CONNECTIONS

Goal: To find relationships among the activities for rockets

Skills: Identifying, comparing, and classifying variables

— Questioning Strategy —

1. In our first activity for rockets, we varied the circumferences of the balloons to see what effect this had on the distance the rockets traveled. What was the experimental variable?

    The size of the balloon or how much it was blown up.

2. What was the dependent variable?

    The distance that the balloon traveled.

3. In the second activity we tested the balloon rocket's flight at a 45-degree angle and straight up and found that the rocket was slower when it went straight up. What was the experimental variable in this activity?

    The path of the rocket—it was either a 45-degree angle or straight up.

4. What was the dependent variable?

    The speed of the rocket.

5. What other variables could we have used as experimental variables in any of the rocket activities?

    Possible answers: different-sized balloons; different cups in the two-stage rocket activity; different types of materials for the flight path (string, fishing line, thread).

UNIT 12— INERTIA AND THE FLIGHT OF SATELLITES

Background Information

Imagine that you're sitting in an airplane ready for takeoff. Your body is at rest. When the plane rushes down the runway to reach a speed high enough to be able to take off, you feel like you're being pushed back into your seat. This is an example of the first part of **Newton's First Law of Motion – The Law of Inertia**. **Inertia** is the tendency of a body at rest to remain at rest unless a force acts on it.

Imagine that you're driving home from school. A pile of books and papers is on the seat behind you. Suddenly a dog runs out into the street and you abruptly step on your brakes. What happened to your body? What happened to the books and papers that were behind you?

This is an example of the second part of Newton's Law of Inertia. Inertia is also the tendency of a moving object to continue moving in a straight line, at the same speed, unless a force stops it. The car and everything in it moves along the street at the same speed. When the car stops quickly, everything in the car has the tendency to continue moving at the speed it had been moving. You feel like you're pushed forward toward the windshield. Your books and papers fly forward, hitting the back of your seat.

This tendency of a body to continue to move in a straight line, at the same speed, until a force is exerted on it directly relates to the flight of the space shuttles described in the previous unit. As the shuttle moves into outer space, the pull of Earth's gravity decreases. Since the shuttle is in motion at about 18,000 mph, it has the tendency to continue in a straight line at that speed. The force required for the shuttle to continue to its orbital pathway decreases proportionately to the decrease in the pull of gravity.

When the shuttle reaches the altitude of its orbital path, usually around 300 miles above Earth, it rolls over into the path. At this time, the shuttle's engines are turned off and the shuttle orbits the Earth at around 17,500 mph; it's coasting in free flight in an elliptical orbit. So what happened to the part of Newton's Law concerning the tendency of a body to stay in motion in a straight line? The orbit of the shuttle is curved.

Two major forces keep the shuttle in orbit: the pull of gravity and the tendency to remain in motion at the same speed. These two forces act against each other. As inertia tends to keep the shuttle moving in a straight line out into space from any point in its orbit, the Earth's gravity pulls the shuttle back to Earth, balancing its tendency toward inertia (see figure A).

If gravity were exerting a stronger force on the shuttle than inertia, the shuttle would slow down, which would result in a smaller orbit. If the tendency for inertia were greater than the pull of gravity, the shuttle would fly straight out into space at a constant speed.

One other factor is considered when planning for a shuttle's orbit. **Orbital velocity** is the sideways speed the shuttle needs to stay in orbit. If the design of the shuttle flight called for an orbital altitude of 300 miles (480 km), the shuttle would need an orbital velocity of about 18,000 miles (29,000 km) an hour to stay in orbit. A shuttle's orbital velocity needs to be exact so the force of gravity and the effect of inertia are balanced.

The same conditions are true for satellites orbiting the Earth, for planets and asteroids orbiting the sun, and for moons orbiting planets.

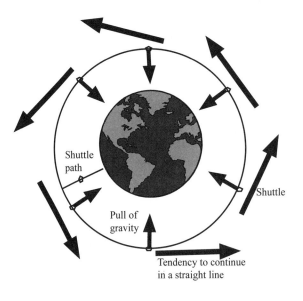

Shuttle path

Pull of gravity

Shuttle

Tendency to continue in a straight line

figure A

Unit 12—NATIONAL SCIENCE EDUCATION STANDARDS

- *Unifying Concepts and Processes*—Students should develop understanding and abilities with regard to systems, order, and organization; evidence, models, and explanation; constancy, change, and measurement; and evolution and equilibrium.

- *Science as Inquiry*—Content Standard A: Students should develop the necessary skills to do scientific inquiry and develop an understanding about scientific inquiry.

- *Physical Science*—Content Standard B: Students should develop an understanding of the properties of objects and materials; position and motion of objects; properties and changes of properties in matter; and motions and forces.

- *Earth and Space Science*—Content Standard D: Students should develop an understanding about the earth in the solar system.

- *History and Nature of Science*—Content Standard G: Students should develop an understanding of the nature of science and of science as a human endeavor.

ACTIVITY 53: INERTIA – RIDING IN CARS

Goal: To understand that inertia is the tendency of all moving objects to keep moving and of all motionless objects to remain motionless (This is Newton's First Law—The Law of Inertia. This activity demonstrates the first part of the law.)

Skills: Observing, inferring, generalizing, hypothesizing

Materials: For each pair of students:
      An open-top toy car (i.e., a convertible, jeep, etc.) which students can bring from home
      A cutout figure from page 197
      A textbook

If students cannot bring in enough cars so there is one for each pair, or you feel they will get too "rambunctious" playing with the cars, you may choose to do this activity as a demonstration (although rambunctiousness can be minimized by setting a tone for the students; for example, they are young scientists and should maintain proper "scientific behavior").

Preparation:
  1. Duplicate page 197 and give one copy to each pair.
  2. Have the students choose and cut out the figure on page 197 that will fit in their car.

Preparation Time: 5 minutes

Lesson Time: 10–15 minutes

— Procedure and Questioning Strategy —

1. Let's see what we have here. What do you suppose the figure you cut out is supposed to represent?

   A person.

2. Now, put your person in the car and put the car near the edge of your desk (or a table if your desk is not flat). Put the book on the opposite side of the desk/table.

Demonstrate this for the students as shown in the drawing below.

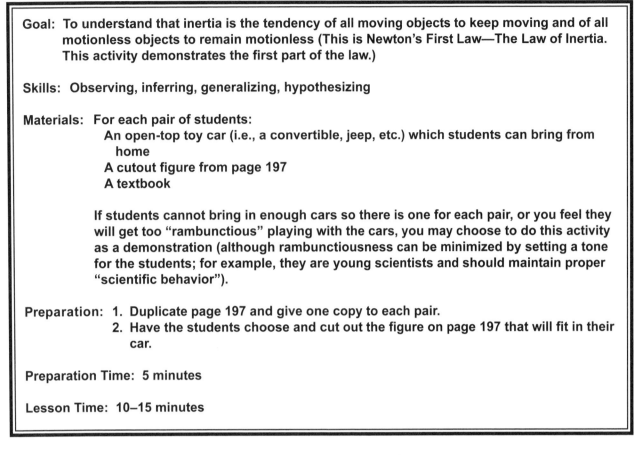

3. When I tell you to begin, roll your car across the top of your desk so that it hits the book "head on." Do this several times, taking turns. Experiment by rolling your car at different speeds. Carefully observe your little "person" each time.

Give the students a few minutes to experiment.

4. Now what did you observe?

> (Among their observations may be:
>
> The car stopped immediately when it hit the book.
>
> The person fell forward when the car stopped.
>
> The faster the car was moving, the more tendency the person had to fall forward.
>
> If the car rolled slowly, the person fell forward only slightly.
>
> The person fell out of the car some of the time.
>
> When the car stopped, the person sort of kept going.)

5. Now let's try to generalize. When the car was immediately stopped, what did the person tend to do?

> Fall forward. Keep going.

6. So when a person or object is moving, what do they have a tendency to do?

> Keep moving.

7. And what caused the "person" to fall forward?

> Its tendency to keep moving when the car was stopped.

8. Does anyone know what we call this tendency?

> (If no one responds, give them the term INERTIA.)

INERTIA is the tendency of a moving object to continue moving unless a force stops it.

— Practical Application —

1. Now let's suppose you're riding in a car. The car in front of you stops suddenly, your car hits it and also stops suddenly. What will happen to you?

> You will keep moving forward. If you have a seat belt on, you will not move forward very far.

2. Why will you keep moving forward?

> Your inertia makes you want to keep moving.

3. So why are seat belts so important when you're riding in a car?

> If you should stop suddenly, the seat belt keeps you from going forward and crashing into the windshield or dashboard. It stops your inertia.

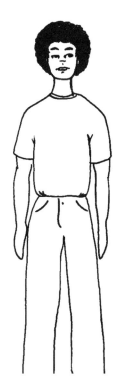
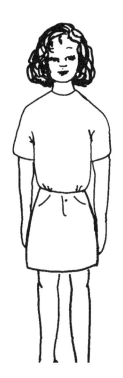

ACTIVITY 54: THE NICKEL, THE CARD, AND THE CUP

Goal: To understand inertia, which is a property of motionless objects that makes them want to remain motionless (This is the first part of Newton's Law of Inertia—Newton's First Law.)

Skills: Observing, predicting, hypothesizing, comparing, generalizing, inferring

Materials: 3" x 5" card
5" x 8" card
Transparent drinking cup
Nickel
Quarter

Preparation: 1. Place the 3" x 5" card on the cup.
2. Place the nickel on the card as shown in the drawing below.

Preparation Time: 1 minute

Lesson Time: 10–15 minutes

— Procedure and Questioning Strategy —

Display the nickel, card, and cup as shown in the drawing.

1. Look at the materials we have here. What do you see?

   A card sitting on a cup with a nickel on it.

2. I am going to flick the card. (You may initially want to demonstrate flicking the card *without* the nickel on it.) What will happen to the nickel?

   (Answers will vary.)

Flick the card.

3. What did you observe?

   The nickel fell into the cup.

4. Let's try it again. This time I'll use the quarter. What do you think will happen now?

   (Answers will vary.)

Flick the card again.

5. What did you observe this time?

The quarter also fell into the cup.

6. What if I try a larger card?

    (Many students will now predict that the coin will fall into the cup.)

Flick the larger card with the nickel, then repeat the activity with the quarter.

7. What kind of pattern do we see here?

    In each case, the card flew off the cup when you flicked it and the coin fell into the cup.

8. Let's try to make a generalization about objects that are standing still.

    Objects that are standing still want to remain standing still.

9. Why did the card move?

    We flicked it.

10. The flick was a what?

    A force.

11. So when do objects move?

    When a force acts on them.

12. Otherwise, what do they do?

    They remain standing still.

— Practical Application —

1. Your neighbor has been washing the car and she/he forgets a bucket on the driveway. How long will the bucket remain there?

    Forever, unless something moves it, such as the wind or someone picking it up.

2. Why will it remain there forever?

    It is standing still, and because of its inertia, it wants to remain standing still. It will never move unless a force moves it.

ACTIVITY 55: TRICKY NICKELS

Goal: To apply the Law of Inertia, which is a property of motionless objects that makes them want to stay motionless

Skills: Observing, predicting, comparing, generalizing, explaining, hypothesizing

Materials: 5 nickels
5 quarters
Marking pen

Preparation: Stack 4 of the nickels as shown in the drawing below.

Preparation Time: 1 minute

Lesson Time: 15–20 minutes

— Procedure and Questioning Strategy —

Display the stack of nickels as shown in the drawing.

1. I am going to flick this nickel into the stack that you see in front of you. What will happen to the stack of nickels?

     (Students will offer a variety of predictions.)

2. Let's try it.

Flick the nickel into the stack (this may take a little practice).

3. What did you see?

     A nickel came out and the others dropped down.

4. Which nickel came out?

     The bottom one.

5. How can we be sure it was the bottom one?

     We could mark it and try it again.

Mark one of the nickels with a marking pen.

6. Okay, we've marked the nickel; let's try it.

Put the marked nickel on the bottom of the stack and repeat the experiment.

7.   What did you see?

> The bottom nickel came out.

8.   What do you suppose will happen if we repeat the activity with quarters?

> (Answers will vary, but at this point several students will predict that the bottom quarter will come out and the rest of the stack will fall straight down.)

Based on the activity with the nickels, students may at this point suggest that you should mark the bottom quarter. If they do not, ask the following question.

9.   What should we do to be sure it is the bottom quarter that comes out?

> We should mark it with the pen.

Do the activity using the quarters.

10.   What did you observe?

> The bottom quarter came out and the rest of the quarters fell straight down.

11.   How does this activity compare to the one with the nickel, card, and cup?

> In this activity, the nickels and quarters fell straight down when we flicked the bottom one out, and in the nickel, card, and cup activity, the nickel and quarter both fell into the cup when we flicked the card out from under them.

12.   Let's form a generalization about objects that are motionless.

> They want to remain motionless unless something acts directly upon them.

— Practical Application —

1.   My car has run out of gas and I have to push it to the service station a block away. When will I have to push the hardest—to get the car started rolling or to keep it rolling once I get it started?

> You will have to push the hardest to get it started rolling.

2.   Why?

> Because of its inertia when it is standing, it wants to remain standing. Once I get it moving I have overcome its inertia (its tendency to remain at rest) and it is easier to keep it going.

ACTIVITY 56: THE GLASS OF WATER AND THE PAPER

Goal: To understand an application of the Law of Inertia, which says that objects that are standing still want to remain standing still

Skills: Observing, predicting, inferring

Materials: For each student:
Sheet of notebook paper
Plastic drinking glass
Water
Book

Preparation: Fill the drinking glass with water.

Preparation Time: 1 minute

Lesson Time: 10–15 minutes

— Procedure and Questioning Strategy —

Place the sheet of paper on the edge of a table and put the glass of water on the paper. (The water is used merely to add a little "drama" to the demonstration.)

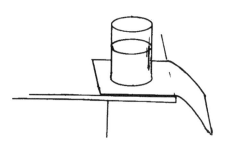

1. What do I have here?

    A glass of water sitting on a piece of paper.

2. I'm going to yank on the piece of paper. What will happen to the glass?

    (Predictions will vary. Based on the two previous activities, some students will predict that the glass will remain sitting on the table.)

Yank the paper out from under the glass (this is easier to do than it seems). Be careful to keep the paper from getting wet, otherwise the glass may "stick" to it and the glass will be pulled onto the floor.

3. What did you observe?

    The paper came out and the glass of water was left on the table.

4. Why did the glass of water remain on the table?

    The glass of water was standing still, and because of its inertia, it wanted to remain standing still, so it didn't move.

5. Now let's all try a similar activity. Put the paper on the edge of a flat table or desk and put the book on the paper. What will happen when you yank on the paper?

> (Most students predict the paper will come out and the book will remain on the table or desk.)

Have them try it.

6. What did you observe?

> The paper came out and the book stayed on the table/desk.

7. Why did this happen?

> The book was standing still and, because of its inertia, it wanted to remain standing still, so it didn't move.

8. How could we make the book move?

> Apply a force to it such as pushing, pulling, or lifting.

Some students may suggest that the force of friction is acting on the glass or book. This is true, and if the paper were pulled slowly, the glass or book would be pulled along with it as a result of the friction. Yanking the paper overcomes the force of friction and the glass or book remains standing.

— Practical Application —

1. We may have seen a magician place a stack of dishes on a tablecloth and "magically" pull the tablecloth out from under them without moving the dishes. Let's explain how this "magic" works.

> The dishes are standing still (motionless) and, because of their inertia, they want to remain standing still. Just as the nickels, quarters, glass, and book remained still, the dishes remain still when the tablecloth is pulled out from under them.

ACTIVITY 57: THE SOCK ON THE STRING

Goal: To understand inertia, which is a property of moving objects that makes them want to continue moving in a straight line (this is the second part of Newton's Law of Inertia—Newton's First Law)

Skills: Observing, inferring, predicting, hypothesizing, generalizing, explaining

Materials: A sock (such as an athletic sock) folded into a ball
String or light twine
Tennis ball

Preparation: 1. Roll the sock into a ball-like shape.
2. Cut a piece of string about 1 meter long.
3. Tie the sock ball to one end of the string.

Preparation Time: 5 minutes

Lesson Time: 15–20 minutes

— Procedure and Questioning Strategy —

Have a student face the other students and swing the string with the sock attached in a circular motion around his/her head.

1. Where do you predict the sock will go when (student's name) lets go of the string on his/her right side?

    (Predictions will vary.)

2. Move to the place in the room where you think the sock will land and be ready to catch the sock.

Have the student swing the sock around a few times and release it at a point directly on his/her right side.

3. Where did the sock go?

    In a straight path from the circle.

4. Let's draw the sock's path on the board.

5. Where do you predict the sock will go if (student's name) releases it when the sock is directly in front of him/her? Move to the place in the room where you think it will land. Be ready to catch it.

6. Let's draw the path that the sock took this time.

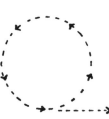

7. What keeps the sock in the circular path around our heads?

    The force of the string pulling it in.

8. What will happen if we swing the sock faster?

    It will still travel straight, but faster, and will fly farther.

Have the student swing the sock faster and let it go. Then draw a circle about 3 feet in diameter on the chalkboard.

9. Now look at the circle I have drawn on the chalkboard. (Student's name), try to hit the circle with the sock. Everyone else watch where (student's name) lets go of the sock in order to hit the circle.

Have the student try it. He/she will likely miss the first time. Have him/her try it a few times and have the other students watch the point of release carefully and offer suggestions. When the student hits the circle or comes close, ask the following question.

10. Where did (student's name) let go of the sock in order to hit the circle?

    Right here (as shown in the drawing).

Let several students try to hit the target, maybe even from different positions in the room. When one does hit the target, ask the student to tell his/her thinking behind the decision about where to release the sock.

11. What can we say in general about the way moving objects travel when they are released from a circular path?

    Moving objects want to move in a straight line.

— Practical Application —

1. We now want to apply our principle to other situations. I'm going to roll this tennis ball along the floor. How will it move?

    It will move in a straight line.

Roll the ball along the floor.

2. How did it move?

    It moved along in a straight line.

3. When will it stop?

When it hits something or when friction eventually slows it down.

4. Suppose there is no such thing as friction and the ball doesn't hit anything. How long will it roll?

   Forever if the floor is level.

5. Sometimes when cars travel too fast they "miss" a curve and go off the road. Let's explain why this happens.

   The car wants to travel in a straight line. The only thing that keeps it on the road is the friction between the tires and the road and the bank of the road (if it is banked). If the car travels too fast, its inertia overcomes the friction and the car goes off the road.

6. Earth travels around the sun much like the sock traveled around (student's name). What does Earth want to do?

   Fly off in a straight line.

7. What keeps Earth in its path around the sun?

   The force of gravity between Earth and the sun.

8. What compares to the force of gravity in our example with the sock and the string?

   The string.

9. How about the moon traveling around Earth? What does it want to do?

   It also wants to go in a straight line, but gravity again keeps it in its path.

10. What behaves like gravity—the sock or the string?

    The string.

11. What behaves like Earth or the moon?

    The sock.

12. When we wash clothes in a washing machine, how do the clothes look after the spin cycle stops?

    The clothes are "stuck" up against the sides of the washer tub.

13. Why are they stuck that way?

    The tub spins during the spin cycle. As it spins, the clothes and the water in the tub want to travel in a straight line due to their inertia. The holes in the tub let the water out, but the sides of the tub make the clothes travel in a circle so they get stuck to the sides.

ACTIVITY 58: WHIRLING WATER!

Goal: To understand an application of inertia, a property of moving objects that makes them want to move at a steady speed in a straight line

Skills: Observing, comparing, explaining, hypothesizing

Materials: Transparent drinking cup
String
Transparent tape

Preparation: 1. Tie the string around the cup as shown in the drawing.
2. Tape the string to the sides of the cup to prevent it from sliding off.
3. Fill the cup nearly full of water.

Preparation Time: 10 minutes

Lesson Time: 10–15 minutes

— Procedure and Questioning Strategy —

1. I am going to whirl the cup of water around my head the same way (student's name) whirled the sock around his/her head in the last activity. What do you think will happen to the water in the cup?

    (Predictions will vary. Some say the water will spill. Others say the water will stay in the cup.)

Swing the cup around your head in the same way the student swung the sock and the string in Activity 57.

2. What did you observe?

    The water stayed in the cup.
    The cup and water moved in a circle around your head.

3. Why did the cup and water behave that way?

    The water wants to go in a straight line (because of its inertia) but the cup won't let it, so it stays in the cup.

4. What will happen to the water if I twirl the cup faster?

    It will still stay in the cup.

Twirl the cup and water again to confirm their predictions.

5. When will the water fly off?

> When you twirl the cup so fast that the string breaks, or when you let go of the string. Then both the cup and water will fly off.

6. Do you think the water will spill out of the cup as it is flying off?

> (Answers will vary.)

You may choose to do this activity outdoors; you could then try to check the student's predictions.

7. How is this activity like the sock and string activity?

> The sock wanted to go in a straight line and it did when you let go of the string. The cup and water want to go in a straight line and also would if you let go of the string.

— Practical Application —

1. Imagine that you're in one of those carnival rides where you whirl around in a circle, then the floor drops out. What happens to you?

> I am "pinned" up against the wall.

2. Why are you pinned against the wall?

> Because of my inertia, I want to travel in a straight line, but the wall won't let me so I "feel" pressed against the wall.

3. When do clothes being washed in a washing machine act in a similar way?

> In the spin cycle, when the clothes end up sticking to the sides of the washer.

4. Can you think of any other everyday examples?

> When the food in a blender or food processor ends up sticking around the sides of the container.

ACTIVITIES 53–58: CONNECTIONS

Goal: To understand the relationships between the characteristics of inertia

Skills: Comparing, explaining

— Questioning Strategy —

1. Let's compare the activities that we did. What did the nickel, card, and cup, the tricky nickels, and the drinking glass and the paper all have in common?

    In each case the object or objects were standing still. The nickel on the card was still, the stack of nickels was still, and the glass of water on the paper was still.

2. When we flicked the card and the nickel and yanked the paper, what happened?

    The nickel fell straight down, the stack fell straight down, and the glass didn't move. (The small amount of movement in each case was due to friction. No other force on the objects tended to make them move forward or backward. They moved down because of gravity.)

3. Why didn't they move?

    Objects standing still want to remain standing still.

4. When we are riding in a car and the car suddenly speeds up, we are "scrunched" back into the seat. How does this relate to what we said about the nickels and the cup?

    The nickels and the cup want to remain still. Our bodies also want to remain still. When the car accelerates, it pushes against our bodies to make us move. The sensation we get is that we are being scrunched into the seat.

5. Now suppose the car stops suddenly. What happens to us?

    We continue moving unless something, such as a seatbelt, stops us.

6. Why do we continue moving?

    Any moving object wants to continue moving. This is part of the law of inertia. Because we are moving, our inertia wants to keep us moving.

7. How is this like the sock and the string?

    We are moving in the car and the sock is moving on the end of the string.

8. How is it different?

    We are moving in a straight line and suddenly stop. The sock was moving in a circle, but it wanted to move in a straight line, so when we let it go, it went straight. It stopped when it hit the back of the room.

9. Sometimes when we have water on our hands, we shake them to "shake the water off." Let's try to explain how shaking the water off works.

> When we shake our hand, it moves and then suddenly stops. The water that is moving with our hand wants to keep moving, so it shakes off. (Wet dogs do the same thing instinctively.)

UNITS 13 & 14—SURFACE TENSION and BUBBLES

Background Information

Have you noticed condensation on the bathroom mirror after you take a hot shower? Or drops of water on a leaf or on the waxed surface of a car? What is the shape of a water drop? Are drops always circular? The surfaces of the water drops on the leaf in figure A are dome shaped. There are billions of water molecules in a drop of water. How do they stay together and form a dome? If you look closely, it looks like there is a "skin" on the surface of the water.

figure A

Actually, all molecules attract each other. When molecules of the same substance are attracted, it is called **cohesion**; the molecules hold together well enough to be able to hold a dome full of water. This is an example of **surface tension**.

If the attracted molecules are of different substances, it is called **adhesion**. The drops of water actually stay on the leaf because of adhesion. The molecules of water adhere to the molecules of the leaf so firmly that the drops don't run down the leaf.

Soap and detergent can break the bond formed by molecules. Imagine that you are washing dishes. Some plates have the remains of eggs stuck on them, an example of adhesion. Trying to wash the plate with water doesn't dislodge the egg particles, so you soak the plate in warm water and detergent. Later, the egg rinses right off the plate. How did the detergent affect the adhesion of the molecules? Water mixed with detergent feels quite slippery. It causes the hold that molecules have on each other to loosen, and the egg slips right off the plate.

Different solutions for making huge bubbles are explored in Activities 64 and 65 to extend the concept of surface tension. The amount of detergent added to water has an effect on the amount of surface tension, the strength of the outer surfaces of the bubbles. Addition of a small amount of liquid glycerin to the solution actually makes the water wetter because it keeps the water from evaporating. The addition of too much glycerin reduces the surface tension.

Units 13 & 14—NATIONAL SCIENCE EDUCATION STANDARDS

- *Unifying Concepts and Processes:* Students should develop understanding and abilities with regard to systems, order, and organization; evidence, models, and explanation; and constancy, change, and measurement.

- *Science as Inquiry*—Content Standard A: Students should develop the necessary skills to do scientific inquiry and develop an understanding about scientific inquiry.

- *Physical Science*—Content Standard B: Students should develop an understanding of properties of objects and materials, and properties and changes of properties in matter.

- *History and Nature of Science*—Content Standard G: Students should develop an understanding of the nature of science and of science as a human endeavor.

ACTIVITY 59: DOMED PENNIES

Goal: To observe that drops of water assume a dome shape when they settle on a surface; that many drops together form a larger dome shape; that something that looks like a "skin" on the top of the water seems to keep the water in a dome shape; that the way water is dropped on the dome affects the number of drops that can fit without spilling over

Skills: Observing, predicting, identifying variables, hypothesizing, generalizing

Materials: For each pair of students:
       Penny (pennies should be in different states of wear)
       Magnifying glass (optional)
       Glass or paper cup with water
       Eyedropper
       Paper towel
       6" x 6" piece of waxed paper

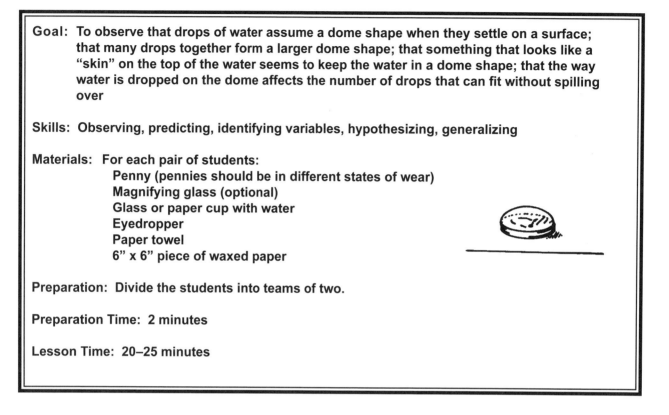

Preparation: Divide the students into teams of two.

Preparation Time: 2 minutes

Lesson Time: 20–25 minutes

— Procedure and Questioning Strategy —

Ask one student from each pair to gather the materials for the activity. Then explain to students that they will need to do the following.

- Predict how many drops of water they think will fit on the heads side of a penny, writing their prediction on a piece of paper.
- Find an even surface to use and put their penny on a paper towel, with the head of the penny facing up.
- Choose one member of the pair to drop water from the eyedropper onto the penny while the other watches and counts each drop that fits without spilling off the penny.
- Turn the penny over and, switching jobs (using the eyedropper and observing/counting), see how many drops will fit on the tails side of the penny.
- Compare predictions with the number of drops that actually did stay on the penny.
- List the variables that may have affected the number of drops that fit.

Ask each team the following two-part question.

1. How many drops fit on the heads side of your penny; how many fit on the tails side?
   (Answers may vary from 15–50 drops.)

Now ask all students the next questions.

2. What variables may have had an effect on the number of drops you could fit on the penny without the water spilling over? (List answers on board.)

> (Possible answers: how far the eyedropper was from the penny; the time allowed between the release of each drop; the size of the drop released; the size of the eyedropper opening; the place on the penny or dome on which the drops landed; the condition of the penny [worn or new]; the height of the rim on the penny; the side of the penny—heads or tails).

3. What was done to fit more drops on the penny?

> (Possible answers: the eyedropper was held closer to the penny; more time was given between drop releases; smaller drops of water were used; a smaller eyedropper opening was used; drops were placed around the middle of the penny or dome; a newer penny was used.)

4. What did you observe when the water landed on the penny?

> (Possible answers: the first drop assumed a dome shape; the drops looked like they were grabbed into the water already on the penny; the dome jiggled, then settled back into dome shape.)

5. What did you notice about the surface of the water as the dome shape of the water grew larger and higher?

> It seemed like something on the surface of the water held the water together, like a "skin."

6. What do you think happened to allow the water to spill over the rim of the penny?

> The amount of water became too much for the skin on the surface of the water to hold together.

— Practical Application —

1. How are the water drops you dropped like falling raindrops?

> They are similar in shape.

2. When a raindrop lands on the waxed surface of a car, what shape does it take?

> A dome shape.

3. What shape do you think a drop of water would take on a piece of waxed paper?

> A dome shape.

Try it.

4. What do you think would happen if you dropped water drops right next to each other on the waxed paper?

Try it to show the tendency of water drops to merge into one large drop due to the cohesiveness of water molecules.

══════ **ACTIVITY 60: STICKY WATER!** ══════

Goal: To understand that surface tension is the attraction of water molecules to each other on the top of water and that these water molecules form a kind of "skin" on the surface of the water

Skills: Observing, inferring, predicting, hypothesizing, generalizing

Materials: Transparent drinking glass, plastic or glass
Container of water
60–100 pennies

Preparation: 1. Set the materials on a level table where all students can see them.
2. Pour water into the glass until the glass is filled to the rim. Have students tell you when it's full to the rim.

Preparation Time: 2 minutes

Lesson Time: 15–20 minutes

— Procedure and Questioning Strategy —

1. How full is this glass of water?

   It's up to the top.

2. How many pennies do you think we could put into this glass of water without the water spilling over?

   (Estimates of the number of pennies usually vary from 1 to 20.)

Slowly start putting pennies into the water, one at a time. Usually it works best to hold pennies vertically and let each penny drop gently as it touches the surface of the water in the middle of the glass. Continue questioning as you add pennies.

3. We have 20 pennies in the glass of water. What does the water look like at the surface?

   It's starting to look like a dome.

4. What do you think will happen if we add more pennies?

   The water will run down the side of the glass.

5. There are 40 pennies in the water. Describe what is happening at the surface of the water.

   The dome is getting taller.

Invite groups of students to watch the surface of the water as you gently touch the top of the water with the penny and let it go.

6. Describe what the surface of the water looks like as the penny pushes down on it.

    The penny makes a dent in the surface, then it breaks through the surface and falls to the bottom of the glass.

7. What do you think is the reason that the water doesn't spill over the edge of the cup?

    It seems to have a "skin" on the top of the water to help it hold its shape.

Tell students that the skin on the top of the water is formed by SURFACE TENSION, which is the attraction of the molecules of a liquid to each other on the surface of a liquid.

8. The attraction of the molecules of a liquid to each other means that the molecules are COHESIVE. It's like the molecules are attached to each other and don't want to be separated.

Keep adding pennies, slowly, until some of the water spills over the side of the glass. Approximately 50 pennies should fit.

9. What happened to the cohesiveness of the water molecules?

    The molecules were cohesive until there was too much water pushing up from under the skin, then the skin of the water separated and let some water out.

— Practical Application —

1. When drops of water fell on our waxed paper, what shape did they take?

    Sort of a dome shape.

2. How does this relate to our experiment with the pennies?

    The water drops have the same shape as the water at the top of the glass.

3. Are there any liquids you can think of that might take a more ball-like (spherical) shape than water?

    Some kind of thick syrup like a corn syrup. Liquid mercury makes the most ball-like shape.

The next experiment is a good follow-up activity.

ACTIVITY 61: LESS STICKY WATER!

Goal: To understand that the surface tension of water can be lessened by adding detergent to the water

Skills: Observing, comparing, inferring, predicting, generalizing

Materials: Transparent drinking glass, plastic or glass
Container of water
50–100 pennies
Small amount of liquid dishwashing detergent

Preparation: 1. Set the materials on a level table where all students can see them.
2. Pour water into the glass until the glass is filled to the rim. Have students tell you when it is full to the rim.

Preparation Time: 2 minutes

Lesson Time: 10–15 minutes

— Procedure and Questioning Strategy —

1. Describe the amount of water in this glass.

   It's full right to the top.

2. Is it just about as full as it was in our last experiment?

   Yes.

Tell the students what you're doing as you add about ten drops of dishwashing detergent in the center of the water's surface.

3. How many pennies do you predict will fit into the glass?

   (Students usually guess around the same amount as they found fit into the glass full of plain water.)

Start putting the pennies into the water, slowly, one at a time, in the center of the surface of the water as in the previous experiment.

4. There are 20 pennies in the glass. Compare how the surface of the water with detergent in it looks to the surface of the plain water with 20 pennies in it from Activity 60.

   It does not have a dome shape like the plain water did. The surface is kind of flat.

Invite groups of students to watch as you gently put a penny into the water.

5. Describe what you see.

    The penny drops right through to the bottom of the glass.

6. Compare the way the surface of the water with detergent in it looks with how the surface of plain water looked when a penny was pushed down into it.

    The penny does not make a dent in the surface as it did in the plain water.

7. How many more pennies do you think will fit?

    (Answers vary.)

Continue putting pennies into the glass until some water spills over the side.

8. What do you think is the reason that less pennies fit into this glass?

    It must be because of the detergent. That's the only thing we changed.

9. What do you think the detergent does to the water?

    It makes it so the skin doesn't stay together as well as it does on plain water. The detergent makes the water molecules less cohesive.

— Practical Application —

1. Think about how water with dish detergent in it feels. Compare how this feels with how plain water feels. (If some students don't know, have them try it.)

    The water with detergent feels more slippery.

2. Do you think this slipperyness has something to do with the cohesiveness of water?

    Yes, if the detergent makes the water slippery, the water molecules aren't able to hold onto each other very well.

3. How could you relate this to the reason we use dish detergent to wash dishes?

    The detergent makes the water slippery so it helps food slide off the dishes.

4. What is the reason that the shower floor gets slippery when you take a shower?

    The soap mixed with the water makes the floor slippery.

ACTIVITY 62: THE FUNNEL AND SOAPY WATER

Goal: To understand that liquids tend to take the smallest shape possible

Skills: Observing, inferring, generalizing

Materials: Small bowl or other container
            Water
            Small amount of dishwashing detergent
            Small funnel
            Paper towels

Preparation: 1. Put 1" of water into the bowl.
             2. Add about 10–15 drops of detergent.
             3. Mix the detergent into the water.
             4. Swish the large end of the funnel around in the soapy water.

Preparation Time: 2 minutes

Lesson Time: 8–10 minutes

— Procedure and Questioning Strategy —

Ask students to observe the action of the soapy water in the funnel. Lift the funnel out of the water and hold it horizontally. The soapy water should leave a "skin" that stretches to fill in the large end of the funnel. The skin quickly draws up to the small end of the funnel. Make sure all students see the action of the skin of the soapy water in the funnel.

1. Describe what you see happening.

    The bubble went down in the funnel.
    The skin of the soapy water travels from the large end of the funnel to the small end.

2. What do we know about what the water molecules do on the surface of the water?

    They are attracted to each other and hold onto each other.

3. Why do you think the skin of the soapy water in the funnel traveled to the small end of the funnel?

    It kept moving to a smaller area until it could cover the smallest surface area possible.

4. What was in the funnel besides soapy water before the soapy skin moved down the funnel?

    Air.

5. What happened to the air in the small end of the funnel when the soapy skin traveled down the funnel?

    It was pushed out of the small end of the funnel.

6. What do you predict will happen if I cover the hole at the small end of the funnel tightly with my finger?

    The soapy skin won't travel down the funnel.

7. Why do you think that will happen?

    The air trapped in the funnel won't be able to go out of the funnel. The air will hold the skin in the large end of the funnel.

8. Let's try it.

Have students observe as you hold your finger tightly over the small end of the funnel, swish the large end in the soapy water, and hold the funnel up to show the skin over the opening.

— Practical Application —

1. Think about the way the shape of the water drops looked when we dropped water on the waxed paper. What is the similarity between the surface of those drops and the action of the water in the funnel?

    The water on the surface of the drops and the soapy water in the funnel took the smallest shape possible.

2. What was the shape of the water drops on the waxed paper?

    A dome shape.

3. How is that similar to the water skin in the funnel?

    It was already in the shape of a circle, so it made the smallest circular shape possible.

ACTIVITY 63: RACING PEPPER!

Goal: To apply students' understanding that the addition of detergent to water lessens water's surface tension

To understand that objects tend to stay on water where there is greater surface tension

Skills: Observing, predicting, inferring, generalizing

Materials: Round pie dish or other large round container
Water
Ground black pepper
Few drops of dishwashing detergent

Preparation: 1. Set the container on a table so it can be seen by all students.
2. Pour water into the container until it is about 2/3 full.
3. Sprinkle pepper over the surface of the water. (As you sprinkle the pepper on the water, students should be far enough away that they will not accidentally breathe it in or get it into their eyes.)

Preparation Time: 2 minutes

Lesson Time: 8–10 minutes

— Procedure and Questioning Strategy —

1. What do you observe?

   The pepper is floating on the surface of the water. A few pieces of pepper sank to the bottom.

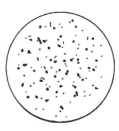

2. What do you think is the reason for this?

   The surface tension of the water keeps most of the pepper from sinking.

3. What do you predict will happen if I drop a little bit of dish detergent into the middle of the water?

   (Answers will vary.)

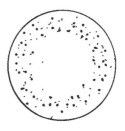

4. What happened?

   The pepper that was in the middle, where the detergent was dropped, sank. The pepper that was around the area where the detergent was dropped stayed on the surface of the water.

5. How do you think the addition of detergent affected the surface tension of the water? Did it make it stronger or weaker?

   It made it weaker.

6. Do you think the detergent weakened the surface tension all over the surface?

It seems to be weaker near the middle where the detergent was dropped.

7. Where do you think the surface tension of the water is the strongest?

Near the sides of the container.

8. So where did the pepper tend to stay?

On the surface of the water where the surface tension was the greatest—near the sides.

ACTIVITIES 59–63: CONNECTIONS
— Questioning Strategy —

Goal: To find relationships among activities for surface tension

Skills: Comparing, explaining, inferring, supporting inferences with observations

1. Let's think about the two activities we did with the glassful of water and the pennies. In which activity did the water have more surface tension—the one in which we dropped pennies into plain water or into water with a few drops of dishwashing detergent added?

    The activity with plain water.

2. How do you know that?

    The dome shape was more flattened and didn't build up into as tall a dome when we added dishwashing detergent.

3. Think about these two activities: the one in which we dropped water from eyedroppers onto pennies to see how many drops would fit before spilling over, and the one in which we dropped pennies into a glassful of water. In these two activities, what was the same about the shape of the water just before the water spilled over?

    The water was in a dome shape.

4. What did we do to make the dome shape on the pennies?

    We dropped water onto the pennies.

5. So, we added water in this activity?

    Yes.

6. What did we do to make the dome shape on top of the glassful of water?

    We dropped pennies into the glass.

7. So, we added pennies?

    Yes.

8. Why didn't the water build straight up from the sides of the cup or the penny, then have a flat top on the water?

    Surface tension causes water to take the smallest shape.

9. What causes that?

    The molecules of water hold onto each other tightly at the surface of the water; they're cohesive.

10. What does cohesiveness do?

    It makes the top surface of the water curve into a dome shape.

ACTIVITY 64: BIG BUBBLES

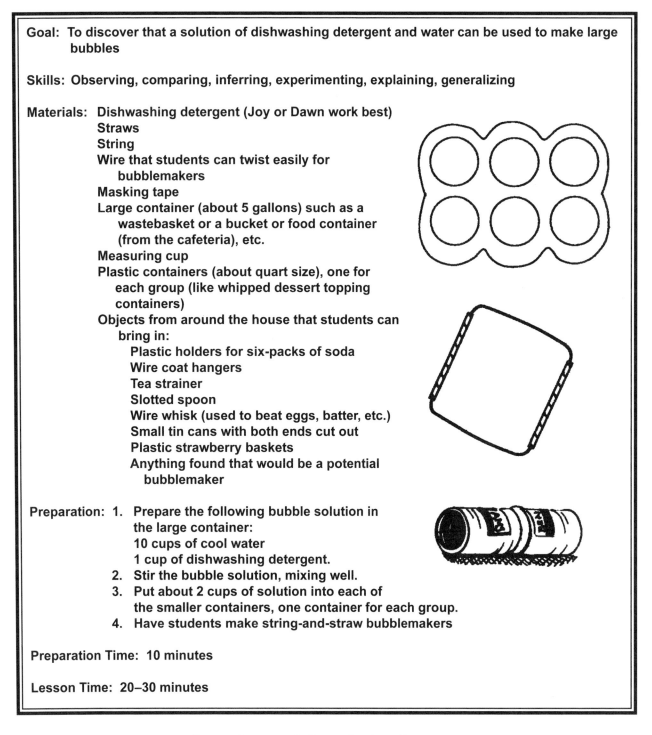

Goal: To discover that a solution of dishwashing detergent and water can be used to make large bubbles

Skills: Observing, comparing, inferring, experimenting, explaining, generalizing

Materials: Dishwashing detergent (Joy or Dawn work best)
Straws
String
Wire that students can twist easily for bubblemakers
Masking tape
Large container (about 5 gallons) such as a wastebasket or a bucket or food container (from the cafeteria), etc.
Measuring cup
Plastic containers (about quart size), one for each group (like whipped dessert topping containers)
Objects from around the house that students can bring in:
  Plastic holders for six-packs of soda
  Wire coat hangers
  Tea strainer
  Slotted spoon
  Wire whisk (used to beat eggs, batter, etc.)
  Small tin cans with both ends cut out
  Plastic strawberry baskets
  Anything found that would be a potential bubblemaker

Preparation: 1. Prepare the following bubble solution in the large container:
   10 cups of cool water
   1 cup of dishwashing detergent.
2. Stir the bubble solution, mixing well.
3. Put about 2 cups of solution into each of the smaller containers, one container for each group.
4. Have students make string-and-straw bubblemakers

Preparation Time: 10 minutes

Lesson Time: 20–30 minutes

— Procedure and Questioning Strategy —

1. Ask the students if they have blown bubbles. What did they use? How did they do it? How big were the bubbles? How long did they last?

Have the students take the containers of bubble solution, with the bubblemakers they have made and collected, outside for exploration. Put all the bubblemakers, along with the string, masking tape, and straws, in a central spot for all groups to use. Let the students explore bubblemaking with as many bubblemakers as possible. As the students are trying out the bubblemakers, go around asking various questions, for example:

2. What do you think will happen if you change the shape of the wire or coat hanger?

3. What if you tape two tin cans together, end to end, with masking tape?

4. What if you blow into the tin cans from about a foot away?

5. What makes the smallest bubbles? The largest?

When the students have tried as many bubblemakers as time permits, gather them together and ask questions to help them tie together their experiences. For instance:

6. Which of the things we brought in as bubblemakers actually worked?

7. How did you make them work?

8. Which made the largest bubbles? The smallest?

9. Which bubblemakers made the most bubbles at one time?

10. What kinds of things did you do that made the bubbles last longer?

11. What objects weren't bubblemakers?

12. Why do you think they didn't work?

13. What's the same about all of the bubblemakers that worked?

— Practical Application —

1. Could you make bubbles like these with just water?
    No.

2. What did we add to the water that helped make the bubbles?
    Dish detergent.

Run the water hard in a sink with the drain closed.

3. Does the water form bubbles?
    Yes.

4. How big are they?

> Not very big.

5. How long do they last?

> Not very long.

Add dishwashing detergent to the water while running water into the sink.

6. How does the addition of detergent make the bubbles different?

> The bubbles are larger.
>
> There are more bubbles piled up on each other.

7. Could you design and make a bubblemaker that makes enormous bubbles—one that doesn't need to be dipped into bubble solution because it has an attached container for bubble solution which lets just enough solution in to blow a bubble? See what you can create.

Have students bring in these bubblemakers for the next activity. OR . . . for ENORMOUS BUBBLES, you and your students can make the bubblemakers shown in the next activity. This kind of bubblemaker can make bubbles about 8 to 10 feet long . . . maybe even longer.

ACTIVITY 65: ENORMOUS BUBBLES

Goal: To extend Activity 64

Skills: Observing, comparing, inferring, experimenting, experimenting with variables, explaining, generalizing

Materials: Directions for Enormous Bubblemakers on page 228, one copy for each group
For bubble solution:
   2 large containers (about 5 gallons each)
   Water
   16 oz. of liquid dishwashing detergent (Joy or Dawn)
   Liquid glygerine (found at drug stores)
For each bubblemaker (one for each group of 2–3 students):
   Narrow strip of cloth or lengths of decorative trim (about 1 1/2 yards)
   Wooden dowel rods, 1/2" in diameter (found at hardware stores)
   3" piece of soft plastic tubing, 5/8" or 3/4" in diameter (sold in hardware stores by the yard)
   Cafe curtain ring
   Thumbtack

Preparation: 1. Make the bubble solution in the two large containers using the recipe from Activity 64.
2. Have students, in groups, make bubblemakers using the directions on page 228.

Preparation Time: 20 minutes

Lesson Time: 20–25 minutes

— Procedure and Questioning Strategy —

Demonstrate the making of bubbles.
   – Close the loop of the bubblemaker before dipping it into the bubble solution.
   – Let the excess solution drip off into the container.
   – Open the loop of the bubblemaker.
   – Move the bubblemaker slowly through the air or walk slowly with the bubblemaker loop open.
   – Close the loop when you have a bubble the size you want OR just before you think the bubble will burst.
   – Keep foam on the solution to a minimum.

Give the students time to explore different ways to make enormous bubbles, ways to keep bubbles from bursting, and ways to make bubbles that rise in updrafts of air.

—Practical Application—

1. Try differing amounts of dishwashing detergent added to the same amount of water for the bubble solution. Keep records of the amounts of detergent used and the approximate

sizes of the bubbles produced. Draw conclusions about bubble solutions and the bubbles produced, for example, which solution makes the largest and/or longest lasting bubbles?

2. Which sizes of bubbles actually rise quite high in the air?

   The small and medium bubbles.

3. What happens to the enormous bubbles?

   They float just above the ground.

4. Why do you think that happens?

   They are too heavy to float up high.

5. Try adding 1–2 tablespoons of liquid glycerine to the bubble solution. Certain amounts of glycerine should make the bubbles last longer since it helps keep the water from evaporating. Does too much glycerine make the bubbles pop faster?

6. Record the amount of time bubbles take to pop. What did you do to make them last longer?

7. Bernoulli's Principle says that the faster air flows, the less pressure it exerts. Can you move your hand over a smaller bubble? Does the bubble rise? What's happening?

8. Design your own bubblemakers. Can you design one that makes a bubble within a bubble? One that makes a lot of bubbles at once? One that makes two bubbles that are attached?

HOW TO MAKE AN ENORMOUS BUBBLE BUBBLEMAKER

1. Use scissors to cut a square about 1/2" x 1/2" from one side of a 3" length of flexible plastic tubing.

2. Thread one end of the cloth strip or trim through one end of the piece of tubing so it comes out the square.

3. Slip the plastic tubing over the dowel rod.

4. Thread the curtain rod ring on the cloth strip or trim. Attach both ends of the cloth strip or trim to one end of the dowel rod with a thumb tack.

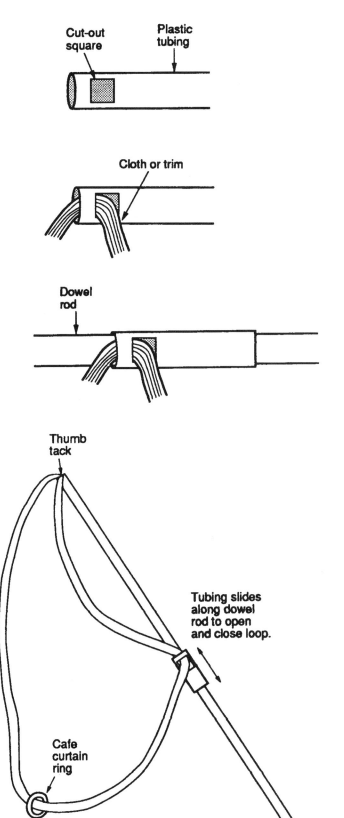

UNIT 15—SOUND

Background Information

Sound is a form of wave energy. When a form of matter rapidly moves back and forth, or vibrates, sound is produced. When the vibrations stop, the sound stops.

Think about what happens when a guitar string is plucked. The string vibrates as it moves back and forth. Each time the string moves to one side, it pushes against molecules of air, crowding the molecules together, producing a **compression wave**. When the string moves back, it leaves a space with fewer molecules that are farther apart. This space is called a **rarefaction**. A **sound wave** is one compression and one rarefaction that makes one vibration. As the guitar string vibrates back and forth, it produces a stream of compressions and rarefactions (figure A).

figure A

As the compression wave moves outward, it pushes against the molecules of air next to the string. The push travels along, from air molecule to air molecule, passing energy from one molecule to the next, producing sound in waves that are carried through the air. We hear sounds when the waves strike our eardrums and vibrate our eardrums. These vibrations are carried by the auditory nerve as impulses to the brain, where the impulses are translated into sound.

The speed of the vibration and the thickness and length of a guitar string affect the pitch of the sound it produces.

- The faster a guitar string vibrates, the higher the pitch
- The thinner the string, the higher the pitch
- The shorter the string, the higher the pitch

Sound waves can also travel through liquids and solids. Sound waves travel the fastest through substances with molecules that are close together because the molecules don't have as far to travel to pass on a vibration to other molecules. Sound waves travel the slowest through substances with molecules that are far apart. For example, sound travels the fastest through steel and the slowest through air. Sound travels about four times as fast through water than it does through air; nine times as fast in wood than in air; and fifteen times as fast in steel than in air (see figure B). Sound does not travel in a vacuum because there are no molecules to vibrate.

MEDIUM	SPEED OF SOUND IN FEET	SPEED OF SOUND IN METERS
AIR	1100 feet per second	336 meters per second
WATER	4800 feet per second	1464 meters per second
SOLID	10,000 feet per second	3000 meters per second

figure B

Unit 15–NATIONAL SCIENCE EDUCATION STANDARDS
• *Unifying Concepts and Processes:* Students should develop understanding and abilities with regard to systems, order, and organization; evidence, models, and explanation; constancy, change, and measurement; and form and function.
• *Science as Inquiry*—Content Standard A: Students should develop the necessary skills to do scientific inquiry and develop an understanding about scientific inquiry.
• *Physical Science*—Content Standard B: Students should develop an understanding of the properties of objects and materials; position and motion of objects; properties and changes of properties in matter; motions and forces; and transfer of energy.
• *History and Nature of Science*—Content Standard G: Students should develop an understanding of the nature of science and of science as a human endeavor.

ACTIVITY 66: SOUND VIBRATIONS

Goal: To understand that vibrations produce sound, and when vibrations stop, sound stops

Skills: Observing, comparing, classifying, inferring, predicting, generalizing

Materials: Ruler
Rubber bands
Aluminum baking pan
Pebbles
2 1/2" x 1/4" strips of paper, one for each student

Preparation: Cut the strips of paper.

Preparation Time: 5 minutes

Lesson Time: 20–25 minutes

— Procedure and Questioning Strategy —

1. Touch the sides of your throat. Keeping your mouth lightly closed, hum a long note. What do you feel?

    It feels like something inside my throat is moving.

2. What does it feel like when you stop humming?

    The movement stops.

3. What is inside your throat that moves or vibrates?

    Vocal cords.

4. You are blowing air between your vocal cords when you are producing sounds. Hum loudly, then softly. Which time were you using greater force to blow air between your vocal cords?

    When humming loudly.

5. Hold your mouth as if you are going to whistle. Hum a long note. What do you feel?

    It makes my lips tickle.

6. Why? What's vibrating?

    My lips.

7. Let's try this. Clap your hands lightly, then clap them harder. Which clap was louder?

    When we clapped harder.

8. What caused the noise when we clapped our hands?

    Vibrations.

9.   What vibrated?

Our hands.

Hold one end of a ruler so about 6 inches extends over the side of a table or desk. Pull the extending end up, then let it go.

10.   What did you observe?

I heard sounds.
The end of the ruler kept hitting the table.

11.   What happened when the ruler stopped moving up and down or vibrating?

The sounds stopped.

SOUND is a form of energy caused by something that is moving back and forth or vibrating.

Stretch a rubber band between two chairs. Pluck the rubber band.

12.   What did you observe?

The rubber band moved up and down. The rubber band moved back and forth.

13.   What did you hear?

The hum of the rubber band.

14.   Do you still hear the hum of the rubber band?

No.

15.   What is the reason the sound stopped?

The rubber band isn't moving now.

16.   What do all of the things we just did have in common?

Something moved back and forth or up and down.
When there was movement, we heard sound.
When the movement stopped, there was no sound.

Put pebbles in the aluminum baking pan. Stretch a rubber band over the pan.

17.   What do you think will happen if I pluck the rubber band?

The rubber band will move up and down/back and forth. The rubber band will make a sound.

18.   What will happen to the pebbles in the bottom of the pan?

They may move around in the pan and make their own sounds on the pan.

Pluck the rubber band many times so all students can see it and the pebbles moving.

19. What happened?

>The rubber band did move and make a sound.
>The pebbles jumped around on the pan and made sounds.

20. When something moves up and down or back and forth it vibrates. What vibrated when we used the pan?

>The rubber band and the pebbles.

21. What caused the sound in each of the activities we did?

>Something vibrated.

22. Summarize what we have learned about sound.

>Vibrations cause sound. When the vibrations stop, the sound stops.

— Practical Application —

Distribute a 2 1/2" x 1/4" strip of paper to each student. Tell them to hold the paper between two thumbs and blow on it to find out if they can make sound.

paper
"reed"

1. How did you make sound?

>By blowing air past both sides of the paper. The air caused the paper to vibrate.

2. We have actually made a reed similar to the reed in some instruments. The reed is usually made of a thin piece of wood or plastic and is in the mouthpiece of the instrument. What kinds of instruments have reeds?

>The clarinet, oboe, and bassoon (woodwind instruments).

3. What vibrates and makes sound on a guitar or other stringed instrument?

>The strings.

4. What causes the strings of a guitar or banjo to vibrate?

>The strings are plucked with a pick or with the fingers.

5. What about the strings of a violin or cello?

>Usually (but not always) a bow is drawn across the strings causing them to vibrate.

6. What parts of other instruments vibrate to make sound?

>The material that is stretched over the top of a drum vibrates when it is hit. The solid metal parts of a triangle or cymbals vibrate when they are hit. The air column vibrates in brass instruments (e.g., trumpet and tuba) and the reed vibrates in woodwind instruments (e.g., clarinet and oboe) when someone blows into them.

ACTIVITY 67: TRAVELING SOUND

Goal: To understand that sound travels better through a solid or a liquid than it does through a gas

Skills: Observing, comparing, classifying, inferring, experimenting with variables, predicting, generalizing

Materials: Wooden yardstick or meterstick
Ticking watch
Deep wide-mouth glass container
2 metal spoons
Water
The drawings on page 237

Preparation: 1. Fill the glass container 3/4 full of water.
2. Make a transparency from the drawings on page 237.

Preparation Time: 1 minute

Lesson Time: 15–20 minutes

— Procedure and Questioning Strategy —

Ask many students the following two questions.

1. Do you think that sound will travel better through a solid, a liquid, or a gas?

2. What reason do you have for predicting that?

Have a student close his/her eyes. Hold the ticking watch to the student's ear for a moment so he/she can recognize how it sounds. Then hold the watch about a yard (or meter) away from the student's ear. Ask the student to tell you when he/she hears the sound of the watch ticking. Slowly move the watch closer to the student's ear until the watch is heard. Let many other students listen for the sound from the watch in the same manner.

4. When I was holding the watch away from your ear, was the sound traveling to your ear through a solid, a liquid, or a gas?

   A gas—the air.

5. Let's try listening through a solid.

Set the back of the watch on one end of the yardstick (or meterstick).

Have a student hold the other end of the stick on the bone just behind his/her ear.

6. Tell me when you hear a sound from the watch.

    (Many students hear the watch at the end of the yardstick; others hear it at a shorter distance.)

Slowly move the watch down the yardstick until the student indicates that he/she can hear the watch ticking. Repeat this procedure until quite a few students have listened for the ticking through the yardstick.

7. Compare the distance from which the watch was heard through the air and through the yardstick.

    We could hear the ticking at a greater distance through the yardstick.

Click together two metal spoons. Have students listen to the sound. Submerge the spoons in water in the glass container and click them again. Have the students compare the sounds they hear. Have some students, one at a time, put their ears to the container and listen to the spoons click.

8. Compare the sounds made by the spoons in air and in water.

    The sound is louder and clearer in water.

9. Summarize what we've learned about how sound travels through different substances.

    Sound travels better through a solid than a gas.
    Sound travels better through a liquid than a gas (four times faster in water than in air).
    Sound is louder when heard through a solid or liquid than through a gas.

— Practical Application —

Put the transparency of the listening Native Americans on the overhead projector.

1. Native Americans used to put an ear on the ground to listen for hoofbeats or put an ear on a train rail to hear a train coming. What have we learned that helps us understand the reason they listened through the ground or a rail?

    We have learned that sound travels better through a solid than through the air.

2. What reason would Native Americans have for wanting to hear these sounds better?

    They could hear hoofbeats or a train coming toward them from farther away through a solid; this would give them more time to make plans about what they wanted to do.

Metals are the best conductors of sound. In some metals, sound travels 16 times as fast as it does through air.

3. Do you think that sounds would be louder on foggy days or clear days?

 Foggy days.

4. How would you explain that?

 There is more water in the air on foggy days and sound is louder in water than in air.

ACTIVITY 68: VARIATIONS IN SOUND

Goal: To discover how the pitch of a sound can be changed

Skills: Observing, comparing, classifying, experimenting with variables, explaining, inferring, predicting, generalizing

Materials: For each group of four students:
    3 rubber bands of the same length but different thicknesses
    A small cardboard box without a cover, like a school box or shoe box
    Various stringed instruments (these can be toy instruments brought in by students)

Preparation: 1. Cut three grooves in the top edges of the short sides of the boxes.
     2. Stretch three rubber bands of the same length but different thicknesses lengthwise around each box. Place them in the grooves to keep them from sliding.

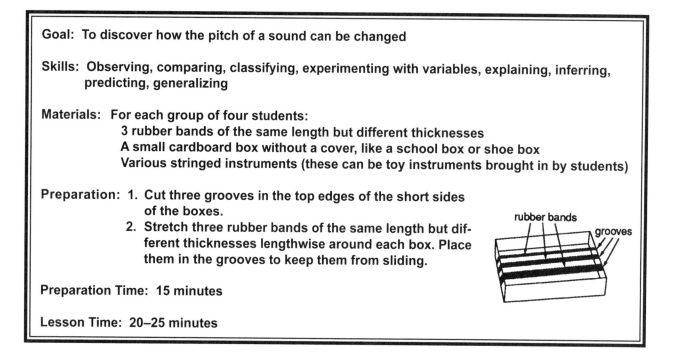

Preparation Time: 15 minutes

Lesson Time: 20–25 minutes

— Procedures and Questioning Strategy —

Before distributing the "stringed instruments" you made to the groups of students, show them that the rubber bands around each box are the same length but different thicknesses.

1. If you pluck these three rubber bands, do you think the sounds they make will be the same or different?

  (Students usually predict they will be different.)

2. If you think the sounds will be different, how will they differ? If they are plucked the same way, will the thickest one be softest or loudest, lowest or highest?

  (Accept all answers as predictions.)

Distribute the boxes to the groups of students.

3. Pluck each rubber band, or string, of your instrument with the same amount of force. How do the sounds of the three strings compare?

  (Possible answers are: the thickest string has the lowest sound [pitch]; the thinnest string has the highest sound [pitch]; one string does not seem to be louder than another.)

4. Pluck each string again to see which one seems to vibrate the fastest.

    The thinnest string.

5. What can we say about the speed of the vibrations and the sound that is produced?

    The faster the string vibrates, the higher the sound or pitch.
    The slower it vibrates, the lower the sound.

6. Pluck one string and listen to the pitch. Then hold the string down at the middle and pluck one side of it. How is the pitch different when only one side is plucked?

    The sound is higher when one side is plucked.

7. What have you done to the length of the string?

    Made it half the length.

8. Try the same thing with the other two strings. What happened?

    When the string was shortened, the pitch was higher.

9. Pluck one string and listen to the pitch. Then pull the string at one end to make it tighter. Pluck it and listen to the pitch. How do the pitches compare?

    The pitch was higher when the string was tighter.

10. Summarize what we have learned about strings and the sounds they produce.

    The thicker the string, the lower the pitch.
    The thinner the string, the higher the pitch.
    The faster the string vibrates, the higher the pitch.
    The shorter the string, the higher the pitch.

— Practical Application —

1. Let's see if what we have discovered about producing different pitches with rubber band strings is true for the strings of instruments.

Have students experiment with either a real or a toy instrument.

ACTIVITIES 66–68: CONNECTIONS

Goal: To understand that vibrations produce sound, and when vibrations stop, sound stops

Skills: Observing, comparing, classifying, inferring, predicting, generalizing

— Questioning Strategy —

1. Let's think about our vocal cords again. What happens to the pitch of your voice when you have a cold?

   The pitch is lower.

2. When you have a cold, your vocal cords swell and get fatter. Compare your vocal cords to the strings of an instrument.

   The fatter the vocal cords, the lower the pitch.

   The thicker the string, the lower the pitch.

Hold a ruler on one end and let four inches of the ruler extend over the edge of the table. Pull up on the extended end of the ruler and let it go.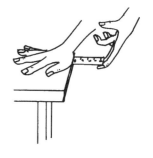

3. Listen to the pitch of the sound.

4. What do you predict will happen to the pitch of the sound if we make the part of the ruler extending over the edge of the table longer?

   The pitch will get lower.

Hold the ruler so six inches extend over the table's edge. Pull up on the ruler's end and let go.

5. Compare the pitch of the first sound to the one we just heard.

   The pitch was lower this time.

Let eight inches of the ruler extend over the table's edge. Pull up on the ruler and let it go.

6. What happened to the pitch this time?

   It was lower.

7. Relate the lengths of the ruler extending over the edge of the table to the pitch of the sounds.

   The longer the ruler, the lower the pitch.

8. Compare the way we changed the pitch of the ruler's sound to our rubber band "stringed instruments."

   The longer the strings, the lower the pitch.

ACTIVITIES 66–68: FURTHER CONNECTIONS

Materials: **Five 12- or 16-oz. soft drink bottles, all the same size, freshly washed**
Water
Measuring cup

— Procedure and Questioning Strategy—

Pour 1/4 cup water into one of the soft drink bottles. Pour 1/2 cup of water into the second bottle, 3/4 cup of water into the third bottle, and 1 cup of water into the fourth bottle. The fifth bottle can remain empty.

1. If we blow over the mouth of each bottle, which one do you think will have the lowest pitched sound?

Distribute the four bottles to four students. Tell them to press the top edge of their bottle against their lower lips and blow a fast stream of air across the top of the bottle.

2. Which bottle had the lowest pitch?

    The one with the least water in it.

3. What does something need to do in order to make sound?

    Vibrate.

4. What would we be vibrating when we blow air across the top of the bottles—the air or the water in the bottles?

    The air.

Explain that the bottle with the least water has the longest column of air (measured as the distance between the surface of the water and the top of the bottle).

5. Which bottle had the highest pitch?

    The bottle with 1 cup of water.

6. What is the reason it had the highest pitch?

    It has the shortest column of air.

7. What if we try a bottle with no water in it? How will its pitch compare with the other bottles?

    It will be lower than the bottle with the least amount of water in it.

Have the students, one at a time, blow across their bottles in order from the lowest pitched bottle to the highest pitched bottle.

8. Compare the length of the columns of air in these bottles to the pitch of the sound they produce.

    The longer the column of air, the lower the pitch. The shorter the column of air, the higher the pitch.

9. See if you can play some tunes.

10. Vary the amounts of water in the bottles. Can you adjust the air column so you can play the scale?

This can be related to the pitch of the vibrating air columns of some instruments. In the clarinet and saxophone, the air column is lengthened or shortened by pressing down on the keys. In a trombone, it is changed by moving the slide in and out.

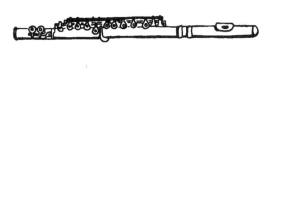

UNIT 16—REFLECTION AND REFRACTION OF LIGHT

Background Information

Light is a form of energy that is given out by the sun, stars, a flame, electric lights, and by other light-producing sources. If an object does not produce its own light, it only can be seen by **reflected** light. For example, light from the sun or a lamp shines on a person and is reflected or bounced off the person. Then the light travels to our eyes so we can see the person. If there were no source of light, we could not see the person.

Imagine you were the person looking at this cat drinking water from the faucet. How would you see the cat? The electric lights in the room shine on the cat; the light is reflected off the cat to your eyes. The light is also reflected off the cat to the mirror. The light changes direction when it hits the mirror and is reflected from the mirror to your eyes. If there were no source of light in the room, you would not be able to see the cat.

figure A

Light travels in straight lines. Even when light is reflected and changes direction, it still travels in straight lines.

Light can travel through air and water, but unlike sound, it cannot travel through an opaque solid such as wood or steel. Sound travels by molecules vibrating and passing on the vibration to nearby molecules. A light source needs no molecules to pass on the light. It can travel the fastest through outer space where there are very few molecules of air. It can't travel through a dense, opaque material like steel because the molecules are packed together so tightly the light rays can't pass through.

Is the spoon in figure B broken? It looks as if it's broken at the surface of the water in the glass.

Light rays travel through a transparent substance in a straight line at the same speed. In this picture, light rays are passing through the air in a straight line, but when the rays reach the surface of the water, they slow down because the water is more dense than the air. When the light rays enter the water at a slant, the rays are **refracted** (bent) and travel in a different direction. This gives the appearance that the spoon is bent. The speed of the light rays depends on the density of the material it enters. The more dense the material, the slower the light rays pass through it.

When light rays pass at a slant from a dense material to a less dense material, for example, from water to air, they speed up and bend as they come out of the water and enter the air.

figure B

Unit 16–NATIONAL SCIENCE EDUCATION STANDARDS

- *Unifying Concepts and Processes:* Students should develop understanding and abilities with regard to systems, order, and organization; evidence, models, and explanation; and constancy, change and measurement.

- *Science as Inquiry*—Content Standard A: Students should develop the necessary skills to do scientific inquiry and develop an understanding about scientific inquiry.

- *Physical Science*—Content Standard B: Students should develop an understanding of the properties of objects and materials; position and motion of objects; light, heat, electricity, and magnetism; properties and changes of properties in matter.

- *History and Nature of Science*—Content Standard G: Students should develop an understanding of the nature of science and of science as a human endeavor.

ACTIVITY 69: HOW WE SEE OBJECTS

Goal: To understand how we see objects
To know that some objects give off their own light

Skills: Observing, explaining, hypothesizing, supporting inferences with observations, generalizing

Materials: Flashlight
Candle
The drawing on page 247

Preparation: Duplicate the drawing on page 247, one for each student. (You may also want to make a transparency of it to display on the overhead.)

Preparation Time: 10 minutes

Lesson Time: 15–20 minutes

— Procedure and Questioning Strategy —

1. Look around the room. What observations can you make?
   (Students will make a variety of observations.)

Now darken the room; the darker the better.

2. Now look at (student's name).

3. What do you observe now?
   (Observations will vary; among them will be: he/she is hard to see.)

4. Why is he/she hard to see?
   The lights are off.

5. What would happen if the room were completely dark?
   We wouldn't be able to see (student's name) at all.

Shine the flashlight on the student.

6. Now what do we observe?
   We can see (student's name) more easily now than before.

7. Why can we see him/her?
   The light is shining on him/her.

8. So what do we need to see objects?

We need a source of light, such as a flashlight, to shine on the object.

Light the candle and display it for the students.

9. Now let's look at the candle. What do you observe?

    Possible answers: it is burning; we can see it; it is giving off light.

10. We couldn't see (student's name) very well in the dark, but we can see the candle. What is the difference?

    The candle gives off its own light. We had to shine a light on (student's name) to see him/her.

11. Give me some other examples of things that give off their own light.

    Possible answers: the sun; light bulbs; fluorescent lights; a flashlight; a fire or anything burning.

In case students ask about stars, planets, and the moon, stars give off their own light, but the moon and planets do not. We don't see stars in the daytime because the sun is so bright that it "masks" the starlight.

12. If an object doesn't give off its own light, how do we see it?

    Light comes from somewhere, such as the flashlight, and bounces off the object.

REFLECTION is the bouncing of light rays off objects.

13. What did we see that supports that answer?

    We couldn't see (student's name) because he/she didn't give off light. We could see him/her when we shined the flashlight on him/her.

— Practical Application —

1. Look at the drawing I handed out (or display the transparency). What do you see in it?

    The sun, a dog, and a person.

2. Now, draw the path of the light that shows how the person is able to see the dog's nose.

    (The students' drawings should appear as shown in the diagram to the right. The light goes from the sun, to the dog's nose, then to the person's eye.)

3. During the evening (after dark) if we happen to look across the street we can often see a neighbor inside his/her house, but we can't see him/her during the day. Why do you suppose there is this difference?

    In the evening the house lights are on, they reflect off the person, and we can see him/her. During the day the lights are off (or most of them are off), so there is not enough light to reflect off the person in the house.

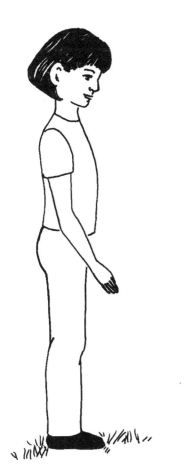

ACTIVITY 70: THE PATH OF LIGHT

Goal: To understand that light travels in straight lines

Skills: Observing, inferring, comparing, supporting inferences with observations

Materials: For each group of three students:
Three 6" x 6" squares of firm cardboard
Light bulb and holder
Three small pieces of modeling clay (to support the cards)
Two hand mirrors
The drawing on page 251

Preparation: 1. Cut a hole 1/4" in diameter in the center of each of the cards.
2. Duplicate the drawing on page 251, one for each student.

Preparation Time: You may choose to have each student make a hole in the center of a card. Have them measure to be certain they get the hole exactly in the center. In this case, the preparation time will be about 10 minutes.

Lesson Time: 20–30 minutes

— Procedure and Questioning Strategy —

Display the lighted bulb for the students.

1. What do you observe?

    (Observations will vary; among them will be: the bulb is bright; it is giving off light; we can see it.)

2. Now your task is to arrange the light bulb and cards so you can see the light through the holes in the cards. You may hold the bulb in any position you wish and you may move the cards around.

Direct each group of students to assemble the cards and clay as shown in the drawing. Have one person move the light, a second look for the light through the holes, and the third move the cards back and forth. Have them perform the activity and make observations.

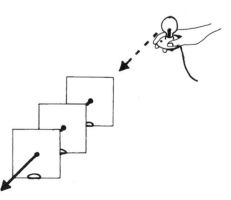

3. What did you observe?

    (The students will make a variety of observations, such as: the bulb had to be right in front of the hole; my eye had to be in front of the hole; the cards all had to be fixed so the holes were in line.)

4. Let's try to figure out what these observations tell us about the path of the light rays.

   The light must be traveling in a straight line.

5. How do we know?

   The holes had to be in line for us to see the light. If the light could go in a curve, the holes wouldn't have to be in line.

6. We hear a person talking outside the door, but we can't see him/her. How does that compare to what we've been discussing?

   Light can only travel in straight lines. Since the person is around the corner, the light would have to bend around the corner if we were going to see him/her.

7. Let's think hard now. What might we do to see someone outside the door, knowing that light only travels in straight lines? (Hold up the mirror if no one answers.)

   We could use a mirror.

8. Let's see how the mirror would work. Let's have (student's name) step outside the door and the rest of us gather near the front of the room. Then I will move the mirror around and you tell me when you can see (student's name).

You will need to stand in the doorway to position the mirror so the students can see their classmate. Then the students can return to their seats.

9. Now let's try to figure out how we saw (student's name) in the mirror. To review, from our last activity (Activity 69), how do we see people and objects if they don't give off their own light?

   Light travels from a source, such as a light bulb or the sun; it bounces off the object and travels to our eye.

10. What was the light source when (student's name) was outside the door?

    The lights in the hall or the sun.

11. So, what was the path of the light?

    It went from the hall lights or the sun to (student's name).

12. Now think hard. Where did the light go after it bounced off (student's name)?

    To the mirror.

13. How do we know?

    We saw (student's name) in the mirror.

14. After the light hit the mirror, where did it go?

> To our eyes. That's how we saw (student's name).

— Practical Application —

1. When we comb our hair we sometimes use two mirrors to see the back of our head to be sure that we're combing our hair properly.

Use the two mirrors to demonstrate this for the students.

2. You have a drawing that shows the light in a bathroom, a boy, the mirror in his hand, and the mirror in the bathroom. Draw the path of the light that will allow him to see the back of his head. Remember now, how does light always travel?

> In straight lines.

3. And how do we see objects?

> Light goes from the source to the object, then it goes from the object to our eyes.

Have the students draw the path of light rays on their handout of page 251. You may have to provide some guidance as they proceed. The correct path is shown in the drawing below.

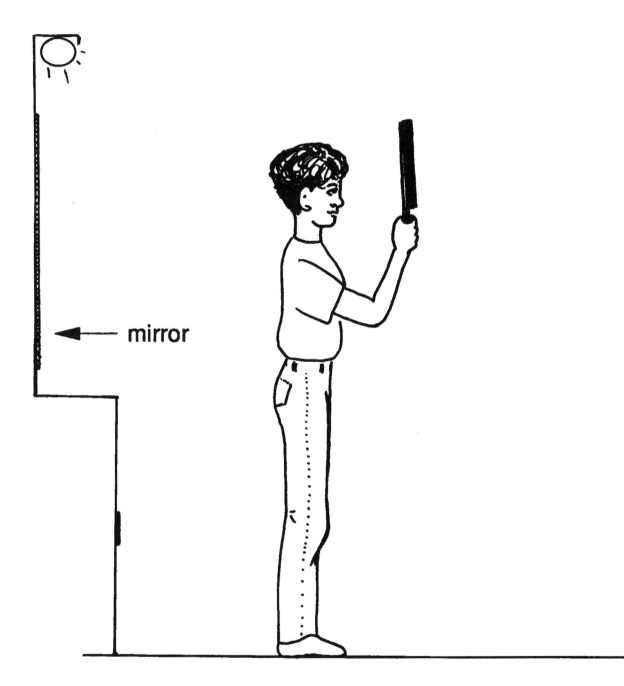

mirror

ACTIVITY 71: THE RISING NICKEL

Goal: To understand that light bends (refracts) when it goes from one substance to another

Skills: Observing, inferring, supporting inferences with observation, controlling variables

Materials: The drawing on page 256
          For each group of three students:
              Opaque shallow dish or bowl (for example, a cereal bowl)
              Nickel
              Water
              Hand lenses or magnifying glasses

Preparation: Make a transparency of the drawing on page 256.

Preparation Time: 5 minutes

Lesson Time: 20–30 minutes

— Procedure and Questioning Strategy —

Begin the activity by demonstrating it for the students. Place a shallow bowl on a table and put a nickel in the center of the bowl. Then have a student (the observer) back up until the nickel is out of sight beneath the rim of the dish. Pour water into the dish. Have the observer tell the class what happens (he/she should be able to see the nickel after the water is added).

Now have the students do the experiment. Have one student in each group be the observer, a second pour the water, and the third watch as the water is being poured to confirm that the nickel doesn't actually move. Then have the students alternate until each has been in all three roles.

Now I see the nickel!

1. What did you observe before we poured water into the bowls?

    We couldn't see the nickel. It was below the rim of the bowl. It was out of sight.

2. Then what did we do?

    We poured water into the bowl.

3. What did you observe then?

    We could see the nickel.

4. Let's try to explain why we couldn't see the nickel when there was no water in the bowl but could see it when water was added to the bowl. What do we remember about the way we see objects?

> Light comes from the source, reflects off the object, and travels to our eyes.

5. What path do the light rays take?

> They travel in a straight path.

Display the top half of the transparency for the students.

6. What do you observe in this drawing?

> The light came from the source. It hit the nickel. It reflected off the nickel and hit the dish. It bounced away from us.

7. So, can we see the nickel?

> No.

8. Does this look like a drawing of before or after we poured the water in the bowl?

> Before. We couldn't see the nickel before we poured the water in, and this drawing shows the light ray bouncing away from us.

9. What must have happened to the light ray when the water was poured in the dish?

> It must have bent.

10 How do we know?

> In order for us to see the object, the light ray had to get to our eyes, and if it went straight, it hit the side of the dish, so it must have bent.

11. How do we know the nickel didn't move?

> We watched and saw that it didn't move.

Display both the top and bottom halves of the transparency for the students.

12. Now what do we see in the drawing, especially in the detail of the bowl at the bottom?

> The light ray is bent down when it hits the water, and it is bent again when it comes back out of the water.

13. What does this bending do?

> It lets us see the nickel.

14. We call this bending REFRACTION.

REFRACTION is the bending of light when it passes from one substance to another. The bending is caused by the two substances being of different densities.

15. We know that water makes light refract, and we said that refraction occurs whenever light goes from one substance to another. What are some other substances that would cause light to refract?

> Two common examples are glass and plastic. Air of different densities also causes refraction.

— Practical Application —

1. Look around the room. What are some of you wearing that others are not wearing?

> (Answers will vary. Eyeglasses may be among them.)

2. Why do we wear glasses?

> It helps correct our vision.

3. Based on what we've done in this activity, what do you suppose the glasses do?

> When light comes from an object, the glasses bend (refract) it so that it comes into our eye at the right spot.

Have the students examine several objects with the hand lenses/magnifying glasses. Conduct the following discussion after they have completed their observations.

4. How did the objects look when you examined them with the lenses?

> They were larger (magnified). If we moved the lens back and forth, the size of the objects seemed to change.

5. Did the size of the objects really change, or did it just appear to change?

> It just appeared to change.

6. Based on what we've done in this activity, how do lenses make objects appear larger?

> When light is reflected off the objects, and the light comes through the lens, the material in the lens bends the light and makes the size of the object look different.

7. Do all lenses make the size of objects look different?

> No.

8. How do you know?

> Our eyeglasses don't make objects look larger. They just make the objects look clearer.

Show the students a pair of glasses and a lens.

9. How do these two compare?

> (Students will give a variety of answers; among them will be that there is a difference in the shapes of the lenses.)

10. So, what determines how the light is bent?

     The way the lens is shaped.

11. What else?

     Where you hold the lens.

12. How do we know that where we hold the lens is important?

     We made the size of objects look different by moving the lens back and forth.

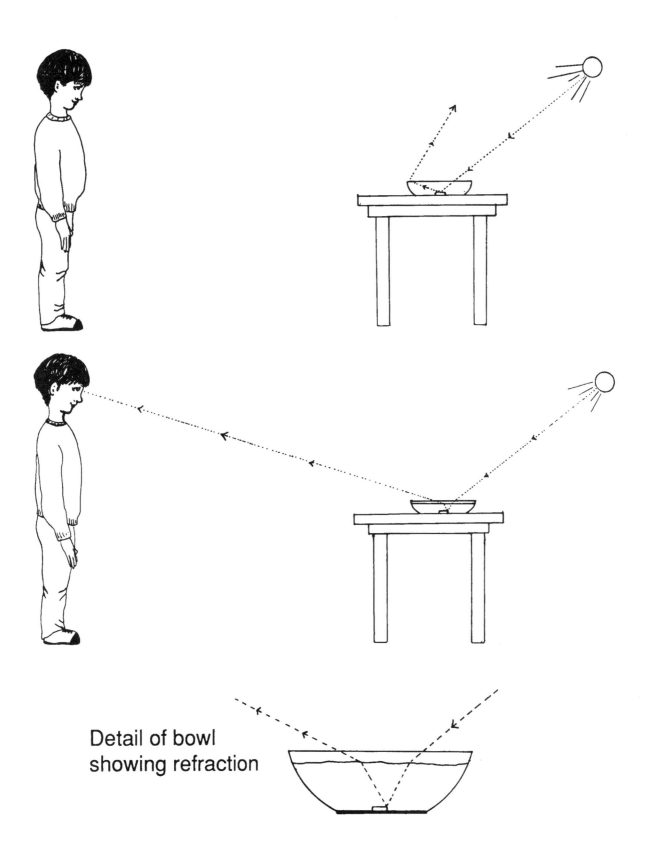

Detail of bowl
showing refraction

ACTIVITY 72: THE BROKEN PENCIL

Goal: To understand an application of light refraction
To make a series of careful observations

Skills: Observation, isolating variables, hypothesizing, inferring

Materials: For each pair of students:
Clear plastic drinking cup
Pencil
Water

Preparation: None

Preparation Time: None

Lesson Time: 15–20 minutes

— Procedure and Questioning Strategy —

Have the students fill their drinking cups 3/4 full of water.

1. You all have a cup of water in front of you. When I tell you to begin, put the pencil in the cup of water and make as many observations as you can. Look at the cup, water, and pencil both from the top and from the side.

Have the students put the pencil in the water as shown in the drawing on the right. Give them a few minutes to make their observations.

2. Let's look now. What are some of the observations that you made?

   (They will make a variety of observations; among them should be: when you look at the pencil from the top, it looks bent; the farther back you get, the more bent it looks; if you turn the pencil upside down, it still looks bent; when you look at the pencil through the cup from the side, it looks like it is broken into two pieces; the part of the pencil that is in the water looks closest to the side of the cup.)

3. Now let's experiment a little. Put the pencil in the cup vertically, slowly move it back and forth and from side to side, and make as many observations as you can.

Give them a few minutes to make their observations.

4. Now, what did you observe?

(They will make a variety of observations; among them should be: when we slid the pencil around the back side of the cup, the part of the pencil in the water didn't seem connected to the part out of the water; the part of the pencil in the water appeared larger when it was at the back of the cup than it did at the front of the cup; the part of the pencil in the cup is magnified compared to the part out of the water.)

5. Let's try to explain all these observations. Why does the pencil appear this way?

   When the light goes into the water, it is refracted (bent). Because we are seeing the part of the pencil that's in the water by refracted light, it appears different from the part of the pencil that is out of the water.

6. Why does the pencil appear larger at the back of the cup than at the front of the cup?

   The water in the cup behaves like the lens we worked with in the last activity. The light is refracted and makes the pencil appear larger.

7. We said that substances such as water, glass, and plastic all refract light. How can we be sure that it is the water and not the plastic of the cup that is refracting the light?

   The part of the pencil that is in the cup above the water line doesn't look bent compared to the part of the pencil that is above the rim of the cup. So the plastic must not be refracting enough light to change the appearance of the pencil.

8. What could we do to further test whether it is the water or the cup?

   We could pour the water out of the cup, put the pencil in it, and see what we observe.

9. Let's try it.

10. What do you observe?

   The pencil doesn't appear bent when there is no water in the cup.

— Practical Application —

1. When we see the sun up in the sky, it looks like a bright white ball, but when we see it on the horizon as it is going down (at sunset), it sometimes looks larger than when it is up in the sky. Based on what we've studied in this activity, why do you suppose it appears different?

   The air close to the earth (on the horizon) is different from the air high in the sky (it is more dense on the horizon), so the light is refracted more when it is on the horizon. This makes the sun appear larger, just as the water made the pencil appear larger.

2. When we look up into the night sky, we often see the twinkling stars. What do you suppose makes the stars twinkle?

   The light from the stars is being bent (refracted) back and forth when it comes through the atmosphere. This bending back and forth is what we see as twinkling.

3. How do we know that it is the light bending that is causing twinkling?

   The only thing the light passes through on its way from the star to us is our atmosphere, so it must be the atmosphere that causes it.

4. Now let's think carefully. Suppose we were on the moon. Would we see the stars twinkle there?

   No.

5. Why not?

   There is no atmosphere on the moon.

Students may wonder why the moon doesn't "twinkle." The amount of light reflected from the moon is too great. Technically, the light reflected from the moon is refracted, just as starlight is, but we don't notice it because there is so much light reflected from the moon.

ACTIVITY 73: CHANGING AN ARROW'S DIRECTION

Goal: To understand an application of refraction

Skills: Observation, isolating variables, inferring, supporting inferences with observations

Materials: The drawing on page 262
For each pair of students:
A clear plastic drinking cup
Water
A 3" x 5" card
A marking pen

Preparation: 1. Make a transparency of the drawing on page 262.
2. Have one student from each pair draw the arrow shown to the right on a 3" x 5" card. The arrow is 1 1/2" long.

Preparation Time: 10 minutes

Lesson Time: 20–30 minutes

— Procedure and Questioning Strategy —

Have each pair of students fill their drinking cup 3/4 full of water.

1. Today we want to make some more observations of light refraction. Experiment by holding the cup, putting the card under it, and looking at the arrow on the card through the water in the cup. Hold the card against the cup, then gradually move it away from the cup. Make as many observations as you can.

Demonstrate for the students as shown in the drawing on the right. Then give them a minute or two to make observations.

2. What did you observe?

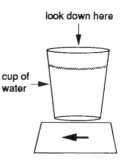

(Students will make a variety of observations; among them should be: we could see the arrow very clearly through the water; as we moved the card away from the cup, the arrow appeared to get smaller; if we held the card so we could see part of the arrow through the water and part directly, the parts didn't look connected; when we jiggled the cup, the arrow seemed to wave back and forth.)

3. Now let's try it again. This time look through the side of the cup. Experiment again by holding the card against the cup then moving it away and back and forth. Make as many observations as you can.

Demonstrate again for the students, as shown in the drawing on the right and give them a minute or two to make observations.

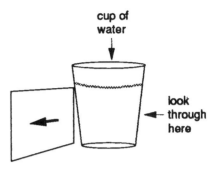

cup of water

look through here

4. **What did you observe this time?**

    (The students will make a variety of observations; among them will be: when the card was against the cup, the arrow looked longer than it really was; as we moved the card back and forth, the arrow moved; when we moved the card away from the cup, the head of the arrow pointed in the opposite direction; if we moved the card around, we could sometimes see two arrows; as we moved the card away from the cup, the arrow got smaller.)

5. **You have made many good observations. Now, to review, why have these things happened?**

    The light is refracted when it passes through the water and, as a result, the images of the arrow look different.

6. **You said that the arrow changed direction when you looked at it through the side of the cup but didn't when you looked at it through the top. Why do you suppose there was a difference?**

    The cup and the water were curved when you looked at the arrow through the side, but they were flat when you looked at them through the top.

7. **How do you know it was the fact that they were curved and not something else?**

    The curvature was the only thing that was different, so it had to be that.

— Practical Application —

Show the students the transparency of the drawing on page 262.

1. **Look at the drawing of the eye. What do you observe about the lens of our eye?**

    It's curved.

2. **We saw that the cup was curved. What did it do to the arrow?**

    It made it seem to point in the opposite direction.

3. **So, what might our eyes do?**

    Turn the objects we see upside down.

Confirm this with the drawing. You may want to tell students at this point that our brains turn the images back around. Further, if we wore glasses that reversed the objects we see, our brains would soon readjust and turn them "right side up" again.

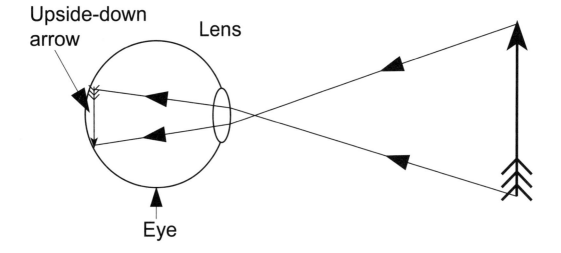

ACTIVITIES 69–73: CONNECTIONS

Goal: To understand the relationships between light and sound

Skills: Comparing, explaining, supporting explanations with observations

— Questioning Strategy —

1. Let's make some comparisons now about sound and light. How are they alike and how are they different?

    They are both forms of energy.

    Sound will travel around corners, but light only travels in straight lines unless it is refracted (bent) by going through some material.

    Sound speeds up when it goes through objects. Light slows down when it goes through objects. This is what makes it bend.

    Light only goes through transparent objects (objects we can see through). Sound travels through objects we can't see through (like the meter stick).

2. How do we know that sound goes around corners, but light doesn't?

    We can hear people talking when we can't see them.

3. Which travels faster—light or sound?

    Light.

4. How do we know?

    We hear of airplanes traveling faster than sound, but nothing travels faster than light. (You may want to tell students that sound travels at about 750 miles per hour while light travels at 186,000 miles a second. They may also have had the experience of hearing a band play and seeing the drumstick hit the drum but hearing the sound of the drum slightly later. Also, thunder comes later than lightening.)

5. How do we know sound travels through objects we can't see through, but light doesn't?

    Sound went through the meter stick.

    The way we see objects is for light to either come from them or be reflected off them. If a person were standing on the other side of a wall and light went through the wall, we would be able to see him or her, but we can't. So the light must not go through the wall. We can see people through a window though.

UNIT 17—MAGNETISM AND ELECTRICITY

Background Information

Magnetism is an invisible force that can push or pull. Magnetism can produce electricity. **Electricity** is energy based on the movement of electrons. Electricity can produce magnetism.

Magnets come in different shapes: horseshoe, bar, rod, and circular.

A **magnetic field** is the magnetic force that fills the space around a magnet. The pulling force attracts magnetic objects made of iron, steel, nickel, or cobalt; the pushing force repels these objects. A magnet can attract or repel these objects without touching them. A magnet can exert its force through materials that are not magnetic; for example, air, paper, transparencies, aluminum, and wood.

A magnet exerts its strongest force at its ends, called **poles**. One end of the magnet is usually called the north pole; the other end is the south pole. Like poles of a magnet repel each other; unlike poles attract each other. The middle of a magnet exerts force, too, but it isn't as strong as the poles. If we put the poles of two magnets close together, cover the magnets with a piece of paper, then sprinkle iron filings on the paper, we can see the magnetic fields of the magnets. We can also see the attraction of a north pole to a south pole (figure A) and the repulsion of like poles (figure B) by using iron filings to show the fields.

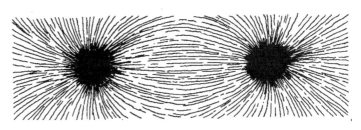

figure A

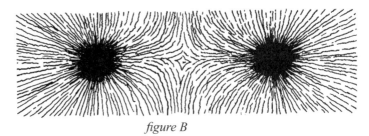

figure B

When a magnet is suspended, the north-seeking pole points to the magnetic north and the south-seeking pole points to the magnetic south. The magnetic north or south is not in exactly the same place as the geographical north or south.

Magnets can be kept strong by storing them with unlike poles (north/south) on top of each other or next to each other and then by putting a keeper across the poles. If horseshoe magnets are stored separately, a keeper should also be placed across the poles.

Magnets can lose their magnetism in three ways: by heating them, by dropping them on a hard surface, and by storing them with similar poles (north/north or south/south) placed on top of each other or next to each other. Magnets can produce an **electric current** and are used in electric generators and motors, and in compasses and toys. They are also used in cabinets and furniture to keep doors closed.

Electric current is the flow of electrons through a circuit. An **electric circuit** is a complete path that allows electrons to travel from an energy source, like a battery, through a bulb or other electrical device and back to the energy source. See figure C on next page.

figure C

Electric current needs a closed electric circuit with a pathway that is unbroken in order to flow. When you turn on your lights with a switch, the switch closes the electrical circuit. Electric current flows as electrons move from one place to another through a wire. When electrons move through a light bulb, the bulb lights. When you turn the switch off, the circuit is broken, the electrical current will not flow through the wire, and the light will not light. Electricity is useful because it can flow along wires and be changed into other form of energy—light, heat, and movement. Electrical appliances such as radios, toasters, washers and dryers, stereo systems, computers, and cars have electric circuits.

Electricity can also produce magnetism. A piece of steel, for example a steel nail, can become magnetized if it is surrounded by coils of wire that are connected at both ends to a dry cell battery. This is called an **electromagnet**. The coil can keep its magnetic properties for awhile after it is disconnected from the battery. The coil will have a north- and a south-seeking pole. An illustration of an electromagnet is shown in Activity 77. An electromagnet can be made stronger by attaching more batteries. Electromagnets are part of doorbells.

Think about a time when you walked across a carpet, then touched someone or touched a metal doorknob. Did you feel a shock? if you did, it was caused by **static electricity**. Static electricity is a force caused by a buildup of extra electrons on a substance, such as a balloon, wool clothing, a person's body, or even a cloud. The extra electrons can be rubbed off, or they can "jump" off onto another object. The electrons won't move until so many electrons build up that they jump to another substance. Copy machines and generators use static electricity. Lightning is produced by the release of electrical energy that has built up inside thunderclouds. It is caused by a huge discharge of static electricity.

Unit 17–NATIONAL SCIENCE EDUCATION STANDARDS

- *Unifying Concepts and Processes:* Students should develop understanding and abilities with regard to systems, order, and organization; evidence, models, and explanation; and constancy, change, and measurement.

- *Science as Inquiry*—Content Standard A: Students should develop the necessary skills to do scientific inquiry and develop an understanding about scientific inquiry.

- *Physical Science*—Content Standard B: Students should develop an understanding of the properties of objects and materials; position and motion of objects; light, heat, electricity, and magnetism; properties and changes of properties in matter; motions and forces; and transfer of energy.

- *Earth and Space Science*—Content Standard D: Students should develop an understanding of the properties of earth materials.

- *History and Nature of Science*—Content Standard G: Students should develop an understanding of the nature of science and of science as a human endeavor.

ACTIVITY 74: A MAGNET'S POLES

Goal: To understand that like poles of a magnet repel each other and that unlike poles attract each other
To understand that the earth has magnetic poles and behaves like a magnet

Skills: Observing, inferring, generalizing, supporting inferences with observations

Materials: The drawing on page 270
For each group of three students:
Pair of bar magnets with marked poles
Pair of horseshoe magnets
Pair of circle (ring) magnets with holes
Compass
Pencil

Preparation: 1. Make a transparency of the drawing on page 270.
2. Arrange the magnets in packets for distribution among the students.

Preparation Time: 15 minutes

Lesson Time: 15–20 minutes

— Procedure and Questioning Strategy —

Start off the activity by sliding the circular magnets over the pencil and holding the pencil and magnets up for the students to see. (In trying it out beforehand, if the magnets snap together, turn one of them around.)

1. What do you observe here?

    The pieces look like thick washers.
    One is sitting up in the air.

2. These things are actually magnets. What we want to figure out is how one is able to sit suspended in midair. Now keep that question in mind as you do the rest of the activity.

Distribute the packets to the groups.

3. Look at the magnets in your packets. Experiment with the magnets a few minutes to determine how they behave when you put them together. Start off with the bar magnets.

4. What observations did you make?

    (They will make a variety of observations; among them are: there is a letter "N" on one end of the magnet and a letter "S" on the other end; when we put the two N's or two S's together, the magnets didn't stick together, but when we put an N and an S together, they did stick together; even when the magnets weren't touching, the N end of the magnet pulled on the S end.)

5. We call the N the north pole of the magnet and the S the south pole. Let's make a generalization about the attraction of the poles.

> Like poles of magnets repel each other and unlike poles attract each other.

6. Now let's try the same thing with the horseshoe magnets and the circular magnets. Experiment with them and see what you find.

Give them a few minutes to experiment with the other magnets.

7. What kinds of things did you observe?

> These magnets did the same thing as the bar magnets.
> The horseshoe magnets also have a north and a south pole; the like poles repel and the unlike poles attract.
> The circular magnets attracted each other when they were put together one way, but they didn't when we turned them around.

8. What does that tell us about the circular magnets?

> They also have poles.

9. Where are the poles?

> One must be on top and the other on the bottom.

10. How could we figure out which is which?

> We could use the bar magnet. If we held the north pole of the bar magnet against a side of the circular magnet and it stuck, we would know that it was the south pole of the circular magnet.

11. Let's try it.

12. What did you observe?

> The circular magnets also have poles.

13. Now, let's think back to what we saw at the beginning of the activity. Why do you suppose the first magnet sat suspended above the second?

> You arranged the magnets so two like poles were facing each other. They repel, so one was suspended above the other one.

14. Were the facing poles north or were they south?

> We don't know.

15. **Why not?**

   North poles repel each other. So do south poles.

16. **How could we figure it out?**

   We could take a pole of the bar magnet or the horseshoe magnet and see if it stuck. That's what we just did to figure out which pole was which on the circular magnets.

17. **What else do we know about magnetic force?**

   It extends beyond the magnet's poles.

18. **How do we know?**

   One circle magnet was sitting in midair above the other circle magnet.

— Practical Application —

1. Now experiment with the magnets and the compass. Take a minute or two to move the magnets around near the compass and make observations.

2. **What did you observe?**

   The compass always pointed in the same direction until we brought the magnet near it. One end of the compass followed the north pole around when we brought the magnet near the compass. When we switched the poles of the magnet, the compass "flipped around" the opposite way.

3. **What does that tell us about the ends of the compass?**

   They are attracted to the poles of a magnet.

4. If they are attracted to the magnet's poles, why does the compass always point in the same direction when no magnet is near it? (If no one answers, display the transparency.)

5. **What do you observe in the transparency?**

   It looks like the earth. There is a big magnet in it.

6. **So why does the compass always point in the same direction?**

   One end is pointing to the earth's north magnetic pole and the other is pointing to the earth's south magnetic pole.

7. **Are the earth's magnetic north pole and its geographic north pole in the same place?**

   No.

8. **How do we know?**

   The compass isn't pointing straight north. Also, the drawing shows them at different points.

9. Someone you know probably has little magnets that he/she uses to stick things on the

refrigerator door. Do you think these magnets have poles?

Yes.

10. Why do you think so?

All the magnets that we have used so far have poles, so they should also have poles.

11. How could we find out?

We could test them with a bar or horseshoe magnet, just like we did with the circle magnets.

If the students have magnets at home, have them test this idea.

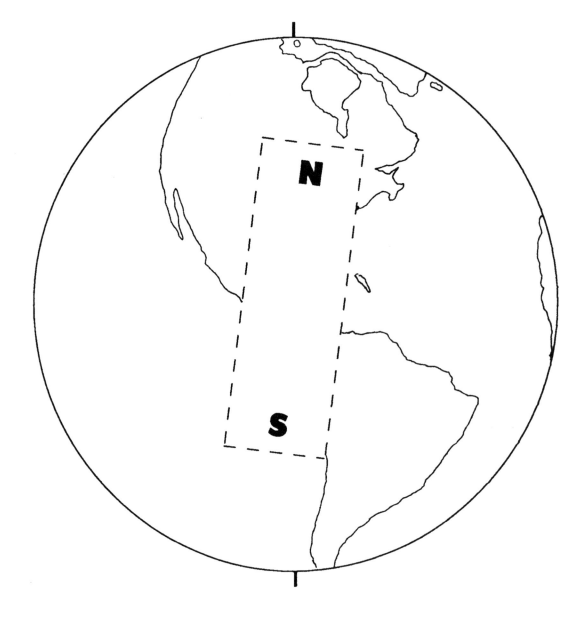

ACTIVITY 75: MAGNETIC FIELDS

Goal: To understand that magnets have a field, which means their attracting
and repelling extends out from the poles of the magnet

Skills: Observing, inferring, comparing, generalizing

Materials: Bar, horseshoe, and circle magnet
Iron filings
Transparency sheet
Overhead projector
3 sheets of notebook paper and a pencil for each student
Drawing on page 274

Preparation: Duplicate the drawing on page 274, one for each student

Preparation Time: 5 minutes

Lesson Time: 15–20 minutes

— Procedure and Questioning Strategy —

Direct the students to take out the paper and pencil and have them ready on the top of their desks.

1. Let's review what we found in the last activity (Activity 74). What did we learn about magnetic force?

    Like poles repelled each other and unlike poles attracted each other. The magnetic force extended beyond the ends of the magnets.

2. How do we know the force extended beyond the ends of the magnets?

    The N pulled the S toward it when they got close enough, even if they weren't touching. One circle magnet sat up in "midair" over the other one. They didn't want to touch.

3. We call this force the MAGNETIC FIELD. (A magnetic field is the magnetic force that extends beyond the ends of a magnet.) We want to observe the magnetic field now and see how it looks. I'm going to demonstrate the magnetic field by putting the magnet on the overhead, covering it with the transparency, and sprinkling these iron filings on the transparency. I then want you to observe carefully and write your observations on a piece of paper.

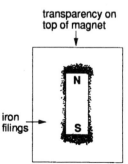

transparency on top of magnet

iron filings

Put the bar magnet on the overhead projector, place a transparency sheet over it and sprinkle iron filings on the transparency. The students will be able to see the shadows of the magnet and the iron filings on the screen. Slide the transparency back and forth slightly to see how this affects the filings.

Give the students a couple of minutes to write their observations.

4. **What did you observe?**

>   Possible answers: the iron filings formed a kind of pattern around the magnet; when you slid the transparency back and forth, the filings got more "compact" around the poles; the filings weren't attracted as much when they were farther away from the poles; they were equally attracted to both the north and south poles.

5. **Where does the magnetic force seem to be the weakest—here (point to area 1 on the transparency) or here (point to area 2 on the transparency)?**

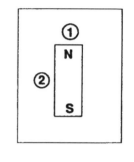

>   It seems to be the weakest at the second place you pointed (area 2 in the drawing).

6. **How do you know?**

>   The iron filings seem to be the least attracted there.

7. **Now we're going to try it again with the horseshoe magnet.**

Lay the horseshoe magnet flat on the overhead projector.

8. **Let's make some predictions about the magnetic field around this magnet. How will the filings look? Where will the field be the strongest? The weakest?**

>   (Predictions will vary.)

9. **Let's try it. I will demonstrate it for you and you write your observations on the second sheet of paper.**

Demonstrate for the students by placing a transparency over the magnet as shown in the drawing. Then sprinkle the iron filings on the transparency. Give them a few minutes to make their observations.

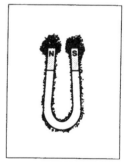

10. **What did you observe?**

>   Possible answers: this magnet's field was also strongest near the poles; the sides of the magnet also attracted the iron filings; the magnetic field seemed to be the weakest at the back of the horseshoe, the point farthest away from the poles; the iron filings were attracted to both poles equally.

11. **Let's try it once more. We're going to use the circle magnet this time.**

Place the circle magnet on the overhead projector with the transparency covering it.

12. **Think hard and draw on your paper the way you think the iron filings will look this time.**

Give the students a few minutes to make their drawings.

13.   Now observe carefully.

Sprinkle the iron filings over the transparency.

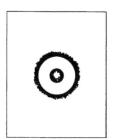

14.   What did you observe?

> Possible answers: the iron filings formed a circle around the magnet; the field seemed stronger around the outside than it did on the inside; the farther away from the magnet you got, the weaker the field seemed to be.

15.   Now we've looked at the fields around all three magnets. Besides the shape, what is one important difference between the field around the circle magnet and the fields around the other two?

> With the circle magnet we were looking at the field around only one pole. With the other two magnets we were looking at the fields around both poles.

16.   How do you know?

> The north pole is on one side of the magnet and the south pole is on the other. One of the poles was facing down and away from us.

— Practical Application —

1.   On the drawing I handed out you see a magnet. You also see some letters. Draw a square around the two letters where you think the magnetic field is the strongest. Draw a circle around the two letters where you think the magnetic field is the weakest.

> (They should put a square around letters A and E. They should circle letters C and G.)

2.   Your cassette tapes have the music put on them magnetically and can be damaged by having magnets around them. Do you have to touch the tapes with the magnet to hurt them, or can you hurt them by just bringing the magnet close to the tapes?

> Just bringing the magnet close can hurt the tapes.

3.   How do you know?

> The magnetic field extends beyond the ends of the magnet, so the magnet wouldn't have to touch the tapes to hurt them.

4.   Let's try it.

Demonstrate this by recording someone saying something. Play it back. Then bring a magnet near the tape. Try playing it again.

5.   What did you hear?

> We couldn't hear (student's name) talking anymore. The magnet ruined the tape.

6.   Computer disks also use magnetic materials. What does this tell us about them?

> They can be damaged by bringing magnets near them.

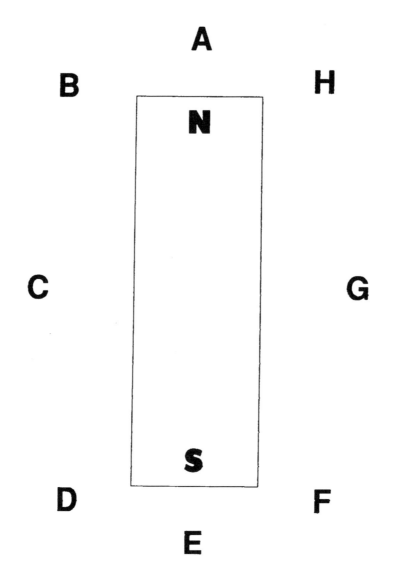

══════ ACTIVITY 76: WHAT KINDS OF OBJECTS ARE MAGNETIC? ══════

Goal: To know what kinds of objects are attracted to magnets

Skills: Observing, classifying, generalizing, inferring, supporting inferences with observations

Materials: For each group of three students:
　　　　The chart on page 278
　　　　Bar magnet
　　　　Set of materials such as the following (you may choose to have the students bring
　　　　　the materials from home):
　　　　　　Penny, nickel, and quarter
　　　　　　Piece of aluminum foil
　　　　　　Soft drink can
　　　　　　Paper clip
　　　　　　Nail
　　　　　　Button
　　　　　　Pen
　　　　　　Eraser

Preparation: 1. Duplicate the chart on page 278, one for each group.
　　　　　　　 2. If the students bring the materials from home, the only preparation is collecting
　　　　　　　　　the magnets. Collect the materials in bags for the next time you do the activity.

Preparation Time: 5 minutes

Lesson Time: 20–30 minutes

— Procedure and Questioning Strategy —

Give each group a bar magnet, a packet of materials, and a copy of the chart.

1. Today we want to determine what kinds of objects are attracted to magnets. Experiment with your magnets to see what kinds of objects are attracted to the magnets and what kinds of objects are not attracted. Touch the objects with the magnets to see if they will stick. Then list the objects that are attracted and not attracted to magnets on the chart that I have given you. After you've checked all the objects, experiment with some other materials you have on you or around your desks, such as a zipper on your shirt or jacket, parts of the desk, a comb or brush, and anything else you can think of.

Give the students a few minutes to experiment with the materials.

2. Now let's make a chart based on your observations. On one side of the chart we'll list the objects that are attracted to magnets and on the other side we'll list the objects that are not attracted to magnets. What did you find?

Ask the students to name objects they found attracted to magnets and other objects not attracted. Write them on a chart on the board. A sample chart might appear as follows:

Attracted to Magnets	Not Attracted to Magnets
paper clip	nickel
nail	penny
	quarter
	aluminum foil
	button
	pen

On the list of objects attracted to magnets will be anything made of iron or steel. Everything else will be on the list of materials not attracted to magnets. For example, some soft drink cans are attracted and others are not; parts of pens are sometimes made of iron so they are attracted; scissors and parts of staplers are attracted; anything made of plastic, rubber, cloth, or wood is not attracted.

3. What have we done by making our lists?

    We have classified the objects into two groups.

4. Let's make some generalizations about the kinds of objects that are attracted to magnets and the kinds that are not attracted to magnets.

    (Students may suggest that metals are attracted to magnets. If they do, ask the following questions.)

5. Are all metals attracted to magnets?

    No.

6. How do we know?

    Aluminum is a metal and it wasn't attracted to the magnet. (If students don't realize that aluminum is a metal, ask them about aluminum cans or aluminum wheels on cars. Also, airplanes use aluminum.)

7. So what generalization can we make about objects that are attracted to magnets?

    Some metals are attracted.

8. What do the metals seem to be made of? Look at the nail and the paper clip.

    They look like they're made of iron or steel (which has iron in it).

9. What else did we find?

> Nothing else was attracted to the magnets. (Technically, magnets are also attracted to the metals nickel and cobalt, but we don't commonly encounter these metals in our everyday living. Nickel coins are not made of the metal nickel.)

— Practical Application —

1. Someone you know probably uses magnets to stick notes and other things to the refrigerator door. What does that tell us about the door?

> It has iron in it.

2. How do we know?

> Magnets are attracted to objects made with iron, but not other metals, so the door must have iron in it.

3. You may have seen little magnets that are made of rubber. What do we know about rubber?

> It isn't attracted to magnets.

4. How do we know?

> We tried it with an eraser (or some other object made of rubber).

5. So what must they have done to the "rubber" magnet to make it magnetic?

> When they made it, they must have mixed in enough iron with the rubber to make it magnetic.

Attracted to Magnets	Not Attracted to Magnets

ACTIVITY 77: MAKING AN ELECTROMAGNET

Goal: To understand how an electromagnet works
To understand how an electromagnet is made stronger

Skills: Observing, generalizing, controlling variables, predicting

Materials: For each group of three students, a packet containing:
D-cell flashlight battery
Nail
Piece of insulated (plastic covered) copper wire, 100 cm. long
Compass
Four #1 paper clips

Preparation: 1. Strip about 1/2 cm. of insulation off the ends of each wire.
2. Gather the materials into packets for the students.

Preparation Time: 30 minutes

Lesson Time: 20–30 minutes

— Procedure and Questioning Strategy —

1. We have been studying magnets and the kinds of materials that are magnetic. Today we want to try to make a magnet using a battery, wire, and a nail. When you get your packets, wrap the wire around the nail the way I am showing you and touch the ends of the wires to the battery. See what happens when you hold the nail next to a paper clip.

Demonstrate how to make an electromagnet for the students as shown in the drawing. Wrap the wire around the nail about 20 times, counting the number of wraps as you go. Then hold the bare ends against the poles of the battery and touch the end of the nail to one of the paper clips. Always release the wires after experimenting with the electromagnet and paper clips. Keeping the wires in contact with the battery for extended periods will quickly run the battery down.

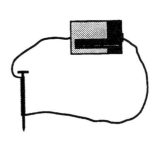

2. Try to make a chain of paper clips behind your electromagnet as shown in the drawing below right. See if it will pull two paper clips.

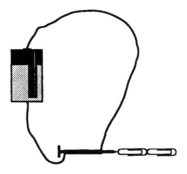

Hand out the materials and let the students experiment with making the electromagnets. Remind them to wrap the wire around the nail about 20 times. Have one student in the group wrap the wire and hold the ends against the poles of the battery, a second make the paper clip chain and test it against the nail, and a third record observations.

3. Now what did you observe?

    (Students will make a number of observations, among them should be: when the ends of the wire were touching the battery, the paper clip was attracted to the nail; the ends of the wire got warm if we held them against the battery too long; if only one end of the wire was touching the battery, the paper clip wasn't attracted to the nail.)

Some differences may occur because of differences in the strength of the batteries, in spite of the fact that they are all supposed to be the same.

4. Now let's review for a moment. What did we find out about magnets in Activity 74?

    Magnets have poles. Like poles repel, unlike poles attract. The north pole of the magnet attracted one end of the compass and the south pole attracted the other end of the compass. The earth is a magnet.

5. Now experiment to see if the electromagnet has poles. Use the electromagnet and the compass. How will we be able to tell?

    We can turn one end of the nail toward the compass and see what happens. Then we can turn the other end toward the compass and see what happens.

6. Go ahead and try it.

Give them a minute to try it.

7. What did you find?

    The electromagnet also has poles.

8. How do you know?

    When we pointed one end of the nail toward the compass, the needle was attracted to it, and when we pointed the other end toward the compass, the needle swung around the opposite way.

9. Let's review what we've learned so far. What have we learned?

    We can make an electromagnet with a wire, battery, and nail. The wire must be connected to the battery for the electromagnet to work. The electromagnet has poles.

10. Now let's try it again. This time we want to experiment carefully. What do you think will happen if we wrap the wire around the nail more times?

    (Predictions will vary. Some students will suggest that the electromagnet will be stronger. Others may disagree since we still have the same power supply—the one battery.)

11. How will we know if it is stronger?

    We can see if it will pull more paper clips. If it pulls two, or even three paper clips, we know it is stronger.

12. Okay, let's try it. First experiment by wrapping the wire around the nail 40 times, see how many paper clips it will pull, then do it again after you've wrapped the wire around the nail 60 times. It's okay to wrap the wire over itself.

Have students try it. Give them a few minutes to experiment.

13. What did you observe?

(Their observations will vary. Possibilities are: the electromagnet now strongly attracted the paper clip; it would pull two paper clips, or perhaps even three or four; now when we released the wires, the nail was still attracted to the paper clip.)

14. What does the last observation suggest?

The nail itself was made magnetic.

15. Do you think it has become a permanent or a temporary magnet?

(Predictions will vary.)

16. How could we find out?

We could check now to see if the paper clip is still attracted to the nail.

17. Go ahead and try it.

Give them a few seconds to see if the paper clip is attracted to the nail without the wires touching the battery.

18. What did you observe?

(Some will say yes. Others may say no.)

For those who found that it was still attracted, tell them to keep this in mind and you can check at the end of the period, or day, or even the next morning. They will find by the next morning that the nail is no longer magnetic, meaning it was only a temporary magnet.

During the course of the activity, some students may ask what would happen if they used two or three batteries. If so, let them try it, or you can demonstrate it by borrowing batteries from some of the groups. Increasing the power (using more batteries) should increase the strength of the electromagnet.

— Practical Application —

1. Electromagnets are an important part of all electric motors and other household items, such as the telephone and doorbell. (If you should happen to have a doorbell among your science equipment, you can show the students the parts that are wrapped with wire. These are the electromagnets.) Let's list some examples of household items that have electric motors in them.

(Answers can include the following: mixer, electric can opener, phonograph turntable, compact disk player, cassette player, fan, refrigerator and/or freezer.)

ACTIVITY 78: STATIC ELECTRICITY

Goal: To understand that static electricity is a force

Skills: Observing, inferring, using models, explaining, supporting inferences with observations

Materials: Wool cloth (such as a wool sweater)
          Balloon
          The drawings on pages 285 and 286

Preparation: Make transparencies from the drawings on pages 285 and 286.

Preparation Time: 5 minutes

Lesson Time: 15–20 minutes

— Procedure and Questioning Strategy —

Inflate the balloon, tie off the end, and hold up the sweater (or other wool item) for the students. Then display the transparency showing the balloon and the sweater filled with + and − charges.

1. What do you observe in the transparency?

    (Among possible observations are: it looks like the balloon and sweater; there are little "pluses" and "minuses" in them; the pluses and minuses seem to be grouped together; they are all over on both the drawing of the balloon and the drawing of the sweater; there are the same number of pluses as minuses.)

2. What you see in the drawings represents little electrical particles. Some have a positive charge and others have a negative charge. The positively charged particles are called PROTONS and the negatively charged particles are called ELECTRONS. Everything that exists is composed of protons and electrons. (Substances also have a third particle in them called neutrons, but they are not involved in this activity.)

3. We see that the balloon and sweater have pluses and minuses. Do you think other things do as well?

    Yes.

4. Why might we think so?

    The balloon and sweater are very different from each other and they have the particles, so other things probably do too.

Confirm that everything is composed of protons and electrons.

5.   You said that the pluses and minuses seem to be grouped together. What does that perhaps suggest about them?

> The pluses and minuses are attracted to each other.
> (If students are unable to answer, prompt them to think about the poles of a magnet and what we found out about them—that north and south poles attract each other.)

6.   Now look carefully.

Rub the balloon vigorously with the wool and bring the balloon near the hair of one of the students (this works best with freshly washed hair that does not have mousse or gel in it).

7.   What do you observe?

> (Student's name)'s hair is standing up.

8. What does that tell us?

> There is a force between the balloon and (student's name)'s hair. This force pulled (student's name)'s hair up.

9.   Let's try to explain why that happened. Look at the transparency.

Display the transparency of the student with the balloon above her head.

10.   What do you see here?

> The balloon has more electrons on it than protons. The person's hair is sticking up.

11.   Where do you suppose the balloon got the extra electrons?

> From the sweater.

12.   How do you know?

> It was the only thing we used to affect the balloon.

13.   And what do we know about the electrons and protons?

> They are attracted to each other.

14.   So, why did (student's name)'s hair stick up?

> The extra electrons on the balloon attracted the protons in (student's name)'s hair, and this attraction pulled the hair up.

15.   We call this buildup of electrons STATIC ELECTRICITY.

STATIC ELECTRICITY is the buildup of extra electrons on a substance such as a balloon, a person's body, clothes, or even in a cloud.

— Practical Application —

1. Let's think now about taking clothes out of a dryer. What sometimes happens to them?

   They stick together. They sort of crackle and pop when you pull them apart.

2. Let's think about what we've learned today and try to explain why this happens to the clothes. As the clothes tumble around in the dryer and rub against each other, what do you think happens?

   The electrons on some of the clothes are rubbed off onto others.

3. Then what happens?

   Because there are more electrons than protons on some of the clothes, those clothes are attracted to the protons in other clothes and they stick together. They crackle and pop when we pull them apart.

The following examples may be a bit developmentally advanced for this age level, so they are described here as a teacher note: The crackle and pop occur when the electrons jump back to the protons to "even out" the number of positive and negative charges. This same thing occurs when we get a shock from walking across a carpet and touch another person or a doorknob. The most dramatic example is lightning. A cloud becomes charged with electrons, and when the electrons jump back to "even out" the numbers, we see lightning.

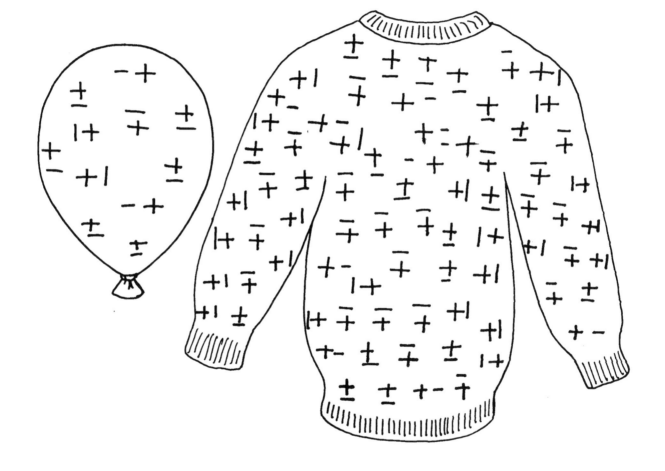

ACTIVITY 79: ELECTRICAL CIRCUITS

Goal: To understand what makes an electrical circuit

Skills: Observing, inferring, comparing, generalizing

Materials: The drawings on pages 290 and 291
For each group of three students, a packet containing:
  D-cell flashlight battery
  Bulb and bulb holder
  Two strips of insulated copper wire, 15 cm. long
  Flashlight

Preparation: 1. Strip about 1/2 cm. of plastic from the ends of the wires.
  2. Arrange the materials in packets for the student groups.
  3. Make transparencies from the drawings on pages 290 and 291.

Preparation Time: 15 minutes

Lesson Time: 20–30 minutes

— Procedure and Questioning Strategy —

1. Today we want to look at another form of electricity. You have in front of you a packet containing a battery, bulb and holder, and wires. First screw the bulb into the holder, then try to arrange the system to light the bulb. As you try to make the bulb light up, keep in mind what you did when you connected the ends of the wire to the battery to make your electromagnet.

Give them a few minutes to experiment with the batteries, bulbs, and wires. After everyone has gotten their bulbs to light up, begin.

2. Let's make some observations. Describe what you did.

   (Among their comments may be: we connected one wire from one end of the battery to one connection on the bulb holder; we connected the other wire to the opposite end of the battery and to the other connection on the bulb holder; the bulb had to be screwed all the way down into the bulb holder in order to light.)

3. Now let's review from our last activity. Everything that exists has what in them?

   Electrons and protons.

4. And what happens to the electrons sometimes?

   They get rubbed off, like the electrons got rubbed off the sweater.

Display the transparency of the drawing on page 290 for the students.

5. What do you observe here?

    It is a drawing that looks like a battery, wires, and bulb. There are a lot of "e"s running through the wire. The "e"s are squeezing through the bulb.

6. In what direction are the "e"s running?

    They seem to be running up the left wire, through the bulb, then back down the right wire and back to the battery.

7. What do you suppose the "e"s in the drawing represent?

    The electrons.

8. And what does the battery do?

    It sort of pumps the electrons through the wire.

9. What makes the bulb light up?

    The electrons squeezing through the thin wire in the bulb.

Now display the second transparency.

10. Now look at this drawing. What is the difference between this one and the first one?

    The electrons are not running through the wire. The wire isn't connected to the battery.

11. So, what have we found out about making the bulb light?

    The battery acts like a pump that pumps electrons through the wire. The bulb lights when the electrons squeeze through it. There must be a complete path for the electrons to travel through, or the bulb won't light up.

12. Does anyone know what we call this?

    (If no one answers, tell them: We call this an ELECTRIC CIRCUIT.)

An ELECTRIC CIRCUIT is a complete path that allows electrons to travel from the battery through a bulb or other electrical device and back to the battery again.

13. And what do we call the flow of electrons through the circuit?

    (If no one answers, tell them, "This is called an ELECTRIC CURRENT.")

An ELECTRIC CURRENT is the flow of electrons through a circuit.

— Practical Application —

Display the flashlight for the students and turn it on.

1. Look now at the flashlight. Does it make a circuit?

    Yes.

2. How do we know?

    The bulb is lit up.

3. Tonight, examine a flashlight at home and try to identify the path for the electrons that allows it to light up. Be prepared to describe the path tomorrow in class.

Plan the following day to discuss with the students the circuit in a flashlight.

4. We have many other electrical circuits in our homes. Give us some examples.

    Turning on any light or appliance is an example. Others, such as radios, electric clocks, and stereos all have circuits in them.

5. Let's think about a lamp that you have plugged into the wall. Describe the circuit.

    The electrons come from the wire in the wall, go through the wire leading to the lamp, go through the wire in the lamp, through the bulb, and back through the wire to the wall.

6. What happens when we turn the lamp off with the switch?

    We disconnect the path for the electrons, just like we saw in the second drawing.

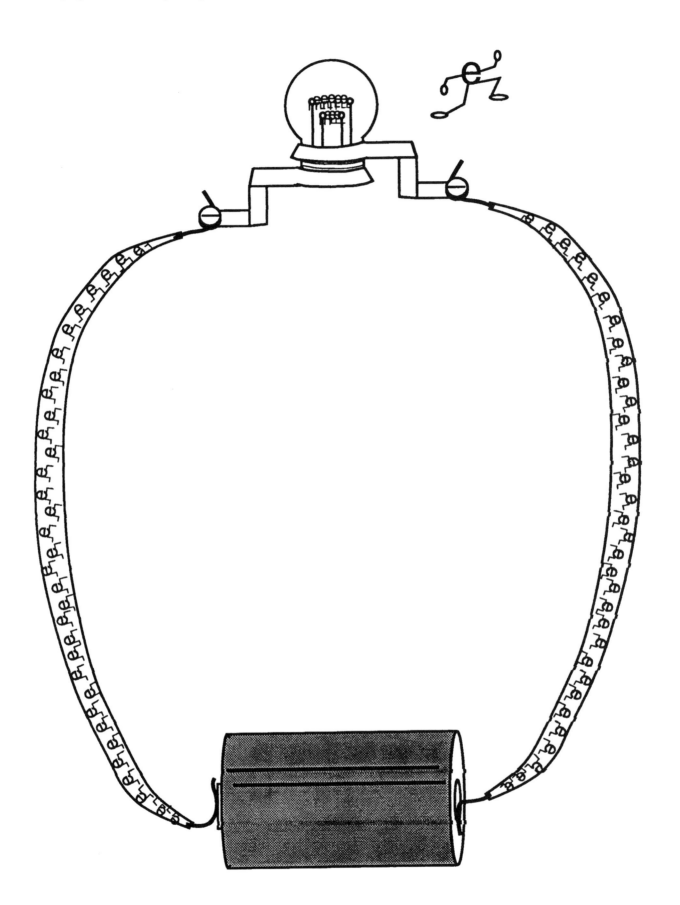

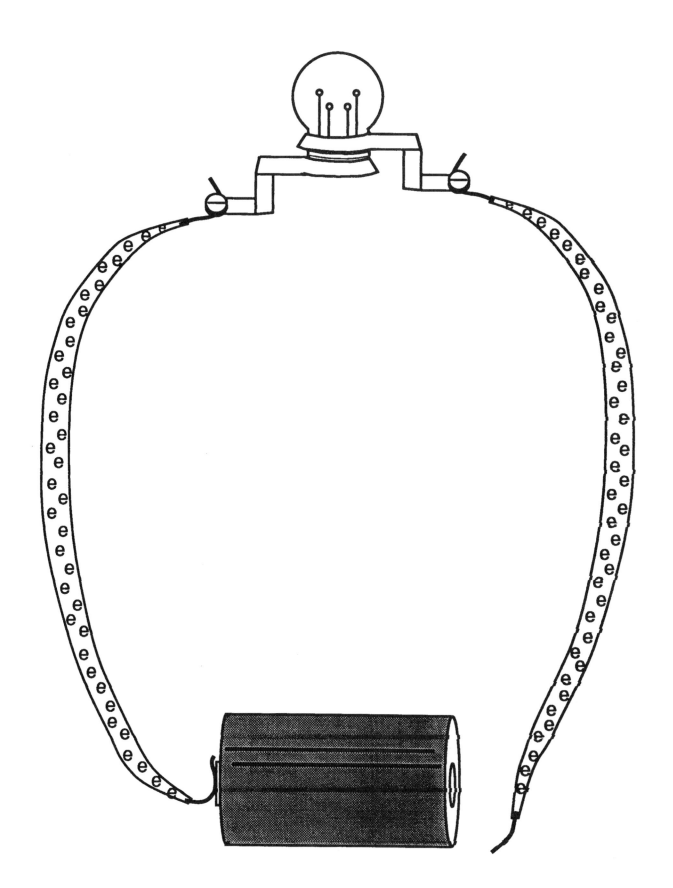

ACTIVITY 80: WHAT COMPLETES A CIRCUIT?

Goal: To understand conductors, which are materials that allow electric currents to pass through them

Skills: Observing, inferring, supporting inferences with observations

Materials: For each group of three students, a packet containing:
> The battery, bulb and holder, and wires from Activity 79
> The packet of materials used in Activity 76 to test for objects attracted to magnets

Preparation: None

Preparation Time: None

Lesson Time: 20–30 minutes

— Procedure and Questioning Strategy —

1. We know how to make a circuit, and now we want to experiment to find out what kinds of materials let electricity pass through them. When I give you your packets, test each object to see if it will allow the bulb to light up. After you've tested the objects in your packet, test anything else that you can find around your desks that can be tested.

Demonstrate how to test the object by holding it against the battery and then holding the wire against the object, as shown in the drawing on the right.

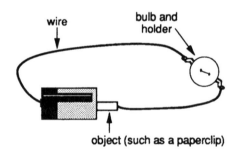

wire   bulb and holder

object (such as a paperclip)

Pass out the packets, and give the students a few minutes to test each of the items.

2. Now let's make a chart to identify which objects completed the circuit.

Make a chart on the chalkboard as students provide the names of objects they tried. The chart may appear as follows.

Completes the Circuit	Doesn't Complete the Circuit
paper clip	button
nail	pen (the plastic part)
nickel	paper
penny	styrofoam
dime	wooden pencil
soft drink can	plastic
aluminum foil	cloth

3. Now let's look at our chart. What kind of pattern do you see?

All the objects that are made of metal completed the circuit. None of the things that weren't metal completed the circuit.

4. What do we call substances that allow electricity to pass through them?

(If no one answers, tell them they are called CONDUCTORS.)

A CONDUCTOR of electricity is any substance that allows the flow of electricity (the flow of electrons) through it. A conductor completes a circuit.

5. Now let's try to make a generalization about conductors of electricity.

Conductors of electricity are made of metal.

— Practical Application —

1. Now let's think of some substances around the house that conduct electricity.

Possible answers: metal cooking ware, silverware, metal serving spoons, tongs.

2. Let's also think of some nonconductors.

Possible answers: plastic and glass cups, plates and other dishes, any cloth, paper, or plastic items.

ACTIVITIES 74–80: CONNECTIONS

Goal: To find relationships between magnetism and electricity

Skills: Comparing, generalizing, supporting explanations with observations

— Questioning Strategy—

1. Let's think about the activities that we did and try to make some comparisons. What are some things about magnetism and electricity that relate to each other?

     Possible answers: north and south poles attract each other; plus (proton) and minus (electron) charges also attract each other; we can make a magnet using electricity by wrapping a wire around a nail and connecting the wire to a battery.

2. We used a nail to make an electromagnet. Do you think anything else would work, and why do you think that?

     A bolt or something else made of iron should also work. Both the nail and the bolt are made of iron which is attracted to a magnet.

3. We tested materials to see if they are attracted to magnets and we tested them again to see if they conduct electricity. What kinds of similarities did you find?

     There were two similarities. Substances made of iron were both attracted to the magnet and conducted electricity. Anything that wasn't a metal neither conducted electricity nor was attracted to the magnet.

4. What differences did you find?

     There were three differences. All metals conducted electricity, but only the things made of iron, or containing iron (like steel), were attracted to the magnet. Also, magnetic force goes through some materials, like plastic, that electricity doesn't. Additionally, magnetic force still affected an object even when the magnet wasn't touching it, but the battery or wire had to be touching the object for it to complete the circuit.

5. How do we know magnetic force travels through objects?

     The magnet attracted the iron filings through the transparency.

6. How do we know magnets affect objects even if they aren't touching the objects?

     The iron filings were attracted to the magnet even though they were a distance away from it. Also, one circular magnet sat suspended in the air above the other one. They weren't touching.

7. We also looked at both current and static electricity. How are they similar?

     They both involve electrons. (Tell students that "electron" is the root word for "electricity.")

8. How are they different?

> With static electricity, extra electrons build up on some materials. The electrons don't move until so many build up that they "jump" to another substance (like a shock from walking on a carpet and then touching something, or like lightning). With electric current, electrons move from one place to another, such as through a wire. When electrons move through a light bulb, it lights up.

GLOSSARY

ABSTRACT
A thought separate from a particular act or thing; not concrete.

ACTION
The doing of something.

AIR PRESSURE
The pressure exerted by the air around us. When there is a difference in air pressure, a high and low pressure area, the higher pressure area moves into the area with lower pressure. Air exerts the same pressure in all directions.

AIR RESISTANCE
The drag experienced when an object moves through the air.

AIRFOIL
A shape, such as a wing, made to move efficiently through the air.

AIR
The gas that is all around us, made up of about 78% nitrogen, 21% oxygen, and 1% other gases.

ASSOCIATIVE REASONING
Seeing the relationship between one thing and another.

ASSUMPTION
Something taken for granted to be true.

ATMOSPHERE
The air that is all around us.

ATMOSPHERIC PRESSURE
Force exerted by the atmosphere; it varies with altitude.

ATTRACT
To make come closer; pull toward oneself.

BERNOULLI'S PRINCIPLE
The faster that air flows over a surface, the less force it exerts on the surface.

CARBON DIOXIDE
A colorless, odorless gas that is not combustible and is slightly heavier than air; can be produced by adding baking soda to vinegar.

CIRCUIT
The complete path along which an electric current can flow; also, any hookup, wiring, etc. that is connected into this path.

CLASSIFICATION
The process of putting objects into groups based on common characteristics or properties.

COHESIVENESS
The tendency of molecules that are alike, for instance water molecules, to stick to one another.

COMBUSTION
The act or process of burning.

COMPARE
To examine things to find out how they are alike and/or different.

COMPRESS
To reduce the volume of something by pressing or squeezing it together, thereby increasing its density.

CONCENTRATE
To focus or become stronger.

CONCLUSION
A summary or judgement based on previous thought; generally the last step in a reasoning process.

CONCRETE
Something, actual or real, that can be perceived by the senses; not abstract.

CONDENSATION
When moisture in the air condenses or forms drops due to cooling.

CONDUCTION
The process of transferring heat within materials where objects are in contact with one another, and the particles of the heated substance do not move from one place to another.

CONDUCTOR
In general: any substance that transmits electricity, heat, or sound. In reference to electricity: any substance that allows the flow of electricity (the flow of electrons) through it. A conductor can be part of a complete circuit.

CONFIRM
To strengthen a belief that something is true.

CONTRAST
To compare in a way that shows the differences.

CONVECTION
The transfer of heat as a result of the particles (molecules) of a warm substance actually moving from one place to another.

CRUDE OIL
Raw, untreated oil which is more dense than refined oil.

DATA
Information gathered from observation by one or more senses.

DENSE
How compact a substance is. For example, when two substances take up the same space and the mass of one is greater, then that one is more dense; when two substances have the same mass and the volume of one is greater, then that one is less dense. Less dense liquids float on more dense liquids.

DENSITY
The degree of compactness; the amount of mass in each cubic unit of space (volume). Density equals mass divided by volume.

ELECTRIC CIRCUIT
A complete path that allows electrons to travel from an energy source, like a battery, through a bulb or other electrical device and back to the energy source again.

ELECTRIC CURRENT
The flow of electrons through a circuit.

ELECTRICITY
A form of energy that comes from the movement of electrons.

ELECTROMAGNET
A magnet created by placing a piece of iron in an electric current-carrying coil of wire. Electromagnets are an important part of all electric motors.

ELECTRONS
Negatively charged particles.

EVAPORATION
The process of liquid turning into vapor.

EXERT
To put into action.

EXPERIMENT
To test an idea through the use of dependent and independent variables by observing and recording information.

FIELD
An area in which an effect exists, like magnetism.

FIRE
The process of combustion manifested in light, flame, and heat.

FLUID
Any gas, like air, or any liquid, like water. Fluids can flow.

FORCE
Any push or pull; an interaction between two or more things.

FRICTION
The force which opposes the movement of one surface sliding or rolling over another with which it is in contact.

GAS
A substance which has the same form as air. A gas can spread out so as to take up all the space open to it or it can be compressed into a small space. A gas can be changed to a liquid by lowering its temperature.

GENERALIZING
Forming a common rule or summary from particular data.

GLYCERINE
A clear, syrupy liquid made from fats and oils and used in skin lotions as a lubricant.

GRAPH
A way of organizing and representing information visually.

GRAVITY
A force that pulls objects down to the surface of the earth. It is the earth's pull on objects.

HEAT
The energy transferred from one material to another because of a temperature difference. Heating molecules makes them move faster.

HIGH PRESSURE
Area of greater atmospheric pressure due to lower (cooler) temperature or less air movement.

HYPOTHESIS
An educated guess; a reasonable explanation of an observation or result of an experiment that is not completely accepted until confirmed by further observations or experimentation.

INERTIA
The property of matter that causes its speed and direction to stay the same unless acted upon by external forces (i.e., to continue moving if it is moving or to remain at rest if it is at rest).

INFERENCE
A conclusion based on observation, where no personal preference or sentiment is involved. May or may not actually be true.

INFLATE
To swell out by putting in air or gas; expand.

INSULATOR
A material that does not readily conduct heat energy. Also, a material that does not readily conduct electricity.

ISOLATE
To set apart from others; place or keep by itself.

LIGHT
The form of energy that acts on the eyes allowing us to see.

LIQUID
A substance that has the same form as water and conforms to the shape of the container holding it. May be changed to a solid by lowering its temperature or to a gas by raising its temperature.

LOW PRESSURE
Area of less atmospheric pressure due to higher (warmer) temperature or greater air movement.

MAGNETIC FIELD
The magnetic force that fills the space around a magnet or current-carrying wire.

MAGNETIC POLE
One of the parts of a magnet that produces magnetic force. Like poles of a magnet repel each other and unlike poles attract each other. The earth has magnetic poles and behaves like a magnet.

MAGNETISM
A class of physical phenomena which include the attraction of iron, cobalt, and nickel to magnets.

MASS
The amount of material in an object.

MELT
To change from a solid to a liquid.

MERCURY
A heavy, silvery metal that is a liquid at room temperature.

MODEL
To produce a representation.

MOLECULE
The smallest particle of a substance that can exist alone without losing its chemical form. A molecule consists of one or more atoms.

NEUTRONS
Particles, with no electrical charge, found along with protons in the nucleus of an atom.

NEWTON'S LAWS
Three statements in classical physics dealing with inertia, force, and action-reaction.

  – NEWTON'S FIRST LAW
Objects at rest will remain at rest and objects in motion will remain in motion unless acted upon by outside forces.

  – LAW OF INERTIA
Another name for Newton's First Law.

  – NEWTON'S SECOND LAW
Change in motion is proportional to, and in the same direction as, the applied force.

  – NEWTON'S THIRD LAW
For every action there is an equal and opposite reaction (i.e., for every action, happening, force, etc. there is a response of equal magnitude in the opposite direction.)

OBSERVATION
Information that is gathered through any of our senses.

OPINIONS
Conclusions based on personal preferences. May or may not be based on observations.

OXYGEN
The colorless, odorless, tasteless gas which forms about 21% of the earth's atmosphere. Oxygen is necessary for something to burn.

PENDULUM
Usually made up of a long piece of wood or metal with a bob (weight) at the bottom.

PITCH
Highness or lowness of sounds. The thicker/longer a string or the longer the column of air, the lower the sound. The thinner/shorter a string or the shorter the column of air, the higher the sound.

POPULATION DENSITY
The number of people per square unit of area.

POPULATION
The number of people in a certain area.

POWDER
A finely ground solid.

PREDICTION
What one thinks will happen.

PRESSURE
The amount of force exerted on a certain area.

PROPERTY
A characteristic of an object that can be used to describe it.

PROTONS
Positively charged particles.

RADIATION
A method of transferring heat by sending the heat energy out in waves from the warm object.

RATE
Speed of moving or acting; how fast something moves or changes in a certain amount of time.

REACTION
An action, happening, etc. in response to some other action, happening, force, etc.

REFLECTION
The return of light or sound waves from a surface.

REFRACTION
The bending of light when it passes from one substance to another. The bending is caused by the two substances being of different densities.

REPEL
To push away.

SOLID
A substance that has a shape of its own. Solids can be changed to liquids by adding heat.

SOLUTION
The dissolving of a gas or solid in a liquid.

SOUND
A form of energy caused by something that is moving back and forth or vibrating.

STATE
The condition in which something is found. Matter commonly exists in three states: solid, liquid, and gas. Matter may change from one state to another.

STATES OF MATTER
Solid, liquid, and gas.

STATIC ELECTRICITY
The buildup of extra electrons on a substance such as a balloon, a person's body, clothes, or in a cloud.

SUBSTANCE
Physical matter; composed of protons, electrons, and neutrons.

SUMMARIZE
To make a statement about all that has been learned in an experiment.

SUPPORT
To find evidence that strengthens what you believe.

SURFACE TENSION
The attraction or cohesion of the molecules of a liquid to each other on the surface of a liquid.

SYMMETRIC
Balanced; two sides the same.

SYSTEM
Has parts that are connected in some way. They don't all have to be visible; for instance, magnetism or gravity can be part of a system.

– CLOSED SYSTEM
A system which is not open to the surrounding air or water.

– OPEN SYSTEM
A system which is open to the surrounding air or water.

TENSION
A stretching or being stretched so as to put or be under strain.

VACUUM
Space that contains no matter.

VAPOR
Steam; moisture in the air.

VARIABLE
A component of an experiment that may be changed.

– CONTROLLED VARIABLE
Something we use or do that remains the same throughout different experiments.

– DEPENDENT VARIABLE
The dependent variable shows the effects of the changes made in the experimental (independent) variable. The independent variable can cause change in the dependent variable.

– EXPERIMENTAL VARIABLE
Another name for independent variable. The experimental variable can cause change in the dependent variable.

– INDEPENDENT VARIABLE
Experimental variable; something we use or a way of doing things that is changed during an experiment.

VENN DIAGRAMS
A graph that uses circles to represent logical relations between sets and operations on sets.

VIBRATION
Rapid motion back and forth. The faster a string vibrates, the higher the sound (pitch). The slower it vibrates, the lower the sound.

VOLUME
The amount of space a substance takes up.

WEIGHT
A measure of the force (pull) of gravity on the mass of a person or object.

WORK
The combination of force and movement. Work is the product of the force used and the distance moved. To a scientist, a force needs to produce movement in order to be considered work.

Reference Materials Available (from Library or Media Center) for Extending Activities and Reinforcing Concepts

Activities _____ through _____

_____

Materials

_____   _____

_____   _____

_____   _____

_____   _____

_____   _____

_____   _____

_____   _____

_____   _____

_____   _____

_____   _____

Observations

Activity _____

_____

I need to change or add the following for better comprehension when I repeat the activity:

The following students need special help:

Notes